Politics and
Government
in California

Politics and Government in California

Fourteenth Edition

Bernard L. Hyink
California State University, Fullerton

David H. Provost
California State University, Fresno

 LONGMAN

An imprint of Addison Wesley Longman, Inc.

New York • Reading, Massachusetts • Menlo Park, California • Harlow, England
Don Mills, Ontario • Sydney • Mexico City • Madrid • Amsterdam

Executive Editor: Pamela Gordon
Acquisitions Editor: Peter Glovin
Supplements Editor: Jen McCaffery
Senior Marketing Editor: Suzanne Daghlian
Project Editor: Bill Mahaffey, Gama Book Incorporated
Text Design: Joel Hatch, Wolfpack Typography
Cover Design: Kay Petronio
Cover Illustration/Photograph: PhotoDisc, Inc. © '95
Full Service Production Manager: Eric Jorgensen
Manufacturing Manager: Hilda Koparanian
Electronic Page Makeup: Wolfpack Typography
Printer and Binder: The Maple-Vail Book Manufacturing Group
Cover Printer: The Lehigh Press, Inc.

Library of Congress Cataloging-in-Publication Data

Hyink, Bernard L.
    Politics and government in California / Bernard L. Hyink, David H.
Provost. — 14th ed.
        p. cm.
    Includes bibliographical references and index.
    ISBN 0-8013-3012-2
    1. California—Politics and government—1951–   I. Provost, David
H.   II. Title.
JK8716.H95   1998
320.9794—dc21   95-33573
                                                              CIP

2345678910—MA—009998

For June and Lollie

in deepest appreciation
for decades of love and
encouragement

Contents

3

The Politics of the 1980s Into the 1990s   *31*

4

Voters, Nominations, and Elections   *60*

5

Referendum, Initiative, and Recall: Democracy Through Petition   *83*

6

The Legislature   *95*

7

The Executive and Administration   114

8

The Judiciary   130

9

Local Government in California   148

Preface

"California is worth fighting for." These were the words of Hiram Johnson, then governor of California, approximately 100 years ago. They appear as an introductory statement before the first paragraph of the first edition of *Politics and Government of California.*

Since that time California has become the most populous state in the nation. It is still growing at a rapid rate with immigrants coming mainly from Mexico, Africa, several Asiatic countries, and some of our own Southern states.

Stretching nearly 900 miles from Mexico to Oregon, it borders the Pacific Ocean. Because of its temperate climate and good soil it is one of the most productive agricultural areas in the world, producing an amazing variety of products. The state also contains many important minerals and its early Anglo population participated in the famous gold rush of 1849. As this edition of the book is written California has come to be one of most important states (some would say *the* most important) in the country in terms of trade, commerce, and industry, exceeding the performance of most of the nations of the world.

Because of its large population it has become the most influential political state, casting 54 electoral votes in U.S. presidential elections. It is to be noted that President Bill Clinton made some 26 visits during his first term in office, 1993–1997. And the Republicans chose San Diego, California, as the host city for their 1996 political convention.

Its large population and big and diverse industry have been the subject of many challenges (some might say problems) in recent years. These include overcrowded cities, problems of water allocations, illegal immigration, inadequate public transportation facilities, racial inequality, a high crime rate, poverty, air pollution, and corruption in industry and government. In addition, California has been subjected to natural hazards such as earthquakes, floods, droughts, massive brush fires, and a disastrous-to-agriculture freeze.

Yet as the recovery in the mid-1990s attests, the enormous resources of the state have allowed it to make significant progress in meeting these challenges. Some have been—if not solved—made less, as is the case with air pollution. Others such as crime have been more intractable. But as the state's people move toward the twenty first century there is evidence they are facing the future with something like the old optimism that had characterized their predecessors before the recession of the early 1990s. A *Los Angeles Times* poll taken in February 1997 found the residents of Southern California, previously disheartened by job losses, base closings, high crime and other societal afflictions, once more expressing satisfaction with their lives and faith in the future.

In doing so, Californians look to government to help in meeting these problems, from reducing gridlock on their highways to dealing with natural disasters. Thus California government has become more involved and more important in assuring a high quality of life for its residents. This edition continues the emphasis of previous editions in paying particular attention to present-day governmental and political issues.

Indeed California is worth fighting for.

This edition contains completely updated material, including the results of the 1996 elections. Changes in the legislative leadership, the composition of the state supreme court, in policies dealing with such issues as gridlock on the state's highways, air pollution, and the quality of education being provided the state's students are here. Developments in civil rights such as affirmative action policies at the University of California, the growing strength of Hispanics in California politics, and changes in criminal procedures under "three strikes and you're out" are also treated. Every effort has been made to assure the reader of as up-to-date material as is humanly possible and to present it in what we trust is a highly readable form. For qualified college adopters, an instructors manual/test bank is available on demand, through your local sales representative.

We are grateful for the assistance of many who have aided in the preparation of this edition, including the following:

Thomas P. Hoeber, publisher of *The California Journal*,

Monica Flowers, executive assistant, California State Department of Finance,

Secretary of State Bill Jones and his staff,

Bruce E. Cain and Roger G. Noll, editors, *Constitutional Reform in California*,

Steven Alan Holmes, Bakersfield College,

Alan D. Buckley, Santa Monica College,

John P. Stead, The Masters College, and

several staff writers of the *Los Angeles Times*.

We also are grateful to a number of state and local government personnel whose help proved once again that bureaucrats are not the slackers and "feeders at the public trough" they are sometimes portrayed as being.

A special thanks goes to the late professor emeritus of political science Karl Svenson of California State University, Fresno, who devoted much time and effort in reviewing the last two editions of this work and made many helpful suggestions for their improvement.

Bernard L. Hyink
David H. Provost

Chapter 1 _____

The California Phenomenon

It has always been difficult to predict the course of California's government and politics, but perhaps never so difficult as it is today. In an earlier edition of this text we indicated that California was a "phenomenon" and perhaps not so much a state of the Union as a state of mind. From the days of discovery through the Gold Rush, the era of Hollywood glamour, the proliferation of aerospace and high-tech industries, it has often been difficult to separate fact from fantasy; like the artificial Christmas trees on Wilshire Boulevard, the fantasy was an essential part of the reality. Today's California faces a harsher reality in many ways. The population booms of the recent past have brought with them increased crime and gang activity, congestion, air and water pollution, a straining of state resources and, in the early 1990s, high unemployment. Despite all its problems, California is fortunate: Its rich resources—abundant talent and its location on the economically booming Pacific Rim—augur well for the future. An understanding of the government and politics of California requires some knowledge of these resources and of the state's dramatic natural and increasingly complex cultural environment.

GEOGRAPHY

California's culture, economy, and polity have been profoundly influenced by its spectacular natural endowments. Stretching along the Pacific Coast for 1,200 miles between the 115th and 124th meridians (comparable to the distance from Charleston, South Carolina, to Boston) with an average width of about 200 miles, California combines the dry heat of the American Southwest, the crisp cool air of the soaring Sierra Nevada Mountains, and precipitation from the Pacific to produce (in its natural condition) one of the most ideal climates in the world. There are extremes: Death Valley, 282 feet below sea level, is frequently hotter than any place in North America. Just 60 miles away, Mt. Whitney, one of the highest peaks, is hardly ever free of snow. But the coastal littorals and adjoining foothills are alluringly temperate. (Los Angeles temperatures average 55° F in January and 73° in July with about 40 days of rain each year; San Francisco temperatures average 50° in January and 59° in July with about 65 days

1

(Courtesy World West Features)

of rain). The warm, dry Central Valley is actually an immense alluvial plain whose fertile soils are irrigated by waters from surrounding mountain lakes and streams.

California's forests, which cover 40 percent of the state, are world renowned for their giant coast redwoods, taller than any other plant or animal life on earth. In addition to being a source of a lucrative timber industry, the forests are crucial for maintaining a sufficient supply of water. Because of the concentration of forests and rivers, Northern California is naturally water-abundant, and Southern California is naturally water-scarce, a situation that has affected the politics of the state in important ways.

The state's geology, dramatized by a history of earthquakes along the San Andreas Fault, has also strongly affected the character of the culture, the economy, and the polity. The lure of gold in the eighteenth century and its discovery in the nineteenth was in the first instance largely responsible for making California a part of New Spain and in the second instance a part of the United States of America. Its oil and natural gas deposits have provided a crucial base for industrial development of the state, and their pattern of exploitation in recent years has been one of the most

'It looks awfully dry here in California. Is there enough water
for 21 missions?'

(Dennis Renault, *Sacramento Bee*)

intense political issues, pitting the ecologists and devotees of conservation against the
developers and proponents of market-determined growth. Commercially exploitable
sources of hard minerals are also a major component of the state's basic economic
strength. The water and forests of the state became political battlegrounds in the
1990s when water was diverted from agriculture to preserve fish in the Sacramento
Delta and timber interests were at odds with environmentalists, in part over the fate
of the famous (or infamous) spotted owl.

DEMOGRAPHY

The Indian Genesis

The Indians encountered by the early Spanish explorers of California lived in separate little communities widely dispersed throughout the area and spoke some 135 regional dialects. This highly decentralized pattern and their generally peaceable nature were probably determined by the climate and the abundance of wild fruit, fish, and game. Small communities could happily live off the land without getting in one another's way. Lacking fighting traditions and alliances, they were easily subjugated by a succession of Spanish, Mexican, and Anglo-American regimes. Their numbers declined drastically from about 150,000 at the beginning of the Spanish period to some 16,000 in the 1880s, not so much from deliberate extermination (although there were some notorious massacres during the early American period) as from diseases that were probably the result of their maladaptation to a less natural way of life. Their indigenous cultures were treated with disrespect by their colonial overlords and virtually destroyed. New knowledge of the advances made by California Indians in agriculture, mining, medicine, and trade, not to mention the astronomical observations of Santa Barbara's Chumish, have rendered the old image of the Indian as "grubber in the dirt" obsolete. They had virtually no impact on the evolution of California's political system, but "savages" they were not.

Hispanic Roots

Upon completing their conquest of Mexico in 1521, the Spaniards under the leadership of Hernando Cortes began a series of explorations up the West Coast in search of the gold-rich "island of Amazons," which, according to a popular Spanish novel, was ruled by a pagan queen, Calafía. Cortes himself got no farther than what is now Baja (Lower) California. Other expeditions followed, most notably that of Juan Rodriquez Cabrillo, who in 1542 explored the coast considerably beyond what is now San Francisco. Actual colonization of the coastal areas north of Mexico, however, was not attempted until the last third of the eighteenth century, when, in fear of Russian encroachment from Alaska and English penetration from Canada, the Spaniards felt impelled to enlarge their empire northward. The Spanish method of colonizing California was essentially that used in Mexico proper: a combination of the sword and the cross. In 1769 a military force under Gaspar de Portolá and a religious expedition under Fra Junipero Serra were dispatched to "civilize" the natives to the north. (On the East Coast the English settlers had long since driven the Indians back behind the Appalachian mountain range and were on the verge of declaring their independence from Britain.)

The three colonizing institutions used by the Spanish religious and military authorities were missions, military forts, and towns built for civilian settlers. In the *missions,* run by Catholic priests, the indigenous peoples were taught the religion, language, and customs necessary to make them good Spanish subjects. They were provided with food, shelter, and clothing and in exchange were often forced to work as slaves for the missions. The Spanish and Indian settlements that grew up around these missions were the embryos of many of today's cities, San Diego being a notable example.

The missions were not always successful in gaining the cooperation of the Indians simply on the basis of economic incentives and religious awe. Some tribes were hostile and had to be subdued by military force; thus the *presidios,* advance outposts protecting the missions, were established. Some of the presidios also attracted settlers and, like San Francisco, grew into cities themselves. The early missions and presidios, having established the feasibility of successful colonization, encouraged the Spanish authorities to sponsor civilian towns, or *pueblos.* Spaniards, Mexicans, and indigenous peoples were recruited as settlers through the offer of land, housing, and supplies. The surplus produce of the settlers would be used to supply the military presidios, and the settlers were subject to military service in emergencies and were required to contribute their labor to public works projects. The vast majority of the Indians lived outside the pueblos but frequently came to town, attracted by the variety of goods and amusements. Limited self-government gradually evolved in the pueblos under an *alcalde* (mayor), appointed by the Spanish military authorities, and a town council, elected in some of the more stable settlements by the citizens themselves.

The indigenous Californians attained their freedom and equality with those of Spanish origin (and a growing population of mixed bloods) in 1822 when Mexico won its independence from Spain, but the entire province *del norte* (to the north) continued to be regarded by the new Republic of Mexico as a colonial appendage. Under the Mexican Secularization Act of 1833 the government seized control of the missions and their lands. Much of the mission property was to have been turned over to the Indians, but governmental instability in Mexico City and the submissiveness of the Indians allowed much of the land to fall into the hands of local politicians. Still, the extension of political democracy during the Mexican period did include the Indians who wanted to become part of the new system.

Although the central government in Mexico City appointed the governor of California, who in turn appointed prefects and subprefects (regional and local administrative officers), the provincial legislature was a popularly elected body with the authority to enact laws concerning commerce, taxes, and education. Moreover, on the local level mayors *(alcaldes),* as well as town councils *(ayuntamientos),* were popularly elected. Given the political turmoil in Mexico City, the Californians were left largely to fend for themselves, and the result in many areas was virtual anarchy.

Thus when westward migrating Anglo-Americans encountered California in the 1830s and 1840s, they found a racially mixed Hispanic society with political traditions of its own, including an evolving democracy with a loose federal structure. However, this rich sociopolitical legacy was not to be integrated as a part of the successor American regime, for the Anglos were by and large contemptuous of the California Mexicans. So the legacy became one of an undercurrent of resentment on the part of the resident Hispanics toward their new overlords and a feeling of alienation from what was once their own land.

California's Rapid Growth in Population

With over 32 million people, California is now home to more than 12 percent of the entire U.S. population. More than nine out of every ten Californians live in one of 45 metropolitan areas, making it the state with by far the largest number of cities with a population of 100,000 or more. In recent years the greatest growth has been in the suburbs, with some of the central cities either static or declining in population. The most populous county in the United States is Los Angeles County, with more than 9 million inhabitants. Well over half of the growth in the last several years has come from natural increase (births over deaths) with the remaining third from immigration—legal and illegal.

The course of California's political history can be written largely as an answer to the question: When and why did they come to California?

From the time that the early Spanish explorers named the northwest coast of New Spain after the land of dazzling wealth portrayed in a novel by Garcia Ordóñez de Montalvo, California has been a beckoning gleam on the horizon—a "great expectation" to millions of people. Some have envisioned adventure, many have hoped to find material security, and others have dreamed of glamour and bright lights.

Each year since the American whalers and fur trappers began arriving in the early nineteenth century, there have been substantially more arrivals than departures. Thus although the population of the United States has been increasing during the past century at an average rate of 40 percent every 20 years, California's population has nearly doubled every 20 years. But the expansion from fewer than 15,000 in 1846, when the American military authorities took California from Mexico, to over 32 million by 1995 has not come from a steady flow of migrants. There have been periods when immigration was comparatively low, but those demographers who predicted that the 1980s would be one of those periods were wrong. Within every 20-year period, however, there has been at least one stimulus to a major population invasion from other parts of the country. By highlighting these major invasions and the explosive pattern of the state's growth, some of the unique political and governmental problems discussed in the following pages can be better understood.

Nineteenth-Century Invasions

The Gold Rush   The news that James Marshall had struck gold on the banks of the American River in January 1848 brought a rush of adventurous young men, most of whom were between the ages of 18 and 25, almost all unmarried. Not all found gold, however, so they went into lumbering, agriculture, and business—and sent for women. By 1860 the population of California was 380,000, and residents born in other states outnumbered the natives two to one.

The Railroad Boom   When the Union Pacific Railroad, built westward from Omaha, was hooked up with the Central Pacific Railroad, built eastward from Sacramento, the trade and migration bottlenecks through the High Sierra passes were cleared. In 1869 the new capitol building was dedicated at Sacramento as if it were a new capitol of the United States. From 1870 to 1880 the resultant increasing land values and commercial expansion stimulated a population rise of nearly 55 percent. This was also the period during which California acquired its large Chinese population, most of whom had been imported into the country by the railroad builders to work as coolie labor. Thousands were laid off in 1876 when the Southern Pacific completed its line down to Los Angeles, but they later became a permanent and productive part of California's workforce.

Twentieth-Century Invasions

The "Black Gold" Rush   Southern California was found to be rich in oil lands at the turn of the century when oil began to displace coal as the major source of industrial power. The state's oil output increased twelvefold from 1900 to 1910. As the geysers spurted skyward so did property values, attracting real estate developers and land speculators into the Los Angeles area by the thousands.

During this period the agricultural areas were converted from grazing lands to wheat fields, orange groves, and truck gardens requiring a large itinerant labor supply. Further Chinese immigration had been stopped by exclusion acts that grew out of the political turmoil of the latter nineteenth century (see discussion of Kearneyism in Chapter 2), so new labor sources had to be found. Farm organizations waged large publicity campaigns throughout the Midwest and South. "Reduced railroad fares, gaudy pamphlets, and silver-tongued traveling salesmen were all part of the pitch to lure white laborers to the coast."[1] Not enough came to meet the demand, so the farmers and ranchers turned to Japan, Mexico, and the Philippine Islands for cheap labor.

With a developing industrial southland and a broad, central farm belt feeding the thriving commercial area around San Francisco, California looked like a sure investment. Young men and women from the older states, eager to stake out a claim in this mine of many untapped veins, boarded trains at Boston, New York, Philadelphia, and Chicago in confident mood. The state's population jumped to 2.5 million by World War I.

The Prosperity Push   Although the population increase slowed during World War I, the prosperous 1920s gave California two million new residents. The value of oil continued to increase. The horse and wagon were pushed to the side of the road by the new gasoline-consuming autos, buses, trucks, and airplanes. California oil producers found the Panama Canal a quick and inexpensive route for shipping oil east to sell at competitive prices. Then, in rapid succession, a series of large new fields was discovered in the Los Angeles area. The Huntington Beach strike in 1920 was followed by the Signal Hill and Santa Fe Springs strikes the next year and the Kettleman Hills bonanza in 1928. People with money to invest descended upon the Southern California area. Refineries were developed to turn the crude oil into gasoline on home grounds. Meanwhile, improved transportation and refrigeration sped California vegetable produce and fancy fruits to Eastern markets, which, in addition to enriching the growers, helped to advertise California.

The most publicity came through the movies and the radio. In snowbound Maine and Minnesota, people heard the radio announcer describe the balmy Rose Bowl weather on New Year's Day, and the local movie screens in Pittsburgh, Cleveland, and Oskaloosa were animated billboards showing palm trees and movie starlets frolicking in the surf. They used to dream of going to Florida, but now California came to be regarded as the nation's playground or a place to spend one's later years lolling in the sun living on dividends and annuities. The young people came for excitement,

---

[1]Kathleen C. Doyle, *Californians: Who, Whence, Whither* (Los Angeles: Haynes Foundation, 1956), p. 29.

the middle-aged came to get in on the ground floor of a sound economic venture, the old came to retire—together they pushed the state's population skyward at a rate of 200,000 a year.

The Dust Bowl Exodus   After the crash of 1929, immigration slowed to a trickle. But in the 1930s a huge migrant labor force from Oklahoma, Arkansas, and other prairie states crowded into California. When the dust blew away the topsoil from their small farms and the Great Depression blew away their small savings, they headed west. They heard that there was fruit rotting on the vines in California just waiting to be picked (it was not picked because it could not be sold), and they came to California with their large families because they had nowhere else to go. This time the state's population growth (three times as fast as the nation's) was not an indication of economic health.

The Siege of the Servicemen   World War II brought many young men to California who might otherwise never have come. Three hundred thousand servicemen who had been stationed there decided to stay after being discharged. Many others went home, talked about the climate and the oranges, and convinced their families it was worth a try. The process was repeated during the Korean War.

The Industrial Boom   World War II, in addition to bringing the servicemen to California, brought heavy industry supported by government subsidies, loans, and cost-plus contracts. The burgeoning of the aircraft industry—Douglas, Hughes, Convair, North American, Lockheed—converted placid suburbs such as Santa Monica and Burbank into humming cities. Allied industries providing parts and supplies to the major aircraft producers were also given impetus. The big steel companies were encouraged by Washington to establish and expand California plants; Kaiser built a huge steel mill in the middle of Fontana's vineyard with the help of a loan from the Reconstruction Finance Corporation. The San Francisco Bay region experienced an industrial revival from the stimulus of wartime shipbuilding. California's oil industry particularly thrived as the state became the fuel station for tankers servicing the Pacific fleet. New electrical supplies, chemicals, and small-tools industries got their start. Civilian employment nearly tripled in manufacturing industries from 1941 to 1945, while other urban employment remained relatively constant. By the end of the war California's population approached ten million.

Peacetime brought stimulus to California's entertainment industry, especially after television began to make use of Hollywood's talent, facilities, and know-how. Simultaneously, California's infant electronics and plastic industries became giants.

The Korean War and the Cold War gave another fillip to heavy industry (for example, Kaiser's $65 million addition at Fontana) and a demand for a larger urban work force—skilled, semiskilled, and unskilled. The great migration of the 1950s was composed primarily of wage and salary workers, and civilian employment in manufacturing registered a 70 percent gain between 1950 and 1958. Manufacturing displaced the retail and wholesale trades as the top employer. California industry had grown considerably during the previous 20 years. The expanded market in California and rising national freight rates brought many manufacturing plants to the state.

The 1970 census showed that the state added about six million people to the 1960 population, a gain of approximately 38 percent—an average of 1,645 new residents every day. In terms of the labor force, 650 workers were added each day, and the state was having more and more difficulty absorbing them. At the turn of the new decade the state's large aerospace industry had to lay off thousands of workers due to the decrease of governmental contracts, driving the unemployment rate to more than 7 percent in 1970.

Slow and Go Toward the Twenty-First Century

The growth slowed in the 1970s, due primarily to the slow economy and concerns over the impact of population growth on the environment. But, even so, the absolute growth in population from 1970 to 1980 still totaled more than 3.5 million people—greater than that of any other state.

Since 1964, when California's population of 18 million made it the largest state in the nation, California's population has grown to over 32 million. The 1980s saw a resumption of massive growth, when the population increased by 26 percent. High rates of growth continued into the 1990s, with nearly 800,000 more residents in 1991 than the year before. The recession of the early 1990s considerably slowed the increase—at least temporarily—cutting that growth in half. If California were a nation, it would rank thirty-ninth in the world, just behind France. There is, however, a cloud not before seen on the growth horizon; while the population has continued to grow and grow rapidly, for the first time more people were leaving California to go to other states than were coming from those states. The loss of jobs, especially in the defense industry in Southern California, proved a major factor in reversing the long and unbroken history of Americans moving into the state. By the mid-1990s, however, a rebounding economy was creating over 350,000 new jobs a year and the Golden State once again appeared to be taking on its previous image as a land of opportunity. The Census Bureau projects California will have a population of 49.29 million by the year 2025. There is nonetheless a question as to just how many people the state can support. Clogged highways, deteriorating schools, crime-ridden inner cities, overcrowded prisons, and overloaded public services such as libraries and museums that have had their hours cut (or in a few cases eliminated entirely) with others such as hospitals stretched to the breaking point—all these and more point to a state facing major problems. As one environmentalist pointed out, if the population booms of the 1980s were to continue, the state would have 302 million people in it in the year 2092. Energetic and idealistic leadership is required to alert an already concerned population fully as to the seriousness of the situation and mobilize an effective response.

SOCIOLOGY AND CULTURE

California is a state of great ethnic variety and is becoming more so each year. One out of every four Californians is of Hispanic origin. One out of every 12 is black. About three million persons of Asian ancestry—more than a third of those living in the United States—live in California. The state's native Indian population, second only to Oklahoma's, is 242,000. The non-white ethnic groups are closing in on 50 percent of the population and the combination of continued high in-migration with birth rates averaging considerably higher than those of whites points to a Third World majority by the start of the twenty-first century. Los Angeles and San Francisco have already become cities with a non-white majority.

The most dramatic increases have been in Asian immigrants, particularly those from Southeast Asia and the Pacific. Between the 1980 census and 1990 census, the Asian/Pacific Islander population grew 127 percent, reaching 2.71 million or 9 percent of California's population. That made the group the second largest ethnic minority. One in every three Asian/Pacific Islanders in the country lives in California. The largest absolute increase was among Hispanics, bringing their total to 7.69 million in 1990 with projections that they will constitute 44 percent of the population by 2030. The slowest-growing group was blacks, who increased to 2.1 million.

The most substantial growth, then—from immigration plus reproduction—is among new Californians of foreign ancestry from Asia and Latin America, who are not only visibly distinct from the "Anglo" majority but who also speak different languages. These characteristics are turning California cities into a series of ghettos, not the mythical "melting pot" wherein the immigrants are assimilated into the majority culture, but a collection of little Guadalajaras and little Saigons. The impact on local governments has been enormous. While immigrants have added greatly to the cultural "mix" in the state and have in many ways been major contributors to the economy here, in other ways they have added to the problems facing the state (see Chapter 12). In 1993, for example, it was estimated that 92 percent of all farm laborers were foreign-born, contributing very significantly to the farm economy (and keeping food prices down), but that same year 92 percent of the students at Hollywood High School spoke a language other than English at home, requiring more classes in English as a second language. California has certainly been enriched by these newcomers, but there have been at times increases in racial tensions, especially during periods of violence and recession. The targeting of Korean shopkeepers during the 1992 Los Angeles riots is an example. The tide of anti-immigrant fervor during the recession of the early 1990s is another. It is important to distinguish, as many of those on both sides of the immigration question fail to, between legal and illegal immigrants. While most Californians oppose illegal immigrants, as was shown by their approval of Proposition 187 in 1994 (see Chapter 3), the majority are not opposed to immigrants legally admitted to the country.

Along with the new ethnic complexity is a continuation and further complication of California's renowned religious diversity. Practically every religious group in the world has a visible part of its flock in California. Because of its huge Hispanic population there is a larger proportion of Catholics in California than in the nation at large. The recent influx of refugees from Indochina make it the Buddhist center of the Americas. Esoteric cults are, as always, at home here, with groups such as the "People's Temple" and the "Jones cult" having made it their headquarters.

The religious groups have much to keep them busy, given the rising incidence of crime; the exploding numbers of youths in violence-prone gangs, often engaged in drug dealing; the high divorce rate; and a whole host of societal ills that have given rise to antisocial behavior.

The state has much to be proud of with its citizens' contributions to music and the arts, in the entertainment field, in scholarship, and in progressive policies adopted by its leaders. California is a wondrous mix of the good, the bad, and the ugly. The glories of its landscape featuring white sand beaches, towering mountains, and awesome deserts are matched by some of the worst smog, most persistent traffic snarls, and increasing displays of gratuitous violence to be found anywhere in the world. The delight of a concert at the Hollywood Bowl is offset by the growing problem of the homeless. And so it goes. All this and more is to be found in California, land of contrasts.

ECONOMY

With an annual gross output of $1 trillion, California would rank seventh in the world if it were a separate nation, just behind Britain and just ahead of China. With its great economic diversity it has historically been able to weather economic downturns much better than virtually any other state. That proved no longer true in the early 1990s as the nation—and California—were plagued with serious economic woes. In fact, California was slower to come out of the recession than other states, though some

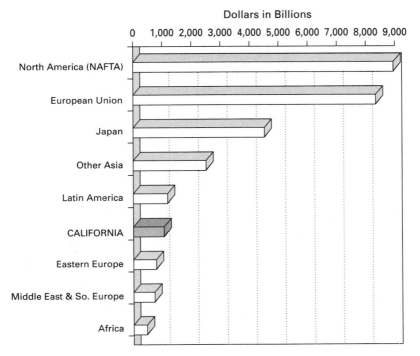

**California Among Worlds Regions
(Gross Domestic Product, 1997)**

(Source: "Budget Summary Highlights," Department of Finance)

aspects—such as tourism, which brought $54.1 billion to the state in 1992—remained relatively strong through the bad times. And agriculture, though briefly damaged by the six-year drought of the late 1980s and early 1990s and a devastating freeze in 1991, rebounded strongly.

Although less than 30 percent of its land area is under cultivation, California consistently leads the nation in gross income from agricultural products ($22 billion in 1996). Forty percent of all fruit marketed in the United States is from California, including 85 percent of the grapes and most of the lemons and apricots. Almost every American olive is a California olive, and the same can be said for almonds, artichokes, dates, figs, raisins, prunes, walnuts, garlic, nectarines, and persimmons. California leads the nation in the production of 53 crops and livestock products, is second in 14, and third in 6. Only Texas exceeds California in hard mineral and oil production, and nearly all of the useful minerals known to humankind have been found here. Only Alaska has more timberland, but California's wood products industry is the largest in the nation.

If some aspects of the economy remained strong, there were others that took a series of major hits with the end of the Cold War. It is estimated that at least 140,000 jobs were lost in the defense industries between 1988 and 1993. California had received 20 percent of defense contracts in the 1980s and the cutbacks were felt especially in Southern California, where over a quarter of the nation's defense jobs were lost in a two-year period. The high water mark for defense contracts came in the late 1980s when spending in the state reached $63 billion a year. But by 1993 that figure

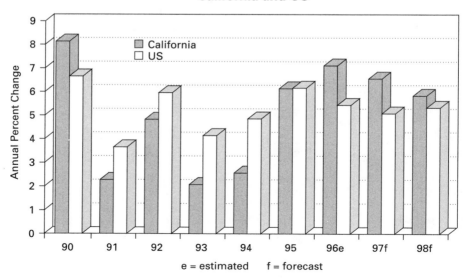

**Personal Income Growth
California and US**

(**Source:** "Budget Summary Highlights," Department of Finance)

had dropped to $50 billion and was projected to plummet to $33 billion by 1997. The impact of these cuts along with the general economic slump was felt in lost jobs, some 750,000 between 1990 and 1993, and 1,000 manufacturing companies that were lost to other states and Mexico during that same period. On top of all that, the Northridge earthquake in January 1994 cost the area an estimated 250,000 jobs.

In 1993 California fought back. In an effort to stem the tide of businesses moving out of the state, the much-maligned workers' compensation system received a major overhaul in 1993 designed to reduce costs to employers and increase benefits to employees.[2] A bipartisan effort led by Speaker Willie Brown and Governor Pete Wilson resulted in significant tax breaks for businesses as well. Both these moves were intended to change an image of the state that had come to be seen as unfriendly to business. As Californians looked toward the twenty-first century there appeared to be quite a lot of light at the end of the economic tunnel.

The fact that California is at the eastern edge of the Pacific Rim offers opportunities not equaled by any other state. Trade with Asia has been on the rise in recent years. The Port of Los Angeles passed New York Harbor in 1995 to become the country's largest gateway for foreign trade. A large portion of the state's $17 billion in exports travels across the Pacific, with Japan its largest trading partner. With United States exports up $71 billion in 1995, California provided 25 percent of the increase. Similar and even larger increases were recorded in exports to Thailand (up 30 percent), the Philippines (40 percent), Indonesia (34 percent) and Malaysia (72 percent).

ECOLOGY

The California way of life has been the product of the felicitous balance on this western slice of the continent among nature's various elements (atmosphere, waters, soils, flora and fauna, and topography) and of the belief that California's vastness (158,693 square miles) and its exposure to the great Pacific Ocean would allow the state to accommodate a virtually limitless expansion of human settlements and industry. Nature's profound equilibrium was unlikely to be perturbed; it would simply absorb the marginal alterations made by the humans.

However, in recent decades the assumption of an unlimited ecological carrying capacity has been severely eroded along with some of nature's crucial structures. Human settlements have not been evenly dispersed throughout the state but have concentrated with high density in the most climate-attractive locations—the seacoast and the foothills. As these areas were developed, overbuilding at such prize locations has undermined the stability of nature's own retaining walls. Landslides and mudslides have begun to convert intendedly permanent structures into mobile homes and entered them, against their owners' wills, in massive demolition derbies. The limits of the absorptive capacity of the air over densely populated urban areas has been

---

[2]Under the old system, workers received only 29.5 cents of each dollar contributed to the fund, the rest going to doctors, lawyers, and insurance companies. The changes were estimated to reduce costs by $1.5 billion a year while raising benefits significantly. Later changes ordered by the insurance commissioner were expected to save an additional $500 million.

painfully evident to smog sufferers since the late 1940s. Important fish-wildlife-plant ecologies along the seacoast are being destroyed by oil drilling and industrial-residential waste runoff, not to speak of the degradation to recreational assets. Similar assaults are being inflicted on the state's lakes, rivers, and streams by overbuilding or excessive diversion and harnessing of their natural flows for agricultural, industrial, and recreational purposes.

The discovery that California's ecology has its own priorities and agendas and will fight back—sometimes viciously—if they are not respected has made the management of California's ecology one of the most controversial, if not *the* most controversial, issues in contemporary California politics.

POLITICAL POWER

California's large population alone translates into potent political clout. It outranks every other state in numbers of representatives in the Congress and in electoral votes. Following the 1990 census, the 1991 congressional reapportionment gave California 52 seats in the House of Representatives.

States with the Most Electoral Votes			
1961–1970	1971–1980	1981–1990	1991–2000
New York (43)	California (45)	California (47)	California (54)
California (40)	New York (41)	New York (36)	New York (33)
Penn. (29)	Texas (27)	Texas (29)	Texas (32)
Illinois (26)	Illinois (26)	Penn. (25)	Florida (25)
Ohio (26)	Penn. (25)	Illinois (24)	Penn. (23)
Texas (25)	Ohio (25)	Ohio (23)	Illinois (22)

Accordingly, the person favored by California's delegation to the presidential nominating convention of either the Democratic or Republican party has an excellent chance of gaining the presidential or vice-presidential nomination. The Republican party nominated a Californian for president in 1960, 1968, 1972, 1980, and 1984, and in the three previous conventions it nominated a Californian for vice-president (one of whom was subsequently chosen to be chief justice of the U.S. Supreme Court). Two of the nominees have been elected president (Richard M. Nixon in 1968 and 1972 and Ronald Reagan in 1980 and 1984). Commenting on the successful 1980 election campaign by Ronald Reagan, the noted political historian Theodore White observed that "California is preeminently the nation's political leader, providing its president and its political style."[3] California has been the leader as the nation moves away from the politics of the traditional machines, away from people voting along predictable class, ethnic, and religious lines. Traditionally, the two key elements of the American political

---

[3]Theodore H. White, *America in Search of Itself* (New York: Harper & Row, 1982), p. 66.

California congressional districts. (Map provided by *California Journal*)

system have been its stability and its predictability. But they have never existed in California, and now they are vanishing from the rest of the country as well.

California benefitted considerably from the presence of a number of the state's citizens in the higher ranks of the Clinton administration during the president's first term. Leon Panetta served as chief of staff, Warren Christopher and William Perry as secretary of state and secretary of defense respectively, and Laura Tyson was the president's chief economic advisor. Mickey Kantor was, first, top trade negotiator and later secretary of commerce. California concerns were likely to be heard more clearly both because of its electoral college clout and because of the presence of such top advisors to the president. With Mr. Clinton's reelection, however, all the foregoing officials decided to retire, leaving a question as to how much of that "clout" California was likely to wield over the following four years.

The natural and acquired endowments that make up "the California phenomenon" impart a unique character to the internal politics and government of the Golden State. The sense of excitement about controversies large and small is part of a heady feeling (fantasy? realistic self-concept?) that the way California deals with its increasingly complex political and governmental problems will set the pace for the nation as a whole.

SELECTED REFERENCES

Barber, Mary Beth, "Can You Make a Buck When Peace Breaks Out?" *California Journal,* January 1994.

———, "Is California Driving Business Out of the State?" *California Journal,* May 1993.

Burdick, Eugene, "From Gold Rush to Sun Rush," *New York Times Magazine,* April 14, 1963.

California Statistical Abstract, Sacramento: State Printing Office, 1993.

Editor, "California 2000: The Next Frontier," *California Tomorrow,* Winter 1983.

Fay, James S., ed., *California Almanac,* 6th ed., Novato, CA: Pacific Data Resources, 1993.

Field Institute, "Living in California," *California Opinion Index,* July 1981.

Kotkin, Joel, and Paul Garbowicz, *California Inc.,* New York: Rawson, Wade, 1982.

London Economist, "California, State of the Future," July 1960.

McWilliams, Carey, ed., *The California Revolution,* New York: Grossman, 1968.

Palmer, Tim, ed., *California's Threatened Environment,* Washington, D.C.: Island Press, 1993.

Quinn, Tony, "The Economy: Gateway to the Pacific," in Thomas Hoeber and Larry Gertson, eds., *California Government and Politics Annual, 1991–1992,* Sacramento: California Journal Press, 1991.

Seidenbaum, Art, *This Is California: Please Keep Out,* New York: Wyden, 1975.

Stall, Bill, "The Problem of People Becoming the Problem," *Los Angeles Times,* August 2, 1987.

U.S. Bureau of the Census, *Census,* Washington, D.C.: Government Printing Office, 1990.

Walters, Dan, *The New California,* 2d ed., Sacramento: California Journal Press, 1992.

Chapter 2

The Development of California Politics and Government

From the state that gave you Hiram Johnson, Earl Warren, Richard Nixon, Angela Davis, Ronald Reagan, Cesar Chavez, Jerry Brown, and Howard Jarvis, it seems as if the only thing predictable about California politics is its unpredictability. A multitude of contradictory impulses—some rooted deep in its past, others shaped by visionary dreams of the future, some ruggedly individualistic, others mystically communitarian, some highly rational and pragmatic, others wildly romantic—contend against one another for the soul of the California polity and are reflected in its constitution, its institutions, and its laws. This has always been the case but now more so than ever, for contemporary California is the product of both its inherited paradoxes and its current complexities. Each generation has contributed its own traumas and complications to the character of California.

THE FORCED BIRTH OF THE GREAT STATE OF CALIFORNIA

California became part of the United States not through an evolutionary expansion of American settlements but through sudden rupture from the mother Hispanic system that nourished its early development. By the 1840s the American government had its eye on the large but weak Mexican province extending up the Pacific Coast toward Canada. Vastly underpopulated (there were estimated to be fewer than 7,000 Mexicans living in the area, only 1,000 adult males, and of those only a hundred or so could read and write), its control by Mexico had largely ceased. The United States was in an expansionist mood, and the idea that Americans had a "manifest destiny" to impart the blessings of their civilization to less fortunate peoples became popular.

Failing to buy California from the Mexican government, the U.S. government made efforts to stimulate "independence" movements which led to the so-called "Bear Flag Revolt" by American settlers in Northern California on June 10, 1846 (they seized some horses belonging to the Mexican governor). Short-lived, it became merely a sideshow to the Mexican-American War (1846–1848).

The Treaty of Guadalupe-Hidalgo formally ended that war on February 2, 1848. Under its terms Mexico ceded all of what is now California, Arizona, New Mexico, and Texas to the United States. But the end of the war hardly brought peace and quiet. The social, political, and economic conditions of the times were highly volatile and were made worse by the gold rush of 1848 and 1849.

News of James Marshall's discovery of gold on the banks of the American River in January 1848 caused soldiers and sailors to desert, shopkeepers to close their doors, and ranchers to leave their livestock. The non-Indian population quadrupled, reaching 100,000 in 1850. The Hispanic culture was drowned in a flood of young Anglos (most were between 18 and 25 years old) seeking instant wealth.

A CONSTITUTION AND STATEHOOD

The foundations of the governmental system now operating in the state were instituted in 1849 and 1850 as California joined the Union.

It was not preordained that California would become an American state so soon after it had been taken from Mexico. There was the option of territorial status, which was preferred by the many Southern Californians with strong Mexican ties, since this would allow a looser connection with the United States. But in the more populous North the predominant sentiment was for statehood, and it was the North that controlled the convention that assembled in Monterey in September 1849 to draw up a constitution. The delegates worked quickly, approving the final document in only six weeks. The proposed constitution was largely a prefabricated structure combining planks from the U.S. Constitution and the state constitutions of New York and Iowa. On November 13, 1849, voters (only white males over 21) throughout California ratified the constitution by a nearly unanimous vote of 12,872 to 811 and chose their first governor, Peter H. Burnett, and other state officers, as well as delegates to the U.S. House of Representatives (although California had not yet been admitted to the Union as a state). The state legislature convened and selected two U.S. senators, John Fremont and William Gwinn, to present the California constitution before the Congress and to request admission as a state.

ECONOMIC AND CLASS CONFLICTS— THE CONSTITUTION OF 1879

Since entering the Union, California's development, though full of surprises, has in the main been in the form of reflections and sometimes magnifications of national trends and traumas. Its responses to the boom and bust cycles in the decades following the Civil War were very much of this character.

An especially severe economic and political reaction to the economic depression of the early 1870s surfaced in California. The thousands of Chinese laborers laid off by the railroad builders upon the completion of the transcontinental lines made the employment situation especially critical and gave a peculiar racist edge to the labor union agitations sparked by the depression. The Workingmen's Party, under the fiery leadership of a young San Francisco drayman, Denis Kearney, campaigned against the railroad menace and the "Yellow Peril." Labor anger intensified in 1876 and 1877 with the arrival of some 25,000 additional immigrants on ships from China, and there were anti-Chinese riots organized by the unions on the streets of San Francisco. Kearney and his men threatened to take over the state.

In addition to demanding legislation to exclude further Chinese immigration, the Workingmen's Party urged state regulation of the railroads and banks, an equitable system of taxation, an eight-hour day, the abolition of contract labor on public works, compulsory public education, and the direct election of U.S. senators. In combination with the rural Grange, which also disliked the railroads and contended that the existing state constitution allowed the monopolies too much freedom, the Workingmen's Party successfully mobilized popular support for a new constitutional convention.

Voters across the state elected delegates of varied political persuasions to the constitutional convention that convened in September 1878: 51 Workingmen, 11 Republicans, 10 Democrats, 2 Independents, and 78 who identified themselves simply as "nonpartisan." The main division was between those who favored considerable state control over the economy and those who stressed free enterprise. The emerging document, ratified by a slim majority of voters in 1879, was less a reformer's Magna Charta than a bundle of compromises. Still, it did incorporate just enough of Kearney's program to take the steam out of his attempts to polarize the state along class lines.

Rather than being completely new, the constitution of 1879 was in large part an elaboration of the 1849 document, with more specific and detailed provisions. But there were a number of important alterations.

The legislature's power was significantly circumscribed. Whereas previously there had been no restrictions on its financial powers, it was now prevented from appropriating state monies to aid private institutions (including religious schools and hospitals), except homes for the blind, orphans, and the indigent. The governor was given the right to convene special sessions of the legislature in which only the subjects mentioned in his call could be considered. This power could be used with pointed effect when a budget bill was up for passage.

The judicial system was completely reorganized. The state supreme court was expanded to comprise a chief justice and six associate justices. County and district courts were to be replaced by superior courts created by the legislature.

The Chinese coolie labor problem received special treatment in Article XIX—a concession to the Workingmen's Party delegates. All corporations were prohibited from hiring Chinese, and their employment "except in punishment for crime" was forbidden on any state, county, or municipal project. The importation of contract coolie labor was made illegal, and the legislature was instructed to discourage any further Chinese immigration. (This article was not completely repealed by the voters until 1952, although the courts had earlier found most of the clauses in violation of the U.S. Constitution.)

There were numerous other provisions written into the 1879 constitution to protect nearly every interest represented at the convention. Thus details such as the maximum number of acres of state-owned land to be granted to one settler and whether noncultivated land was to be counted by tax assessors (properly subjects for simple legislative statutes) were included. The result was a bulky and unwieldy document that required amendment very frequently.

CONSTITUTIONAL REVISION

By 1963 California's constitution had been amended more than 350 times and contained some 80,000 words, becoming the second longest state constitution in the United States. Many of the provisions severely restricted the power of the government to perform its proper functions.

After several unsuccessful attempts at constitutional reform, the state legislature in 1963 appointed a Constitutional Revision Commission made up of 60 leading citizens representing industry, agriculture, education, government, and other civic groups. The recommendations of this Commission, after review by the legislature, were presented to the electorate in a series of constitutional amendments starting in 1966 and continuing through 1980. Most were approved, and the state constitution was reduced to one-third its former length. In addition, several important governmental changes were made, such as the provision for a full-time legislature to replace the former limited terms of legislators. These changes are discussed in following chapters on the legislature, executive, and judiciary.

THE PROGRESSIVES VERSUS THE RAILROAD MAGNATES

In the prosperous 1880s economic power and political power became concentrated in the hands of the railroads' "Big Four": Leland Stanford, Collis Huntington, Charles Crocker, and Mark Hopkins. At the height of their power, according to California historian John Caughey,

> there was hardly an office, from the seats in the United States Senate down through the governorship and the courts to the most inconsiderable town office, in which the right man could not do the railroad a service.[1]

The domination of California politics by the Southern Pacific Railroad went virtually unchallenged from the decline of Kearneyism to the rise of the nationwide Progressive movement at the start of the twentieth century. With the railroad magnates being one of their chief targets, the Progressives, under the national leadership of Theodore Roosevelt and Robert M. La Follette and in California Hiram Johnson, organized themselves into an especially powerful political force in California.

Whereas the railroads brought the Industrial Revolution to the West Coast, and some of its most successful entrepreneurs bequeathed California many of its finest private educational institutions, libraries, and museums, the Progressives brought lasting structural changes into the state's system of politics and government.

---

[1]John W. Caughey, *California,* 2d ed. (Englewood Cliffs, NJ: Prentice-Hall, 1953), pp. 449–450.

Hiram Johnson campaigning. (Courtesy California State Library)

The state's first Progressive legislature made such an impact that Theodore Roosevelt called its work "the most comprehensive program of constructive legislation ever passed at a single session of an American Legislature."[2]

LIVING HIGH BEFORE THE CRASH

The first third of the twentieth century was the period of California's heady adolescence. Much of the lifestyle that was to arouse the rest of the nation's envy (often bitter jealousy) had its origins in this devil-may-care period.

The growth in population slowed somewhat in the immediate postwar period, but the impact of the "black gold" rush continued to increase. As noted earlier, the ease of shipping California's oil to the rest of the nation was enhanced by the construction of the Panama Canal. And of course more and more people were turning from horse-drawn to gasoline-powered transportation. New oil strikes in the 1920s brought more people and with them more development. New preservation techniques meant that California produce could be shipped east as well, a boost to the farmers as well as an enhancement of the state's image.

---

[2]Ibid., p. 464.

Postwar prosperity brought popular complacency toward politics and government. The only significant political rivalries of the time were North-South and rural-urban and focused on the issue of legislative reapportionment.

Although in 1900 Southern California had only 20 percent of the state's population, by 1920 it had nearly 40 percent and was continuing to gain rapidly. The population explosion, especially in Los Angeles, threatened the domination of the legislature by the northern and rural interests. The citizens of Los Angeles, outraged when the legislature refused to redraw the state senate after the 1920 census, qualified an initiative constitutional amendment for the ballot to make reapportionment of legislative seats mandatory on the basis of population. Northern and rural interests countered with their own constitutional initiative, which, while requiring a redrawing of assembly districts to reflect the population changes, instituted a "Federal Plan" for California by making the counties the basis for senatorial districts, thereby assuring a greater number of northern and rural senators. The federal plan carried the day in the 1926 election. The Southern Californians were not able to change the system in their favor until the 1960s.

The effects of the Great Depression of the 1930s were especially severe in California, since many of the state's major industries—motion picture production, tourism, and olive, date, fig, and citrus growing—were nonessential. Despite the lack of jobs, thousands of persons from other hard-hit areas, particularly the Arkansas-Oklahoma dust bowl, flocked to the "Promised Land." As Wilson, in John Steinbeck's *The Grapes of Wrath*, said:

> Oh, but she's worth it. Why, I seen han'bills how they need folks to pick fruit, an' good wages. . . . An' with them good wages, maybe a fella can get hisself a little piece of land an' work out for extra cash. Why, hell in a couple of years I bet a fella could have a place of his own.

The ranks of the unemployed swelled dangerously. Social and political unrest was rampant. Visionary groups such as the Technocrats vied with religious movements such as the one led by Aimee Semple MacPherson whose vision of heaven was much like Hollywood. However, the period did produce movements with definite political impact. The dormant Progressives revived the Democratic Party, which won the governorship for the first time in 40 years and gained control over the state legislature as well. Culbert Olson, a reformer at heart, had the misfortune of becoming governor during the later stages of the Great Depression. His majorities in the legislature diminished and he was faced with fiscal conservatives from both parties (an "economy block") that frustrated many of his initiatives. He managed to gain approval for improvements in the state's penal system and in the areas of youth correction and mental hygiene.

During Olson's administration the "Yellow Peril" was rediscovered. The result: After Pearl Harbor pressure was brought on Olson to aid in the evacuation of all Japanese from the state. He disliked the idea but eventually assisted in the federal actions that removed 94,000 Japanese living here. That this action might be constructed as prejudice was shown by the fact only those Germans and Italians actually suspected of espionage and sabotage were evacuated. *All* Japanese, including American citizens, were ordered to relocation centers in other states. The judgment of historians concerning this episode in the state's history is—understandably—harsh. The following comment is typical:

> In retrospect the evacuation of the Japanese appears both cruel and unnecessary. . . . That Olson took no stronger line (opposing it) than he did is clear evidence that even a man of liberal instincts and genuine humanitarianism could be bewildered by the forces set in motion by the waving of "California's Bloody Shirt."[3]

The most lasting effect on California government from the Great Depression was the blurring of the demarcation among spheres of state, local, and national responsibilities. Federal funds were funneled into the state to provide jobs and stimulate business investment. In partnership with the state, superhighways and giant flood and reclamation projects were started, including the Hoover Dam and the Central Valley Project. Grants-in-aid to local social service agencies were provided by Congress, often tied to the local governments' adherence to nationally legislated rules and regulations for their administration. National regulation of business activity reached into the state under the U.S. Supreme Court's increasingly liberal interpretation of the interstate commerce provisions of the federal Constitution as allowing the hand of national authority to extend to firms manufacturing goods that would later be transported for sale across state lines.

WORLD WAR II: THE NATIONAL GOVERNMENT REVIVES THE CALIFORNIA BOOM

World War II accelerated the enlargement of the national government's role in California. Huge federal subsidies poured into California to support the state's aircraft and other defense-related industries. The revival of the California boom was widely appreciated, but it also had problematical implications. The state's economic well-being was now crucially dependent on decisions made in Washington, D.C. This new situation affected California politics by establishing a common interest between big labor and big business to keep the defense contracts coming in. After the war, particularly in Orange and San Diego counties, labor and business united in sending Cold War hardliners to Congress and electing "moderates" to the state legislature and county councils to preserve an attractive local tax and regulatory climate for the defense industries.

1942–1966:
ERA OF THE MODERATE PROGRESSIVES

Earl Warren, Goodwin Knight, Edmund G. "Pat" Brown—two Republicans and a Democrat, each a strong governor, all part of the popular California fusion of Hiram Johnson progressivism and Franklin D. Roosevelt liberalism—shepherded the state

---

[3]Robert E. Burke, *Olson's New Deal for California* (Berkeley: University of California Press, 1953), p. 206.

into a position of national leadership for coping with the problems of advanced industrialization and urbanization.

Earl Warren always considered himself a Hiram Johnson Progressive. Entering public service in 1919, he rapidly rose to the position of district attorney of Alameda County. In 1936, still only 45 years old, Warren became chairperson of the Republican State Central Committee and led California's delegation to the Republican National Convention. In 1938 he won the nomination of the Republican, Democratic, and Progressive parties in the primaries for the position of attorney general under Democrat Culbert Olson. So began his successful nonpartisan career.

Warren tried for both the Democratic and Republican gubernatorial nomination in 1942, but Olson led in the Democratic primary. In the general election campaign Warren continued to style himself as a nonpartisan and handily defeated Olson, receiving 57 percent of the vote to Olson's 42 percent. If it is a misfortune that "only men of very loose political affiliations, like Warren, can be elected," commented one analyst, "the blame must be attributed to the (Hiram) Johnson crusade which pounded the ruling party into so many fragments that no one has ever put it together again."[4]

Warren's nonpartisanship paid off spectacularly in 1946 when he won the nomination for governor in both the Republican and Democratic primaries. In 1950 James Roosevelt was able to capture the Democratic nomination, but Warren beat him by more than a million votes in the November general election. Warren had a keen awareness of the controlling features of California politics: the large proportion of independent voters and the necessity for a candidate for governor to appeal to the liberal urban vote as well as to the conservative elements in the state. He followed essentially a middle-of-the-road course, which was displeasing to both the extreme right and the extreme left but was agreeable to the large body of voters in between. He was able to retain the support of both organized labor and the business community.

Warren's ten-year governorship—the longest in California's history—was highlighted by a greatly expanded state welfare program, including old-age pensions, workers' compensation, and mental hospital and prison reforms. His political popularity allowed him to press almost anything he requested through the legislature. The outstanding exception was his compulsory health insurance plan, which, after determined opposition by the California Medical Association lobby, was defeated in the legislature.

The popular California governor received the Republican vice-presidential nomination in 1948, becoming the running mate of Thomas E. Dewey. He was considered a leading contender for the Republican nomination for president in 1952 until the Eisenhower candidacy was announced. In 1953 Eisenhower appointed him chief justice of the U.S. Supreme Court.

The Democrats had to wait four more years for their chance to regain the governorship. Lieutenant Governor Goodwin H. (Goodie) Knight succeeded Warren and won election on his own in 1954. Though he continued many of his predecessor's policies, he failed to be reelected in 1958 when he was forced to run for the U.S.

---

[4]Raymond Moley, in *The Politics of California: A Book of Readings,* David Farrelly and Ivan Hinderaker eds. New York: Ronald Press, 1951), p. 220.

Senate instead so as to give Senator William Knowland the opportunity to run for governor, a game of political musical chairs designed to advance Knowland's presidential aspirations. Both lost.

The beneficiary of this Republican debacle was another political progressive, Attorney General Edmund G. (Pat) Brown. For the first time since the 1930s, the Democrats were able to take advantage of their 3–2 lead in registration, in part because the cross-filing system now designated clearly which candidates belonged to which party. (For many years newly arrived voters registered Democrat but voted for incumbents, most of whom were Republican. Having come to the state because of the good things it had to offer, they were inclined to keep those in power in power rather than rock the boat.) The highly pragmatic and nonideological Brown administration was in tune with the mood of the times, and his continuation and gradual expansion of the social-service state erected by his predecessors gave rise to little concerted opposition during his first term. His primary public relations problem was over the issue of the death penalty, which he opposed and most Californians favored. This perceived vulnerability encouraged the entry of the former vice-president, Richard Nixon, narrowly defeated for the presidency by John F. Kennedy in 1960, into the gubernatorial race in 1962. Brown ran stressing his nonideological approach to problem solving (e.g., the state water project, school construction) and clearly was better able to project that nonpartisan image so important in California elections than the highly partisan Nixon. Brown won handily, by 300,000 votes, but at the same time the voters elected a Republican, Thomas Kuchel, to the U.S. Senate, thus demonstrating again the public's nonpartisan mood.

Governors Warren, Knight, and Brown presided over a generally confident California. By the middle 1960s California's per capita income was 20 percent higher than the national average. It consistently led the country in gross income from agricultural products, growing 40 percent of all the fruit marketed in the United States and producing almost as much oil and cotton as Texas. It was the nation's leader in aircraft production and was rapidly gaining on the Eastern industrial states in other heavy manufacturing—steel, fabricated metals, and plant machinery. Almost 90 percent of the 19 million Californians were now living in urban areas, making it the state with the largest number of cities with a population of 100,000 or more.

Industry kept increasing because of the population and resources, and the people kept coming because of the industrial growth. Observers were predicting that by the middle of the 1970s there would be one continuous city from San Diego to San Francisco. Yet underneath the surface of affluence—in part, a reaction to California's prosperous growth—there were rumblings of doubt and discontent. Many, looking at the increasing air and water pollution, the mudslides and landslides from excessive subdividing of the foothills, the congestion on the freeways, and the overcrowding of parks and beaches, began to wonder whether such continual rapid growth was all good and whether the state and local governments were able to handle it. Some looked at the expansion of government that paralleled the state's economic growth and worried that their freedom of enterprise might be unduly circumscribed. Minority groups began to feel their *relative* deprivation more keenly, as evidenced by the eruption of violence among the blacks in Watts (a pleasant middle-class black community). Students at the University of California launched sit-in campaigns against what they perceived to be the dehumanizing rules and regulations of the vast bureaucracy of the state's multiversity.

The Republican Party moved to the political right in 1964, nominating conservative Arizona Senator Barry Goldwater as their presidential candidate. One of his staunchest supporters was motion picture actor Ronald Reagan, who made many speeches (actually the same one, "the speech," many times) urging Goldwater's election and descrying government waste and Democratic policies designed to redistribute the wealth. Though Lyndon Johnson won easily, both nationally and in California (he carried the state by a huge 1.3 million vote margin, though he failed to carry Democratic U.S. Senate candidate Pierre Salinger with him; he lost to conservative Republican George Murphy by 300,000 votes), Reagan's efforts did not go unnoticed. Goldwaterites had gained control of the state's Republican Party and Reagan was their man for 1966. When Reagan defeated San Francisco Mayor George Christopher in the Republican primary, Brown supporters were convinced they could once again preempt the political center and win easily. They both underestimated Reagan as a candidate and misjudged the mood of the electorate.

REAGAN: ANOMALY OR PORTENT OF A CONSERVATIVE TREND?

For the 1966 general election, Ronald Reagan competed with the experienced Brown for the middle-American California voter. He purged his rhetoric of some of the more abrasive Goldwaterisms he had thrown around in 1964 and stuck mainly to the standard conservative complaints against excessive government spending and centralization of control in Washington and Sacramento at the expense of private initiative. He also related effectively to the growing citizen concerns about a spread of Watts-type uprisings among disaffected minorities and student demonstrations on campuses. In promising a more efficient system of law enforcement and an investigation of the University of California he implied that the Brown administration was overzealous in sponsoring civil rights legislation and overpermissive on matters of law and order. Brown was left with little that was new to say and had to content himself with defending his record.

Reagan got 59 percent of the 6,370,000 votes cast. There were only 3,350,000 Republicans registered, as opposed to 4,720,000 Democrats, which means that at least 300,000 registered Democrats crossed party lines and voted for Reagan. The successful gubernatorial candidate brought into office with him the entire slate of Republican candidates for other state executive offices except attorney general, which was won by incumbent Thomas Lynch. The Republicans also severely cut into the Democratic control of the legislature but not enough to take over either the assembly or the senate.

Reelected in 1970 over the former powerful Speaker of the Assembly Jesse Unruh, Reagan had a full eight years to attempt to reverse the long-established trend toward bigger government and higher taxes. He failed, though the rate of increase slowed markedly. He maintained with some justification that many programs were

Governor Ronald Reagan and Jesse Unruh campaigning during the 1970 election.
(Courtesy Wide World Photo)

mandated by law and that Democratic control of the legislature made his efforts much more difficult.

Reagan did succeed in moving the state from some fairly serious red ink into the black during his tenure as governor. He inherited a deficit of $500 million from Pat Brown and left Pat's son Jerry with a $350 million surplus in 1974. While Reagan could claim some of the credit, the booming state economy meant higher revenues from income, sales, and business taxes.

During the Reagan years the numbers of employees on the state government payroll stayed relatively constant—a fact the governor rated as possibly his greatest accomplishment in Sacramento. In the final analysis, however, he failed to reduce the role of government, his paramount goal before achieving office.

EDMUND G. BROWN, JR., AND THE POLITICS OF LIMITATION

It was a measure of the younger Brown's keen political instincts that he latched onto the growing popular sentiment in California that defeated his father and brought Reagan into office—the discontent with big government—rather than attempt to resurrect the Progressive—New Deal liberalism of past decades. Jerry Brown added a new element to the state (and national) trend, however, by propounding and symbolically representing the philosophy that the cause of big government lay in society's materialistic appetites and that the whole "more-is-better" approach to life, typified by the California ethos, would have to be reversed if the hope of reducing the size and role of government was to be realized. Brown's counterculture, "small-is-beautiful" approach, however, did not become evident until after his election.

The 1974 election in California mirrored the mood of a country outraged by the antics of Republican President Richard Nixon over Watergate. Democrats won most statewide offices and increased their majorities in the state legislature and the congressional delegation. Alan Cranston won reelection to the Senate by a whopping 1.3 million votes. Still, many were turned off by the scandal and voter turnout was the lowest in 30 years.

Brown cast himself as a crusader against corruption at a time when corruption was very much on the public's mind. As secretary of state he proposed and as candidate for the Democratic nomination for governor he campaigned for Proposition 9, a reform of campaign spending in the 1974 June primary. By so doing he demonstrated his instinct for anticipating the central issues of the day.

The general election campaign between Jerry Brown and his Republican opponent, State Controller Houston Flournoy, turned out to be primarily a popularity contest, one that Brown won, though narrowly, 52–48 percent. That gave him little in the way of a policy "mandate," little leverage over his party or the legislature.

California voters seldom get what they think they will when choosing a governor, but in electing Jerry Brown in 1974 they were in for more surprises than usual.

He rejected use of the $1.3 million governor's mansion, opting to sleep on the floor of a rented apartment. He refused use of a Cadillac limousine, preferring a Plymouth Satellite. His inaugural address lasted just seven minutes. And he gave a

Suli choir the job of providing the inspirational tone at some official functions. All this and more proved Jerry Brown did indeed march to a different drummer.

THE 1978 GUBERNATORIAL ELECTION

The outcome of the race for governor was not long in doubt. Facing a relatively colorless candidate in Attorney General Evelle Younger, Brown won going away, 56 percent to 36 percent. But Republicans gained considerable solace from victories by George Deukmejian as the new attorney general and Mike Curb as the new lieutenant governor. In both these contests the California voters showed again their proclivity to split their ballots, with both winners garnering ten-point wins over their opponents.

The most heat in the 1978 election cycle was generated by Proposition 13, the Jarvis-Gann initiative (see Chapter 10). Generated by wildly escalating property taxes and an apparent inability of the state government to take corrective action, the proposition was approved by a 2–1 margin. What proved significant was the reversal by Brown on the issue. A staunch opponent before the vote, he performed one of the most deft feats of political acrobatics ever executed by an American politician the day after the primary election. He announced himself a convert. He would, he proclaimed, implement Proposition 13 in the most humane way possible (using "bailout" funds from the state surplus to cushion the blow on local governments). It may have saved his bid for reelection, since before his conversion he had been trailing slightly in the polls; after his switch he pulled steadily ahead.

JERRY BROWN'S RECORD

In several fields the governorship of Jerry Brown made a significant impact, widely regarded as positive. Brown was a strong and effective leader in preserving California's natural environment almost single-handedly saving the California Coastal Commission when it was up for renewal in 1976. He was in the forefront of the effort to attract high-tech industry to the state. He gave active leadership to the search for new sources of energy, stressing solar energy as a means that carried less ecological hazard. Jerry Brown also opened high-level government to Californians who had never before been invited to help run the state. Of the approximately 3,000 appointments made by the governor, one-third went to minorities, and one-fourth went to women.

However, Brown made serious missteps in his career as governor. His midterm run for the presidency in 1980 not only took him away from his gubernatorial responsibilities but injured his image as an effective and popular politician.

Probably the most serious error made by Governor Jerry Brown was his failure to raise taxes during the last two years of his administration. The recession had caused a sharp decline in state revenues, and at the same time large financial grants were still being transferred to local governments to cover their shortfall caused by Proposition 13. All state surplus funds had been expended, and there was insufficient income to meet current expenses. Indeed, the $1.5 billion deficit that had been accumulated by the time Jerry Brown left office proved to be a political disadvantage in his campaign for the U.S. Senate in 1982 and would continue to be a liability to his future political ambitions.

Jerry Brown was more at home with ideas of sociocultural change than concrete actions. However, he did expand considerably the scope of government in the regulatory area with several new agencies including the Agricultural Labor Relations Board and the Energy Commission. His governorship is not remembered for highways, dams, and schools built by the state—of which there were virtually no significant new starts during his regime. He is admired more for what he stood for rather than for what he accomplished. A reporter once asked Brown to evaluate his own performance. He replied, "I did it my way."[5]

SELECTED REFERENCES

Bollens, John C., and G. Robert Williams, *Jerry Brown in a Plain Brown Wrapper,* Pacific Palisades: Palisades Publishers, 1978.

California Secretary of State, *Statement of Vote,* Sacramento: State Printing Office, issued after each general, primary, and special election.

Cannon, Lou, *Reagan,* New York: Putnam, 1982.

Caughey, John W., *California,* 2d ed., Englewood Cliffs, NJ: Prentice-Hall, 1953.

Harris, Joseph P., *California Politics,* Palo Alto: Stanford University Press, 1961.

Hill, Gladwin, *Dancing Bear,* New York: Harcourt Brace Jovanovich, 1968.

Lorenz, J. D., *Jerry Brown: The Man on a White Horse,* Boston: Houghton Mifflin, 1977.

Mason, Paul, "Constitutional History of California," *Constitution of the United States and the State of California and Other Documents,* Sacramento: State Printing Office, 1973.

Mowry, George E., *The California Progressives,* Berkeley: University of California Press, 1951.

Owens, John Robert, Edmond Constantini, and L. Weschle, *California Politics and Parties,* New York: Macmillan, 1970.

Peck, Robert, *Jerry Brown: The Philosopher Prince,* New York: Stein and Day, 1978.

---

[5]Editorial, *Los Angeles Times,* January 9, 1983.

Chapter *3* _____

The Politics of the Eighties Into the Nineties

A recurring question concerning California politics in the 1980s was: Is the Golden State becoming more conservative? As with so many questions about California, the answer is not easy or simple. At first glance the question itself seems a bit strange. Most people, when they think of California, envision a state and people who are innovative, progressive, and—in the minds of some—even a bit "off the wall" in their approach to life. After all, it was Californians who gave the governorship to a motion picture actor with no previous experience in government. And they followed up by electing a governor whose unorthodox style earned him the title of "Governor Moonbeam." Major experiments from the Progressive era of the early twentieth century to the tax revolt of the late 1970s upheld a tradition of trying new ways of dealing with issues. The fact that in many instances other states followed suit gave California a reputation for leadership that was well deserved.

Was California moving to the right, politically? One possible indicator was voter registration, which saw the Democrats' lead drop from 3–2 to 5–4 by the beginning of the 1990s. Many districts became closer in party registration and any district with less than a 60–40 Democratic edge is usually considered "marginal." Polls taken toward the end of the 1980s showed a strong shift toward the Republicans as the party people "identified with" (as opposed to being registered in), a reversal pollster Mervin Field declared a "phenomenal turnaround."

Other indications of a "conservative tide" running in California politics during the 1980s would include George Deukmejian's sweeping victory over moderately liberal Tom Bradley in the 1986 gubernatorial election. "The Duke" won 61 percent of the vote and carried all but 2 of the state's 58 counties en route to a second term. Support for the death penalty has been generally strong but in recent years has become overpowering, a major factor in the defeat of three state supreme court justices thought to be "soft" on this issue. Californians have repeatedly indicated a desire to "get tough" on crime, with their approval of the Victims' Bill of Rights initiative in 1982 often cited as an example. The public has endorsed measures declaring English the "official" language of the state, turning down proposals for stronger controls over handguns, and approving bonds for prison construction, all usually seen as conservative positions.

Despite all this, and Ronald Reagan's victories in the presidential elections of 1980 and 1984, there were some indications that gave hope to the state's Democrats.

- The party continued to dominate both the state's congressional delegation and both houses of the state legislature.
- Democrats continued to win most statewide offices other than governor, usually by big margins.
- Voters supported "liberal" positions such as the right to have an abortion, opposition to censorship of library holdings, the rights of homosexuals, and racial tolerance.
- Even with respect to taxation, the mood seemed to shift toward a more "liberal" stance. Toward the end of the 1980s a Field poll found 71 percent of those surveyed said they would support higher taxes for better government services, such as police and fire protection, schools, and highways.

The early 1990s showed much the same mix. The Republicans continued their hold on the governorship. Democrats held secure majorities in the state legislature and the congressional delegation (briefly interrupted by the national Republican sweep of 1994 but restored in 1996). The public demanded more protection from violent crime and voted for tax increases (a hefty boost in the gasoline tax and continuation of a hike in the sales tax). Of course the Democrats took particular pleasure in carrying the state for their presidential nominee, Bill Clinton, in 1992 and 1996, but he campaigned as a "new" Democrat, presumably more conservative, and went so far in 1996 as to sign into law a welfare reform bill vigorously opposed by liberals, so even here the message was a bit mixed. The 1994 election showed still another reversal, this time punishing Democrats who lost seats in the congressional delegation and, perhaps more surprisingly, in the state assembly where the Republicans gained a whopping eight seats. But in 1996 the voters returned a majority of Democrats to Washington, D.C., and gave control of the assembly back to the Democrats. In all likelihood what we are seeing is a continuation of Californians' long tradition of refusing to be categorized, the captives of no one point of view. If so, that may provide one answer as to why California politics, perhaps more than that of any other state, is so intriguing.

Successful California politicians know that there is indeed a political map of the state with definable pockets of deep concern on particular issues. As a start they know that there are at least four regions, defined by socioeconomic characteristics and special interests. The following is a rough approximation of the major geopolitical areas.

1. *The San Francisco, Berkeley, Oakland Complex,* plus coastal regions up to the Oregon border and down to the Tehachapis (about 22 percent of the state's population), is predominantly cosmopolitan, intellectual, civil libertarian, internationalist, and environmentally conscious, with a visible supply of militants who can be mobilized to get out the vote or take to the streets on a variety of issues.
2. *The Southern California Sunbelt,* including Orange, San Diego, and the six other Southern California counties but excluding the city of Los Angeles (about 53

percent of the state's population), is a mostly middle-class and upper-middle-class population comprised of families employed by or indirectly dependent on the research and development and electronics industries of Southern California. The large proportion of engineers, executives, and highly paid blue-collar technicians are for the most part owners of single-family homes and have an intense interest in the property tax, inflation, and other middle-class concerns.

3. *Metropolitan Los Angeles* (about 13 percent of the state's population) is a melange of black and chicano ghettos, blue-collar whites, pensioners, media and academic elites, investment and savings-and-loan executives and their middle-income, white-collar entourages. This is a politically volatile area subject to bitter divisions along class and ethnic lines.

4. *The Interior Agricultural Plateau* (about 12 percent of the state's population), dominated by the immense Central Valley, is the breadbasket of California and is highly dependent on government-run hydroelectric, irrigation, and agricultural programs. It is also the area that employs the most migrant Mexican farm workers and has been the scene of much labor-agribusiness conflict in recent years.

Latching onto these diverse and often opposed interests in a way that appeals to a majority of the state's voters is a high political art. Candidates for statewide office must be able to engender confidence on the part of a wide variety of constituents and, more than any of their opponents, must be capable of satisfying (or, at least, of not damaging too greatly) all of their interests. It is no wonder that any successful gubernatorial candidate in California is automatically considered a potential presidential candidate. It is not only that California, being the most populous state, has the most electoral votes in the presidential election but also that anyone able to satisfy California's vast and complex electorate, by that feat alone, acquires the charisma of a master politician.

Analyses of the most recent California elections—who won and how they did it—can therefore tell us even more than what to expect in the form of policy initiative and output from the current set of public officeholders. Such analyses also help us (*and* the officeholders) to understand what the electorate is like and what its various elements most value or oppose.

ELECTIONS IN THE 1980s

A fairly clear pattern emerged from the elections of the 1980s. The Republicans captured the governorship and carried the state for their presidential candidates. They won several key battles over ballot propositions. The Democrats held onto most of the other statewide offices while continuing to hold fast to their control over the state legislature and the congressional delegation.

The 1982 Gubernatorial Election

That certainly was the pattern in 1982 when George Deukmejian ended eight years of Democratic control of the governorship by defeating Los Angeles Mayor Tom Bradley in what proved to be both a fairly dull campaign and an extremely close election.

Bradley had outdistanced a dozen competitors in the primary while "the Duke," as Deukmejian was known, won a hard-fought contest with former Lieutenant Governor Mike Curb. In the general election campaign, each stressed "jobs, jobs, and more jobs." Bradley appealed to environmentalists while Deukmejian called for abolition of the Coastal Commission, which has responsibility for protecting land along the Pacific coast from overdevelopment. Deukmejian opposed it on the grounds that such decisions are best left to local government.

Two very different issues attracted attention during the campaign. The fact that Bradley would have become California's first black governor raised questions concerning a "hidden" racist vote. When Bill Roberts, campaign manager for Deukmejian, publicly stated there was a hidden antiblack vote of at least 5 percent he was fired. Still, given the closeness of the outcome, several analysts blamed Bradley's defeat on his color. Other analysts saw the presence of Proposition 15 on the ballot as crucial. Supported by Bradley and opposed by Deukmejian, it would have placed strict limits on the sale and possession of handguns. Sixty-three percent of the voters opposed it and some may have gone to the polls primarily to defeat it, staying around long enough to vote against one of the more vocal proponents. Given the closeness of the outcome, Bradley's support for it may have been the difference between winning and losing.

The 1982 Senatorial Election

What sparks were lacking in the contest for governor were amply supplied by the race for the U.S. Senate between outgoing Governor Jerry Brown and San Diego Mayor Pete Wilson. Though Brown had won two terms as governor, his popularity was at low ebb. His runs for the presidency combined with his controversial handling of the medfly crisis, first delaying and then ordering massive spraying to eradicate the dangerous pest, and his unpopular appointment of Rose Bird as chief justice of the California Supreme Court all made him vulnerable. Brown's campaign sought to exploit fears of atomic war with ads portraying Wilson as opposed to a freeze on nuclear weapons and, combined with other attacks, nearly pulled victory from defeat. In the end, however, Wilson won with 51 percent of the vote to Brown's 45 percent. Given the 3–2 registration edge enjoyed by the Democrats, it was clear that many had crossed party lines. Brown withdrew from party politics to emerge again as chair of the state Democratic Party and, in 1992, as a candidate once again for the presidency.

The 1984 General Election

The highlight of the election was, as was to be expected, the battle between President Ronald Reagan and Democratic challenger Walter Mondale. Originally the Mondale campaign "wrote off" California as a state that could not be won due to the enormous popularity of Ronald Reagan in his home state. Democratic leaders in the state saw things differently and urged a strong campaign so as to avert a disaster up and down the ticket. Though Mondale lost the state's 47 electoral college votes by 16 points and 1.5 million votes, the Democrats' losses were otherwise minimal. One seat was lost in Congress (to "B-1 Bob" Dornan in Orange County) and the Republicans managed to win just one additional seat in both the assembly and state senate.

Among the 16 propositions on the ballot, the voters gave the green light to the creation of a state lottery despite widespread opposition from political and religious leaders. Some claimed the lottery would lead to "Chicago-style" organized crime. Others said it would be a regressive means of raising money since those at the lower end of the economic ladder, hoping for instant riches, would risk a higher proportion of their incomes than would those at the middle and upper ends. The voters did approve one other initiative. They gave overwhelming support (71–29) to a proposition that asked that ballots be printed in English only. Arguments were quite heated during the campaign, with proponents seeing a need to avoid a separatism that they thought ballots printed in other than the English language would encourage and opponents arguing that bilingual ballots would increase voter participation and that abolishing them was, consciously or not, racist. In any event, the proposition could only be advisory inasmuch as the law mandating bilingual ballots is federal and cannot be overridden by state statute.

The 1986 Gubernatorial Election

If their first race for governor was dull but close, the rerun between George Deukmejian and Tom Bradley in 1986 was bitter and a rout. From waging a "statesmanlike" campaign in 1982, Bradley went on the attack in 1986 in an all-out effort to prove to the electorate that "the Duke" had not earned a second term. Deukmejian was not challenged in the primary, nor was Bradley, whose popularity coming out of the highly successful Los Angeles Olympic Games of 1984 carried him to a 6 percent lead over "the Duke" in an early poll. Other Democrats thinking about making the race stepped aside. The result was a long and bitter campaign, beginning in the primary and characterized by attacks and counterattacks. An example: When Bradley charged Deukmejian had been "bought off" by polluters because a quarter of a million dollars had been contributed to the incumbent's campaign by companies accused of generating toxic wastes, the response was quick and strong—television commercials citing Los Angeles' violations of federal pollution standards by dumping its sewage in Santa Monica Bay. Bradley faced other problems, some of them self-inflicted. In the 1982 campaign he had come out strongly favoring gun control; in 1986 he opposed it, opening him up to charges of flip-flopping. He had been cochair of a committee supporting Rose Bird's first confirmation as chief justice, but in 1986, with polls showing how unpopular she was with the voters, he declined to take a position on her reconfirmation. In the end the outcome was a foregone conclusion: Deukmejian garnered a whopping 61 percent of the vote in the biggest victory for governor since the days of Earl Warren and cross-filing. Obviously, with the economy flourishing and the people satisfied, voters were in no mood for a change.

The 1986 Senatorial Election

A number of observers claimed that the 1986 election nationwide was the most negative in history. Although that claim can be debated (some campaigns in the nineteenth century got exceedingly rough), there is no denying that attacking one's opponent characterized much of that year's politics. Nowhere was that more evident than in the race for United States senator from California. Not only was it a very expensive campaign, with each side spending over $10 million, but it also featured some of the hardest-hitting rhetoric of any recent race in the state.

The road to the finals was largely unobstructed for Alan Cranston, a senator since 1968. Had he decided to step down, there were a number of aspiring Democrats who would have been happy to take his place, but none wanted to challenge him. For Ed Zschau the story was quite different. His record on a variety of issues such as abortion and the environment brought challenges from several more conservative Republicans led by Los Angeles television commentator Bruce Herschensohn.

Zschau's success in the June primary is testimony to the power of television in this media age. Recognizing he was not well-known, Zschau blanketed the state with a series of radio and television commercials designed to rectify that situation. The strategy worked, and Zschau surprised quite a few analysts by winning the Republican nomination, 37 percent to 30 percent for Herschensohn. The so-called right wing of the party split their votes, and the man from Silicon Valley won the necessary plurality.

The campaign proved a bitter one, with Cranston accusing his opponent of inconsistencies in his voting record (you might not always agree with Cranston but you *always* knew where he stood) and Zschau pointing to Cranston's "extreme" liberalism and, not very subtly, his age. Television commercials featured a young and vigorous-looking Zschau juxtaposed with a picture of a scowling and elderly looking Cranston. Cranston's lead began to slip away but on election day he managed to squeak through by a mere 120,000 votes out of over 7 million cast. That he could win at all when at the same time Republican Deukmejian was swamping Tom Bradley only provides further evidence of Californians' penchant for splitting their tickets.

The 1988 General Election

The 1988 general election saw Californians cast their votes for continuity. They gave the state's electoral college votes to George Bush, heir to and supporter of Ronald Reagan's policies, and returned Pete Wilson to the U.S. Senate for a second term. They made no changes in the partisan makeup of the state's congressional delegation and few in the state legislature. The voters seemed to make a judgment that things were, in general, going pretty well and so no changes were needed.

George Bush won California's 47 electoral college votes from Massachusetts Governor Michael Dukakis in a bruising and sometimes bitterly contested campaign. As in the rest of the country, exchanges of negative television commercials predominated as each side tried to portray the other's candidate as unfit to serve in the nation's highest office. Public reaction was predictable: Many decided neither man deserved to win and stayed home on election day. Turnout dropped to less than half of California's voting-age population.

The race for United States senator was, in many respects, just as negative. Democratic challenger Lieutenant Governor Leo McCarthy charged incumbent Republican Pete Wilson with being the "captive of polluters," and each accused the other of voting to cut Social Security while Wilson noted McCarthy's support for the unpopular former chief justice of the California Supreme Court, Rose Bird. In the end voters apparently did not feel McCarthy had given them sufficient reason to make a change, and Wilson was reelected, 53–44, the first time anyone holding what had come to be known as "the jinx seat" had been returned to office since William Knowland in 1952.

There was no change in the Democrats' 27–18 advantage in the state's congressional delegation as the Burton gerrymander of 1982, which locked party control of virtually all seats continued to work its magic. As for the state legislature, the senate also was unchanged at 24–15 Democratic with one Independent.

For many Californians, interest focused on several of the 29 propositions they found on their ballots.

The initiatives proved much more controversial—and expensive. Topping the list were five that sought to address the auto insurance crisis. The skyrocketing cost of insurance premiums and the apparent inability of the state legislature to deal with the problem led to three propositions sponsored by the insurance industry designed to reduce their costs, one by the trial lawyers to require a reduction in premiums for "good drivers," and a fifth, sponsored by consumer groups, that had the backing of activist Ralph Nader. The last was the most sweeping and included a mandated 20 percent rate reduction for everyone and a further 20 percent cut for "good drivers." A massive media and direct mail campaign was waged by the insurance industry and, to a lesser extent, the trial lawyers. In the end the public adopted a position that might be described as "a plague on both your houses," rejecting their propositions in favor of the least well-financed of them all, the Nader proposal. The insurance industry immediately appealed to the state supreme court on the grounds that, if implemented, they would be forced to operate at a loss. The court upheld the bulk of the measure in May 1989, but placed the rate rollbacks in question by permitting exceptions where companies could show such reductions would deny them a "fair and reasonable return" on their investments.

In other actions the voters approved a 25 cent a pack increase in the tobacco tax, the revenues to be used for a variety of health and public service programs (this despite a multimillion dollar campaign waged against it by the tobacco industry) and adopted a measure sponsored by Superintendent of Public Instruction Bill Honig and the California Teachers Association that established a minimum funding level of 39 percent of the general fund budget for public schools from kindergarten through the community colleges.

ELECTIONS IN THE 1990s

The 1990 Gubernatorial Primary Election

The 1990 campaign for governor began with a bruising battle for the Democratic nomination between two major contenders, Attorney General John Van de Kamp and former San Francisco Mayor Dianne Feinstein. Several moments stood out, most of them favorable to Feinstein. Her strong defense of the death penalty caused her to be booed at the Democratic state convention but cheered by an electorate that has consistently favored it over the years. Taking a stance later to be emulated by presi-

Dianne Feinstein. (Photo courtesy of Senator Feinstein's office)

dential candidate Bill Clinton, Feinstein sought to portray herself as a different kind of Democrat, strong on law and order yet caring. The "caring" aspect was epitomized in an enormously effective television commercial showing her in news footage taking charge following the assassinations of Mayor George Moscone and Supervisor Harvey Milk in 1978. This commercial turned around a campaign that had seemed dead in the water. Indeed, her first campaign manager quit, saying she lacked the necessary motivation to win. After the ad ran for a month in major media markets (at a cost of $600,000), she passed Van de Kamp, never to fall behind again.

Meanwhile, Van de Kamp, the early front-runner, spent much of his time, effort, and money rounding up support for three ballot measures he intended to use as major parts of his platform in the general election. Of course he never made it to the finals; however, the initiatives did. The endorsement he received as the "official" Democratic candidate buoyed him briefly, but failed to ignite his personal campaign, which many found lackluster at best. In June he was soundly defeated by Feinstein, 52–41.

On the Republican side there were no highlight events. The remarkable aspect of the GOP primary was the absence of any significant challenger to Senator Pete Wilson. He had long been heartily disliked by party conservatives as too liberal on

Caucus

by Hügo

Caucus. (Courtesy World West Features)

such issues as abortion and for his support for Gerald Ford over Ronald Reagan in the 1976 presidential primary. The right wing of the party, badly in need of a win to prevent another Democratic gerrymander of election districts following the 1990 census (see Chapter 6), swallowed hard and joined in the effort to get him elected.

The 1990 General Election

The Wilson-Feinstein contest was marked by strong attacks by each side on the other, this despite the long friendship that had grown between them from the time both were mayors of major California cities. Charges and countercharges flew thick and fast. Some bordered on the ridiculous, such as Wilson's claim that Feinstein and her husband had benefited from the savings-and-loan bailout because they "owned" an S&L. That might have stretched matters a bit since Feinstein and her husband, Richard Bloom, held a 1 percent interest in a Medford, Oregon, institution. On the other side, Wilson was accused of being "bought" by the savings-and-loan industry since it had contributed more to him than any other senator. True enough, but more S&Ls are found in California than in any other state and no evidence was ever produced showing Wilson's votes had been influenced. One factor in all this slamming may have been the fact both were moderates and there was not a great deal of difference between them on "hot button" issues. Iraq's invasion of Kuwait may have helped Wilson, a noted hawk on defense issues, and the fact he had millions in campaign funds while Feinstein came out of her hard-fought primary nearly broke also helped. And there was the matter of organization. The Republicans far outdistanced the Democrats by signing up new voters by a margin of 2–1. They did a better job of getting absentee voters to mail in their ballots as well. In any event, Wilson pulled out a close win in November, 49–46.

Other Races in 1990

The other close contest turned out to be between Arlo Smith and Dan Lungren for attorney general. Again, most of the campaigning was negative as each sought to portray the other in a bad light. Lungren was a right-wing extremist, the captive of crazies, while Smith was ineffective as a prosecutor, his record as district attorney demonstrating his poor work. Smith countered by pointing out an undeniable fact: Lungren had never prosecuted a case in his life. In the end the difference turned out to be those absentee ballots. It took over a week to count them all and reverse a 30,000 vote lead for Smith on election day.

As for the other constitutional offices, the Democrats swept, some consolation for losing the two top positions. Eu, McCarthy, Davis, Brown, and Garamendi all won handily. Five supreme court justices up for reconfirmation all won new 12-year terms easily.

The deluge of ballot propositions on the November ballot (a near-record 28 of them) spawned a host of editorials around the state deploring the excess. Space does not permit a full airing of them and so only a few comments will have to suffice. The use of counter-initiatives was apparent. If environmentalists had a proposition, timber interests put one on (see Chapter 5 for more on the counter-initiative). Of all the environmental initiatives, Proposition 128, dubbed "Big Green," was the most ambitious. It was massive, over 10,000 words, and nothing if not comprehensive. It dealt with everything from prohibiting depletion of the ozone layer through pesticide use to polluting of the seas by oil drilling. In one of the more dramatic television commercials, a very young girl, bald from chemotherapy treatments for her cancer, pleaded for voter support of Big Green. No evidence was shown that her cancer would have been prevented by adoption of the proposition's provisions, however. Opponents trotted out a major authority figure in the person of C. Everett Koop, the former surgeon general of the United States, who solemnly proclaimed Big Green would do no good. Whether for that reason or because they did not trust a document so long and complicated, Big Green was rejected by the voters by a whopping 36–64 vote.

Showing a renewed spirit of antitax fervor, the voters overwhelmingly turned down five tax increase propositions, two to boost liquor taxes which involved use of the counter-initiative. The voters also turned thumbs down on most of the bond issues, including a number that in past years had been approved with ease. Among the casualties were bonds for parks, higher education, county jails, and child care, to mention a few. Only veterans' bonds and school bonds survived, and those narrowly.

The 1992 Primary Election

Several things stood out as different about the 1992 primary election, but one constant remained: California's vote had no influence on the selection of parties' presidential nominees. By the time Californians got around to voting, the candidates for November had already long since locked up their nominations, George Bush for the Republicans and Bill Clinton for the Democrats. The failure of the legislature to move the state's presidential preference primary to the first Tuesday in March as proposed by Assemblyman Jim Costa (D-Fresno) once again left the state's major contribution to the selection process one of sending money to other states.

Among the differences was the selection of two women to run for the U.S. Senate. This was made possible by Pete Wilson's resignation from the Senate to become governor and the requirement that a newly appointed senator must go before the voters at the next election. Thus, for the first time since joining the Union, there were two Senate contests. First, the Democrats. In one contest, the one for the so-called "short seat" vacated by Wilson and therefore only the two years remaining in that term, Dianne Feinstein was pitted against Controller Gray Davis. The Feinstein name, familiar now as a result of the close loss in the race for governor in 1990, proved too formidable for the well-financed Davis, this despite charges by the Fair Political Practices Commission of significant campaign reporting violations by Feinstein's campaign organization stemming from the 1990 gubernatorial contest. The so-called "long seat" (a full six-year term was at stake) saw liberal Congressional Representative Barbara Boxer's principal opposition coming from Lieutenant Governor Leo McCarthy, a well-known veteran of state politics, and another liberal member of the state's congressional delegation, Mel Levine, who had the formidable B & D campaign consultant organization in his corner and the largest war chest. However, Boxer campaigned vigorously up and down the state and gradually supporters of McCarthy shifted toward her, this despite revelations she had bounced a number of checks at the House bank (a charge that caused several incumbents to lose their seats elsewhere). Levine spent in the neighborhood of $5 million, most of it on television commercials that proved largely ineffective. Known as the stealth candidate, Levine made few public appearances in contrast to Boxer. The result was a surprisingly easy victory for Boxer (44 percent) over McCarthy (31 percent) and Levine (22 percent).

On the Republican side, John Seymour, who had been handpicked by Wilson to replace him, faced no major opposition for the short seat, though the right wing of the party gave its support to William Dannemeyer, a quite conservative member of the House of Representatives. The long seat proved quite a different matter. Bruce Herschensohn, that conservative Southern California television commentator who lost to Ed Zschau in the 1986 primary, represented a clear choice against moderate Representative Tom Campbell. While the Seymour-Dannemeyer contest was fairly low key, this one was hard-hitting (occasionally below the belt). Each side repeatedly accused the other of lying. Herschensohn claimed Campbell lied in claiming to be a conservative (he was on economic issues but more moderate to liberal on social questions). Campbell accused his opponent of trying to scuttle Social Security (Herschensohn in the past had argued it should be privatized) which Herschensohn denied. It was less than an "elevated" campaign and in the end the fact that Herschensohn was so well known in Southern California where most of the votes are, especially in a Republican primary where more conservatives are likely to vote, gave the nod to Herschensohn.

The 1992 General Election

For only the second time since Harry Truman did it in 1948, the Democrats carried California in the presidential contest. Interestingly, both candidates tried to portray themselves as "new" Trumans, but to no real effect. George Bush's popularity in the state plummeted as the recession was prolonged. In the end, the GOP strategists effectively wrote off the state and the president made no trips to it during the general election campaign. Both Clinton and independent Ross Perot spent time in the state, but the outcome was never really in doubt from Labor Day on. That may have been a factor in the losses suffered by a number of Republicans running for Congress and the state legislature. In conservative Orange County Bush's margin was a third what it had been in 1988. The final tally nearly mirrored the rest of the country with Clinton receiving 46 percent of the vote to Bush's 32 percent and Perot's 22 percent.

The Short Seat   There was little drama in this race between Dianne Feinstein and John Seymour. From the beginning, Seymour faced an unusual situation in that he, an incumbent, was far less well known than his opponent. Despite hard work and long days on the campaign trail, Seymour was never able to break the public's indifference toward him. In the end Feinstein won "going away," 55 percent to 36 percent.

The Long Seat   If Feinstein's victory seemed likely from the start, Boxer's seemed to be—and then was not. She began the campaign with a number of advantages. She, like Feinstein, was a woman in what was forecast to be "the year of the woman" (and turned out to be just that). She was generally seen as being helped by the selection of Bruce Herschensohn as her opponent. Many thought her very liberal record (one observer said she never saw a spending bill she didn't like) would have made her an easy target for the moderate Tom Campbell. For those who like clear choices, this was a contest made in heaven. He was pro-life, she pro-choice. He wanted to drill for oil off the coast, she opposed all such drilling. He wanted no cuts of any kind in defense spending and opposed gun control, she took the opposite positions in both cases. Strategically, Boxer tried to moderate her image by moving toward the center while Herschensohn was unabashedly conservative to the core. That may have helped his credibility as the campaign progressed because his numbers in the polls began to improve and improve steadily. At one time down 20 points, by election day polling types were saying the race was "too close to call." One last-minute allegation may have turned the tide for Boxer. A leading Democrat charged Herschensohn made frequent visits to a bookstore selling pornographic materials. Herschensohn said he bought quite respectable newspapers on his visits. Whatever the effect of this charge, Boxer came out the winner, 48–43.

One of the true surprises of the election was the extent to which Democrats held their own under the new—and presumably more fair—reapportionment. Instead of losing ground, they actually gained a seat in the assembly while holding their own in the senate. As for Congress, it was expected the Republicans would pick up at least 5 of the 7 new seats available. Instead the Democrats won three of them to gain a 30–22

Barbara Boxer. (Photo courtesy of Senator Boxer's office)

edge in the congressional delegation (compared with the 27–18 they had before the election).

Thirteen propositions graced the ballot but most of those considered controversial failed to win voter support. The most successful was Proposition 164, which was overwhelmingly approved (59–42) and set term limits for California's representatives in Congress: three two-year terms for the House and two six-year terms for the Senate. Those favoring the limits for the most part made the same arguments they had in 1990 in gaining passage of Proposition 140, the state officials' limits (see Chapter 6). Opponents also stuck to much the same points, though they questioned the power of a state to set qualifications for federal office. The U.S. Supreme Court sided with the opponents in May 1995, ruling that such state-imposed limits for *federal* office are unconstitutional.

Other propositions approved included repeal of a tax on snack foods that many found irrational in its application (a tax was imposed on popcorn but not on doughnuts) and a proposition put on the ballot by public employees that banned what they termed "raids" on their pension funds in order to fund state programs. Losers included measures to allow assisted suicide, a plan to require employers to provide health insurance, and one by Pete Wilson that would have cut welfare checks and given the governor added power in the event of a fiscal emergency. The last was deemed both an attack on society's most vulnerable and a power grab. Two propositions designed to save two watchdog agencies—the legislative analyst and auditor general, threatened with elimination in the aftermath of Proposition 140's mandated cuts in legislative staffs—also lost.

The November 1993 Special Election

Governor Wilson called a special election for November 1993, the immediate stimulus for which was to provide an opportunity for the voters to decide whether a special half-cent sales tax added in 1991 to deal with the deficit should be made permanent or, as promised when it was adopted, allowed to lapse. Though this seemed likely to be a highly contentious issue when first placed on the ballot, debate over it proved to be relatively mild, especially in contrast to the fierce fight over school vouchers on the same ballot. With Wilson reversing himself (his police allies convinced him the added revenues were essential to public safety), the opposition was largely limited to taxpayer groups opposed to most proposals to increase taxes for whatever purpose. In the end, Proposition 172 extending the tax was approved.

Five of the seven propositions on the ballot were turned down, including one that generated both national attention and high feelings on both sides, the school voucher initiative. Proponents of Proposition 174 argued the public school system was a near monopoly and could be forced to improve its performance by giving it more competition. That competition was to be encouraged by providing a voucher worth $2,600 of public money to mostly private schools for each child they enrolled. Backers pointed to poor test scores, high dropout rates, and violence on campus as reasons to provide parents with a choice of where their children should be educated. Opponents, led by the California Teachers Association and other education groups, admitted the need to improve but said taking good students out of public schools (private schools could refuse to accept difficult students) would only make matters worse. They also pointed out that those already in private schools would shortly qualify for vouchers at a cost of $1.3 billion a year, this at a time when the state budget was in real trouble. Then there were questions of accountability (How would the funds be monitored?), curriculum content (What would be taught?), and qualifications (even a witches' coven could qualify if it gathered 25 warm bodies) that ultimately led to the defeat of the voucher proposal . . . for the time being.

The 1994 Primary Election

There were few surprises in the 1994 primary elections. The contest for the Democratic nomination for governor was expected to go to State Treasurer Kathleen Brown despite the best efforts of Insurance Commissioner John Garamendi. He attempted to "hang" Brown's personal opposition to the death penalty on her campaign and her refusal to explain her position (her response was, "I will enforce the law") frustrated both Garamendi and a number of reporters. That appeared to matter little in the primary and Brown defeated Garamendi 48 percent to 33 percent with 14 percent going to state senator Tom Hayden.

On the Republican side incumbent Governor Pete Wilson expected a free ride only to find himself challenged by multimillionaire Ron Unz, a political neophyte willing to spend several million dollars of his own money in what most thought was a rerun of the old television series *Mission Impossible*. Unz's message: Wilson is too far left to be a real Republican. Cut government, cut taxes, eliminate workers' compensation, drop all nonacademic coursework in schools. Get back to basics all around. The message was attractive to many conservatives and, with an appeal based on his support for tough measures to deal with crime and an equally tough stance with respect to illegal aliens, Unz pulled a not inconsiderable 34 percent of the vote in the June election.

The parties' primaries for the U.S. Senate were interesting in that neither frontrunner bothered to campaign against the competition (something also for the most part true of the gubernatorial primary). Michael Huffington emulated the Zschau campaign in 1986. He bought large amounts of television time to attack Feinstein's vote for President Clinton's budget and in the process made himself much better known. He came from a 7 percent support level in January to 38 percent in May. Feinstein finally responded by pointing to Huffington's failure to pay taxes in California (his business interests and part-time home were in Texas). The results in the primary were a foregone conclusion as Feinstein won 74 percent of the Democratic vote and Huffington got 55 percent to conservative William Dannemeyer's 29 percent of the Republican vote. That Feinstein lost over a quarter of the Democratic vote to two total unknowns was troubling to party leaders, however.

The other contests were far less visible. A Field poll in the latter part of May found most people in the "don't know/don't care" category. That showed up on election day when less than 40 percent of registered voters bothered to cast ballots, the lowest since statistics began being kept in 1916. Interest, to the extent it existed at all, focused on several state officeholders seeking to move over or up to avoid the swiftly descending sword of term limits. Some were successful, others not. If there was a surprise in the other contests it was in the defeat of David Roberti by former Democratic state chairman Phil Angelides of Sacramento for that party's nomination for treasurer. It was widely thought that Roberti had the edge following his well-publicized success in defeating a gun owners' effort to recall him. However, that used up much of his campaign war chest and he was unable to reply to a vigorous (some said vicious) attack in television advertisements depicting him as the friend of those convicted in the FBI "sting." The implication was that he was somehow involved, though no evidence to that effect was found. The Republican candidate, Matt Fong, the son of March Fong Eu and a member of the Board of Equalization, was unopposed.

There were few surprises among the propositions either. Perhaps the exception was the fact that all four bond issues were defeated, including formerly popular ones that were to aid school construction and parks. It was apparent the public was uncomfortable with the total of $5.9 billion they were being asked to approve. They also rejected an effort to restore the renters' tax credit ($60 a year for singles, $120 for couples), probably believing the cost was too high given the state's precarious fiscal condition. A measure (Proposition 179) that raised the minimum term for murder by drive-by shooting from 15 years to 20 years was approved by a whopping 88 percent of the voters, a further indication that crime was at the top of the voters' list of concerns.

One question pondered by political analysts was why only 35 percent of registered voters bothered to cast ballots. There were several explanations. There was little question who was going to win the gubernatorial or senate nominations. There was no "hot" issue on the ballot like gun control or property tax relief to draw people to the polls. And there were many who said the public was simply turned off, turned off by negative campaign commercials and by a system that seemed unable to deal effectively with the problems facing the state.

The 1994 General Election

The campaigns for governor and United States senator never paused for the traditional summer break. Not for these candidates the old maxim that held general election campaigns should kick off on Labor Day. Instead Pete Wilson, Kathleen Brown, Dianne Feinstein, and Michael Huffington spent millions on television advertising over the summer months. In part, that reflects advances in video technology. No longer does it take two to three weeks to respond to an attack; a couple of days will suffice. For example, a Wilson advertisement claimed Ms. Brown did not support his call for "one strike and you're out" for rapists and child molesters. Within a few days she was on screen saying she did and he lied. A few days later he ran a commercial quoting newspapers to the effect his charge was accurate.

The race for governor was of special interest for several reasons. One was the presence of another Brown, Kathleen, seeking to follow in her father Pat's and brother Jerry's footsteps in becoming governor. Second, she would become the first woman to occupy the governor's chair if elected. Third, Pete Wilson was attempting one of the biggest comebacks in state if not national political history. Seen as politically dead in 1993, his rise in the polls (helped by a somewhat inept Brown campaign) gave visions of the phoenix rising from the ashes.

The campaign was largely negative, with each candidate slashing at the stands of the opponent. Brown tried to stress the state's poor economy (comparing recoveries in other Western states with the lack of one in California) and noting 550,000 jobs lost during Wilson's administration. He, however, put her on the defensive on two "hot button" issues: Crime, where her personal objection to the death penalty put her at a disadvantage, as it had in the primary, and illegal immigration, which she was described as failing to see as a major problem while most Californians did. She did support the "three strikes and you're out" initiative, which blunted a bit the Wilson attack on her as soft on crime. Still, polls during September and October indicated Wilson had a significant edge with the voters on most issues, including, surprisingly enough, the economy. Only when it came to education did Brown have a major lead. Critics pointed to Brown's campaign as unfocused in contrast to Wilson's unremitting stress on crime and illegal immigration (with, it should be noted, an occasional foray into economics with claims he had saved jobs that otherwise would have left the state).

In the final analysis Kathleen Brown may have summed up the reason for her 15-point loss when she said "I was in the wrong place and the wrong time with the wrong message."[1] Had she run in 1992, "the year of the woman" when her kind of issues were more prominent, she might have won.

The contest for United States Senate involved a campaign that had actually begun in the primary since both Dianne Feinstein and Michael Huffington had ignored their primary opponents to focus their attacks on one another. As in the gubernatorial campaign, television played an enormous role and with the millionaires going at one another; the attack commercials flew through the airways thick and fast. In the final accounting this was the most expensive campaign in the nation's history with over $41 million spent ($29 million by Huffington, $27.5 million his own money, and $12.5 million by Feinstein, $2.5 million her own money). The strength of the Huffington challenge came as something of a surprise. Feinstein had made a considerable name for herself as a first-term senator, successfully sponsoring several measures that were deemed by most to be impossible to pass. One was a massive desert protection bill that former Senator Alan Cranston had attempted to push through with no success for seven years. Another was a ban on 19 semi-automatic weapons which was narrowly approved by both houses. Huffington, on the other hand, had made no particular impression during his equal time in the House, having decided to run for the Senate a few months after spending $5.4 million of his own money to win election to the lower house. The television blitz nonetheless brought him to within seven percentage points of Feinstein by the time of the primary.

The race was characterized by nasty attack advertisements from both sides. Huffington attacked her as a government-loving liberal who betrayed California with her vote to approve President Clinton's budget. She struck back saying he had done nothing during his time in the House and was, after all, a transplanted Texan who failed to pay state income taxes while maintaining a ghost home in the Lone Star state. Basically, it came down to a candidate who thought government had a role to play in the solution of society's problems versus one who thought much of government at the federal level should be dismantled. By mid-September they were in a dead heat according to the polls. Election day results confirmed the closeness of the contest and it was not until some 700,000 absentee ballots were counted that Ms. Feinstein was declared the winner by 166,000 out of 7.788 million votes cast.

The Republicans did unusually well in both the other statewide races and in the assembly. Attorney General Dan Lungren easily defeated Democrat Tom Umberg 54–39. Umberg's television advertisement that claimed Lungren was responsible for the death of Polly Klass because a new computer tracking system had been delayed by diversion of money to Lungren's public relations fund (a charge vehemently denied by Lungren) was denounced by virtually all the mass media outlets. Gray Davis was an equally easy victor over Cathy Wright for lieutenant governor, winning 52–40. Republican Bill Jones, a member of the assembly representing Fresno, defeated acting Secretary of State Tony Miller for that office and in the process became the first person from the Central Valley to be elected to statewide office. Kathleen Connell successfully survived the Republican tide, narrowly defeating Republican Tom McClintock (48–46). Matt Fong, the son of former Secretary of State March Fong Eu, won the treasurer's position over Phil Angeledes (48–43) but

---

[1]*Los Angeles Times*, November 13, 1994, p. A3.

as a Republican, having left his mother's party. The insurance commissioner slot went to Republican Chuck Quakenbush over Art Torres (49–43) and Delaine Eastin, head of the assembly education committee, defeated Maureen DiMarco, who was Pete Wilson's secretary of education, for superintendent of public instruction. The battle over congressional and state legislative seats was in some cases fierce. The Republicans, feeling the disenchantment of the public with Congress and politics in general, believed they had a great opportunity to pick up several seats in Congress (and hoped to gain control of both houses through similar gains across the nation). The final result was a net gain of four seats, for a congressional delegation of 26 Democrats and 26 Republicans.

In the senate the lineup was modestly changed with Republicans narrowing the Democrat edge to 21–17 with two independents. But the picture was radically different in the assembly where the Republicans anticipated picking up three to four seats and ended up winning eight seats (four involved open seats and four where incumbent Democrats lost) for a 41–39 advantage. It was the first time since 1970 the Republicans secured a majority. It was thought that one consequence would be that Willie Brown would be deposed as speaker, a position he had held for 14 years. However, Paul Horcher, who had feuded with his Republican Party leadership for several years, declared himself an independent and voted for Brown, leading to a 40–40 tie. That led to a great deal of behind the scenes maneuvering and threats of recall (ultimately successful) against Horcher and several Democrats (not successful) who had proclaimed themselves during the campaign as independent of Brown and yet had voted for him.

The reason for the Republican near sweep, many analysts said, was anger at government in general, anger at President Clinton, and the fact Republicans were able to make the election a national referendum on the Clinton presidency. Former Speaker of the House of Representatives Tip O'Neill had maintained "all politics is local" but not in 1994.

There were four major propositions on the ballot that proved contentious. One, Proposition 184, was called "three strikes and you're out" because a third felony conviction led to a sentence of 25 years to life, whichever was greater. Proponents pointed to the incidence of violent crime[2] and what they perceived to be a legislature controlled by those more interested in protecting the rights of criminals than those of their victims. The first time around a bill to enact three strikes failed to get out of committee in the assembly, but with the Klass killing it sailed through both houses later and was signed into law by the governor. Why, then, the initiative? Fear that a new legislature might water down the strict provisions of the law, something much more difficult to do if contained in an initiative.

Opponents said three strikes was far too wide-ranging, that the third strike could be for a nonviolent crime (one famous case involved theft of a piece of pizza), and that our courts would become even more overcrowded with few plea bargains and our prisons jammed (20 new ones were estimated to be needed as a result of this law).

In the end there was no doubt the measure would pass and it did, by a whopping 72–28 margin.

---

[2]The proposition was the result of the killing of Kimber Reynolds of Fresno by a felon released early and given a major shot in the arm later by the kidnap-murder of 12-year-old Polly Klass of Petaluma.

The other truly "hot" issue was Proposition 187, the so-called Save Our State initiative. Its supporters were incensed at the flood of illegal immigrants entering the state and wanted to "send a message" to Washington to do something about it and in the meantime to cut off benefits costing state taxpayers billions of dollars a year. (Estimates ranged between $1.5 billion and $5 billion.) The children of these illegal immigrants were to be shut out of school, only emergency medical care would be provided, and welfare payments would be denied. Opponents responded that this would do nothing to secure our borders, would endanger public health, and unfairly punish children for something clearly not their fault. Some pointed out kids left on the street all day could do a good deal of mischief. On a different level, many charged the proposition was inherently racist and would result in targeting anyone with brown skin. Polls showed early enthusiasm for it waning in the face of opposition from the media, church groups, and others, but apparently many lied to those taking the polls; it passed 59–41. At least nine lawsuits were filed immediately to block its implementation and it seemed clear the legality of the proposition would have to be decided ultimately by the U.S. Supreme Court.

Turnout was far higher than in the primary with 60.45 percent of registered voters casting ballots (or 47 percent of those who could have voted if registered). The popularity of absentee voting continued to grow with 22 percent of voters electing to use them.

The 1996 Primary Election

The state's attempt to become a significant player in the 1996 presidential sweepstakes was less than a rousing success. Despite moving the primary from the first Tuesday in June to the last Tuesday in March, it remained a nonstarter as other states moved their primaries even earlier. The result was that, once again, the party candidates for the presidency were decided before Californians had a chance to express an opinion. President Clinton faced no organized opposition while Bob Dole, the Republican standard bearer, had sewn up that nomination before the end of March.

Propositions on the March ballot failed to stir emotions even approximating those associated with the anti-illegal immigrant initiative of 1994. Two propositions to impose the death penalty on carjackers and drive-by shooters (195, 196) were given overwhelming approval. Another attempt to create no-fault car insurance was easily defeated. A good deal of heat, if little light, was generated by propositions that would have limited lawyers' contingency fees[3]—both were defeated. However, Proposition 202, which would have limited such fees to 15 percent where the effort required by legal counsel was minimal, nearly passed, losing only 49–51. That stimulated another initiative that appeared on the November ballot prohibiting legislative action to put a limit on these fees (see below). Proposition 198, which sought to end the state's use of the closed primary system, though opposed by both the major political parties, won easily (59–41). Details are provided in Chapter 4.

---

[3]Contingency fees are involved when a lawyer agrees to take a case without any guarantee of payment apart from a percentage of whatever award is given by the court. If the case is lost, the lawyer receives nothing; if it is won, he or she gets anything from 15 percent to 40 percent of the money won by the client.

The 1996 General Election

The presidential contest was thought from the start to be "Bill Clinton's to lose". He didn't. Bob Dole never made serious inroads on the president's early lead in California, though, unlike George Bush in 1992, he never stopped trying. Millions of dollars were spent on television advertising in the last month in an effort to win the state—or perhaps to avoid another devastating loss of congressional and state legislative seats such as took place in 1992. In the end the president carried the state 51–38 with Ross Perot gaining a distant 7 percent. Ralph Nader, nominated by the Green Party, did not campaign and received 2 percent of the vote.

Republicans lost three seats in the congressional delegation, all of the incumbents having been closely identified with House speaker Newt Gingrich. Perhaps especially surprising was the loss of conservative Bob (B-1 Bob) Dornan, challenged by a Hispanic woman in an increasingly Hispanic district in normally Republican Orange County. That left the state's congressional delegation at 29–23 Democratic.

A similar pattern emerged in the state legislature. Democrats regained control of the assembly and promptly elected the first Hispanic speaker in the state's history, Cruz Bustamante. In a blow to the conservative leader in the senate, Bob Hurtt, the Democrats enlarged their edge there as well.

A good deal of heat was generated by several ballot propositions. The greatest amount centered on Proposition 209, titled the California Civil Rights Initiative

(Tom Meyer, *San Francisco Chronicle*)

(CCRI) and derided by opponents as an anti-civil rights measure. Those supporting it pointed to practices that gave preferential treatment to minorities and women and argued that such things as admission to college or the awarding of contracts should be based entirely on merit. Those opposed warned of a return to the "old boys network" of earlier times where friends recommended friends and women and minorities were shut out. Though support for the proposition eroded in last stages of the campaign, it eventually passed, 54–46, and was immediately challenged in court.

The other propositions that received significant attention included 215, allowing the medicinal uses of marijuana, 211, tort reform, and 208 and 212, both of which dealt with campaign finance reform.

Proposition 215 asked that private cultivation of marijuana be legalized when use of the drug was approved by a doctor. Anecdotal evidence suggested it was particularly helpful in alleviating nausea in patients undergoing chemotherapy for cancer, helping those suffering from AIDS, and in relieving pressure on the eye from glaucoma. Opponents pointed out the doctor's "prescription" could be oral and that the wording of the proposition was so loose as to permit use of marijuana for a wide variety of maladies, even, they said, for headaches. None of this mattered to the majority of the electorate which voted, 56–44, to approve it. However, the Clinton administration immediately threatened to deny doctors authorizing use of the drug the right to prescribe *anything*, thus preventing them from the practice of medicine, this on the basis of federal law declaring such use illegal.

Campaign finance reform had been an "in" topic for years (see the 1988 general election). With the feeling that no substantial reform was likely to come from the state legislature (the people thinking that those who benefitted from the existing system were unlikely to change it), two measures appeared on this ballot. Proposition 212 was the more stringent in limiting contributions to just $100 for local contests and $200 for statewide elections (compared with 208's limits of $250 and $500) and it set upper limits on contributions from outside the district at 25 percent. What led to its defeat may have been a provision that would have ended the ban on honoraria and gifts established by Proposition 112 (see page. 112). Most newspapers endorsed 208, which was sponsored by the League of Women Voters and Common Cause, among others, and opposed 212. In the end 212 narrowly lost (49–51) and 208 won easily (61–39).

A "sleeper" may have been Proposition 218. It received virtually no media coverage and there was little campaigning on either side. It was approved by a wide margin, 56–44. It requires that all increases in local taxes or fees (for such services as garbage collection, sewage disposal, libraries, parks and the like) must be approved by vote of the public. Taxes or assessments imposed after December 31, 1994, must go to the voters within two years for their approval. It was touted by proponents as closing loopholes used by local government to get around the limitations created by Proposition 13; opponents argued it would cost local governments hundreds of millions of dollars a year and lead to greater costs due to lower credit ratings for municipal bonds. In fact, that happened shortly after passage of Proposition 218 as credit ratings for San Diego and Sacramento were reduced.

The voters also approved bond issues for water supply development and veterans' housing (while defeating one for jails) and continued their "get tough on crime" policy by voting to deny those who got into accidents while committing a felony or while driving drunk or without insurance the right to sue for "pain and suffering" (recovery of actual medical costs was still allowed).

POLITICAL PARTIES

In the 1996 elections eight organizations had legal status as political parties in California: the Democratic Party, the Republican Party, the American Independent Party, the Libertarian Party, the Peace and Freedom Party, the Green Party, the Reform Party, and the Natural Law Party. Legal status as a political party gives an organization the right to have the names of its candidates for public office printed on the official election ballot. Legal status also obligates a political organization to keep its structure and procedures in conformity with explicit provisions in the Elections Code. Without legal recognition a political organization may still run candidates for office, but their names must be handwritten on the ballot by their supporters on election day.

Requirements for Legal Status

Legal recognition as a political party in California is conferred upon an organization that either obtains a registration of at least 1 percent of the total number of registered voters or files a petition signed by a number of voters equal to 10 percent of the vote cast for governor in the preceding election. Once recognized, a party continues to appear on the ballot as long as it passes *both* of the following tests: In any gubernatorial election one of its candidates for statewide office must receive at least 2 percent of the vote cast, and it must maintain at least one-fifteenth of 1 percent of the total registration. Having received 5 percent of the vote for governor in 1978, Ed Clark did not automatically gain legal status for his Libertarian Party, since he was not identified as a Libertarian. Clark and the party protested this technicality and threatened to bring the issue into the courts to compel the secretary of state to confer legal status on what was now the third largest party in the state. (The Prohibition Party and the Communist Party are among those organizations that once were on the official ballot but are now disqualified for failing to meet the state requirement.)

Formal Structure and Functions

To say that California law is explicit concerning the structure and basic functions of political parties is an understatement. The Election Code goes into such detail that it seems as if the only thing left to the discretion of party leaders themselves is the preparation of a menu to be served convention delegates.[4]

State law provides that every recognized political party must hold its *state convention* at Sacramento once every two years. The convention usually lasts two days. Its

---

[4]For example, "The convention shall be called to order at 10 o'clock . . . by the retiring chairman of the state central committee. It shall at once proceed to the election of a temporary chairman by a roll call read from an alphabetical roll. . . ." (Section 2807) "The convention shall . . . adopt a State platform for its party which shall be made public not later than 6 o'clock in the afternoon of the following day." (Section 2809)

principal functions are to draft the state platform and to select presidential elector candidates. The members of the convention consist of all party nominees and holdovers for statewide and congressional offices, and the Republicans add certain party officials to this number.[5]

The day after the state convention has finished its deliberations, the state *central committee* meets, also at Sacramento, to elect the officers of the party's executive committee and to propose certain legislation.

The state central committee is a large body of party leaders composed of all members of the state convention and a number of their appointees. (The Democrats elect additional members by caucus in each assembly district.) The chairpersons of all county central committees and the national committeemen and committeewomen serve as members of the state central committee.

The *executive committee* of each party has the *formal* responsibility to oversee party affairs and campaigns. Occasionally, the committee appoints district campaign committees to assist congressional and state legislative candidates. The day-to-day management of the affairs of the formal party organization is carried out by the chairperson and vice-chairperson. These top offices provide no monetary compensation and have little formal power.

Membership of the executive committee consists of the chairpersons of the 58 county central committees, the cochairpersons of the 45 congressional districts, the state officeholders, and the elected officers of the state central committee—a group of about 160 persons.

Members of the *county central committees* of the party are chosen by the voters in each county. County committees are elected in the *biennial* partisan primaries for terms of two years. In larger counties they are elected by assembly districts; in smaller counties they are elected by supervisorial districts. In addition to the elected members, party nominees for state offices and incumbents living in the county are ex officio members of the committee. County committees vary in size, but none may have fewer than 21 elected members. The total elected from Los Angeles County is about 250, made up of about 7 elected from each of the assembly districts in the county.

There is very little formal connection between the official state parties and the national organizations. The main link is provided by *national committee members* who serve on the national committee. The national committee's operations are largely devoted to presidential election activities. Because of the manner of selecting national committee members, their ties to their official party organization in California may be tenuous.

Factional Organizations Within Parties

Hiram Johnson's Progressives, in their move to curb the power of the railroads over state politics in the early twentieth century, sought to enhance the power of the public at the expense of the railroad-dominated parties. The initiative, referendum, and recall, together with cross-filing, were all aspects of this objective (see Chapter 2).

---

[5]If the party has no holdover incumbents or nominees for a given office, an "appointive delegate" is named by the party committee in the district concerned.

Among several restrictions on party leaders was one that led to the development of a number of "unofficial" party organizations that for years played a major role in determining candidates for partisan office. By law, parties were prohibited from making preprimary endorsements, presumably limiting the leadership's power to decide who should run and enhancing the role of the rank-and-file membership.

Cross-filing made it possible for Democrats to "cross over" and run for the Republican nomination and vice versa. The possibility that a single candidate from the opposition might be able to gain the nomination with a bare plurality of the vote, the remainder being split among "regular" party members, was made more likely by the inability of party leaders to endorse in the primary. Then, too, until the mid-1950s primary ballots carried no indication of party affiliation to alert the voters. "Raiding" was therefore easier. The Republicans pioneered in the development of voluntary and unofficial organizations created to prevent this from happening. In 1933 a number of progressive Republicans formed the California Republican Assembly (CRA) to identify, develop, and endorse candidates in primary elections. The Democrats followed in 1953 with the California Democratic Council (CDC). Since they were "unofficial," they were not prohibited from endorsing candidates in primary elections.

Both organizations became deeply involved in taking stands on public issues, the CRA becoming more and more conservative and the CDC increasingly liberal. At times their positions proved so far out of the political "mainstream" as to be embarrassing to candidates and party leaders. They needed the organizational endorsements and support these groups provided, but they often attempted to distance themselves from the groups' positions. At that, some Republican activists found the CRA too moderate and split, forming the United Republicans of California. More liberal Republicans established the California Republican League.

The influence of these and other unofficial party organizations lessened in the 1970s. The weakness of the state's parties, the tendency of the public to vote for individuals rather than on party lines, the impact of television with its emphasis on personality—all played a role. The reason for the existence of these groups in the first place disappeared in 1984 when a federal judge in San Francisco ruled that the prohibition against preprimary endorsements violated the First Amendment's guarantee of freedom of speech. Upheld by the ninth Circuit Court of Appeals in 1988, this decision has meant that party leaders now may make such endorsements. Republicans have been reluctant to do so, but Democrats have used the primary endorsement power much more generously, including the state party's endorsement of John Van de Kamp over Dianne Feinstein for governor in 1990 (not noticeably very effective).

Additional Party Groups

Other semiofficial party groups are active in elections from time to time. Young Republicans, Young Democrats, women's party organizations, and university groups have played influential roles within the parties. They may do precinct work, assist at fund-raising events, and cover phone banks on election day, and members frequently participate in discussions concerning the positions to be taken by the party and its candidates.

Although these semiofficial or adjunct groups can still play a role in generating support for a party or candidate, the functions they have traditionally performed have grown less important. Walking precincts has, in many cases, given way to the use of direct mail as a principal means of reaching the voter. Stuffing envelopes was a significant—if boring—task in past years. Today, machines perform this same task and much more efficiently. As technology has taken over, many of the routine jobs of campaigning and those who performed these routines have become less and less important to success.

INTEREST GROUPS

Political parties, and even intraparty factions such as the CDC or CRA, tend to be broad coalitions encompassing a number of different interests and points of view. To be elected, parties need to appeal to many different groups or constituencies. If a party comes to be seen as the "captive" of any one group or narrow ideology, its prospects for victory are likely to disappear. Who, then, speaks for these groups? These are organizations variously called special-interest groups, pressure groups, or vested interests (the last especially if the speaker opposes their goals). Rather than attempting, as parties do, to form electoral coalitions with their inevitable set of compromises (if one group gets all it wants, others will get less than the minimum they will accept and be alienated from the party), interest groups focus on the specific needs of their members. They have an interest in parties and candidates but only as the success of one or the other will affect their goals.

That interest is, however, demonstrated in very concrete ways, and it is here that political action committees (PACs) come in. These organizations are created by special-interest groups for the specific purpose of raising money from supporters, money that is then funneled into the campaigns of candidates likely to be favorably disposed toward the parent group's objectives.

Special Interests

When the term *interest group* is used, most people probably think of some very large organization such as the AFL-CIO or the National Association of Manufacturers (NAM), and they are right but only partially. There is an incredible variety of these groups, all dedicated to bring pressure to bear on government in order to achieve at least some of their objectives. (It is that pressure which leads some to prefer the use of *pressure groups* as a more descriptive label for them.) Of course, not all groups qualify as pressure groups since not all try to influence government. Bird-watching societies and model railroad buffs are examples. But thousands of organized groups are registered in Washington, D.C., whose function it is to try to get policies adopted, laws passed, or court decisions made that are favorable to their members.

California has had a long history of special-interest activity, some of it noted in Chapter 2 where the role of railroads in the politics of the late nineteenth century was discussed. One of the ironies of the Progressive Movement's successful campaign to break the power of the Southern Pacific over state government is that in doing so it broke—or severely diminished—the power of political parties. Yet generally it may be said that where parties are weak, pressure groups are strong. Parties can provide protection against pressure group retaliation for an unfavorable vote, but if the parties are weak that protection ceases to exist. If these groups play too influential a role in state politics today, at least some of the blame must rest with Hiram Johnson's Progressives.

Special-interest groups have a bad image, yet they play a constructive role in bringing the views of elements of our society into the political process. For example, there may be no one in the state legislature to present the views of those involved in the wine industry, but groups such as the California Association of Winegrape Growers can and do.

Special interests vary enormously in size, influence, and goals. Some are almost always involved in pressuring government, whereas others do so only rarely. They are numerous. Some 1,100 lobbyists were registered in Sacramento in 1996. They represented large corporations, farm interests, organized labor, women, churches, environmental interests, doctors, banks, minorities, and small businesses, to mention only a few. From the California Manufacturers Association to the Sierra Club and Burger King to the Mountain Lion Coalition, Mexican-American Political Association, and the California Pistachio Commission they all take their respective cases before legislative committees, administration boards and, at times, the courts.

One very effective way of gaining "access" to legislators and other elected officials is through making contributions to campaign war chests. That, at the least, guarantees "the returned phone call" when you need to make your case. In the 1993–94 election cycle, the ten largest contributors were headed by the California Teachers Association with $1.32 million in contributions. The other "top ten" were the Container Supply Company ($1.22 million), Allied Business PAC—now the California Independent Business PAC ($1.08 million), California Medical Association ($1.04 million), California Trial Lawyers Association ($950,728), California Optometrists PAC ($848,018), California Professional Firefighters Association ($575,450), the California State Employees Association ($516,772), and California Dental Association ($504,875).

Citizens' Groups

Organizations of citizens with similar views on a range of public policy issues such as political reforms and improving the environment are also active in the state's political process. In contrast to the special-interest groups, citizens' groups are often broadly based and include members of various occupations and classes. During the past few years citizens' groups have been increasing their membership and carrying more weight with the voters. For example, although the California Taxpayers Association is technically a lobbying group, it performs considerable research toward achieving economy and efficiency in the spending of tax dollars.

Perhaps the best known citizens' group is the League of Women Voters. Born out of the suffragette movement, the League now operates on local, county, state, and national levels. The California League has 15,000 members, most of whom are white homemakers over 30 years old. (Perhaps in deference to "men's lib," the League has now opened its membership to males.) Each member pays annual dues, and this money is divided among each of the four operative levels (national, state, county, and local). The League's main activities include voter services, study programs, and endorsements of legislation (action). Long known for its thorough and unbiased research of issues, the League is widely respected by voters and lawmakers alike. Another well-known nonpartisan citizens' group is Common Cause. Conceived in Washington, D.C., in 1969, Common Cause established its California branch in 1972. Members pay annual dues, which go to the national headquarters. Contributions beyond the regular dues support the state office. Common Cause's program calls for open legislative meetings, lobbying disclosure, conflict-of-interest laws, and public campaign financing. Since its preferred means of change is via the legislature, Common Cause lobbies in Sacramento, using letters of support from its 60,000-plus members as leverage.

Environmentalists have formed some of the most powerful citizens' groups. The Sierra Club is the most prominent, combining thorough research with an effective lobbying team in Sacramento. Other well-known environmental groups include the California Coastal Alliance, Friends of the Earth, and the Environmental Protection Center.

LOBBYING

The process of lobbying has been described as the art of persuasion. The figures just cited clearly show that lobbying is itself a big business. But who are the lobbyists and how do they ply their trade?

As noted above, in 1996 there were about 1,100 lobbyists registered in Sacramento, representing virtually any interest imaginable. Some lobbyists are so-called "in-house" lobbyists, individuals who work for and are paid exclusively by a particular organization such as the McDonnell Douglas Corporation or the California Association of Community Colleges. Others are "contract" lobbyists, sometimes referred to as "hired guns," who will and do work for anyone willing to pay their fees. The number of clients may range from two or three to half a hundred or as many as the staff can handle. Kahl Associates employs eleven full-time lobbyists and represents 54 different clients, including the Loma Linda University Medical Center, Western Wood Preservers Institute, California Chamber of Commerce, Fruit Growers Supply Company, and Western State Petroleum Association (which was the biggest buyer of lobbying services from January 1, 1995, through June 30, 1996, spending $2.8 million). However, the biggest money-maker among lobbying firms during that period was the firm of Carpenter, Snodgrass & Associates with earnings of $3,875,521.[6] At the other end of the scale are numerous lobbying firms with a single lobbyist representing a lone client. Women are making up a larger and larger part of the lobbying corps. In 1977 there were only 44 women registered as lobbyists. In 1996 they accounted for nearly 30 percent. About a third of lobbyists have had some direct experience as members of the legislature or as staff to members of committees. The reason why such individuals are sought out for these jobs may be summed up in one word—access. The first and most important task of any lobbyist is to gain access to the people who hold power over those policies that affect his or her clients.

[6]Office of the Secretary of State, "Lobbying Expenditures and the Top 100 Lobbying Firms, October 1–December 31 and Cumulative Totals for January 1, 1995–June 30, 1996," Sacramento, November 1996.

Knowing the governmental ropes—and the players—personally is an enormous advantage when it comes to gaining access.

The definition of a lobbyist is set down in the Political Reform Act of 1974. If someone "communicates directly" and on a regular basis with a government official "for the purpose of influencing legislative or administrative action," he or she is required to register as a lobbyist. The act goes on to define regular access as when there have been more than 25 direct contacts with officials for two consecutive months. Not everyone does register, and the actual number of those engaged in lobbying is almost certainly much higher than the 1,045 found in the official roster.

How do these men and women exercise their art of persuasion? There are two basic categories of techniques: direct pressure and indirect pressure. Direct pressure involves attempts to convince government officials to adopt policies supported by the group. Indirect pressure seeks to create a favorable public opinion which, in turn, influences governmental decisions.

The Samish case brought the public's attention to the influence lobbyists had in Sacramento. Artie Samish, a lobbyist for the beer industry, was described in 1949 in *Collier's* magazine as more powerful than the governor of the state. It was alleged he had total control over the Public Morals Committee and his influence only ceased upon his conviction for income tax evasion.

This case led to passage of the Collier Act (in 1949), subsequently amended, which required all lobbyists to register and file monthly reports with the legislature regarding their employers.

It was not until 1973 that further serious efforts were made to regulate lobbying. Led by Common Cause, the People's Lobby, and then Secretary of State Jerry Brown, an initiative was placed on the June 1974 ballot. Proposition 9 was approved by the voters and the new regulations went into effect the following January. The proponents won, arguing that the people had a right to know the sources and uses of special-interest money contributed to their elected representatives.

Under current law the definition of "lobbyist" includes any person receiving compensation from nongovernmental sources for activities that influence legislative or administrative actions. These activities must be a substantial or regular portion of the person's job. Each lobbyist is required to register with the secretary of state and regularly file detailed reports on all financial transactions. Employers of lobbyists must file their own financial reports, and all reports are to be made available to the public. A lobbyist is prohibited from spending more than $10 a month per legislator—sufficient for two hamburgers and a Coke, said the supporters of the 1974 legislation. The Fair Political Practices Commission (FPPC), created by the reform act, has responsibility for enforcing these provisions, including the preparation and processing of the reporting forms and the investigation of all complaints of noncompliance. In cases of violation, the FPPC can subpoena witnesses, issue cease-and-desist orders, and levy fines of up to $2,000. The commission has five members: The chairperson and one member are appointed by the governor, and one member each is appointed by the attorney general, the secretary of state, and the controller. Members serve four-year terms.

The lobbying provisions of the 1974 reform act were among the most hotly debated during the campaign for its passage. Opponents of the ballot measure claimed that it reflected a bias that all so-called legislative advocates were crooks and that all lobbying activities were inherently immoral. Another major complaint was that the massive amounts of paperwork and lack of privacy associated with the new reporting regulations would deter even legitimate attempts by interest groups to make their views on legislation known to their elected representatives. Supporters of the measure countered that, although the reforms might cause minor inconveniences, the public's basic right to know the sources and uses of political money required the full-disclosure provisions and that these reforms were needed to restore popular faith in representative government. They also claimed that the stringent expenditure limitation on lobbying, rather than reflecting a bias against "legislative advocates," would actually encourage participation by eradicating the advantages of lobbyists with large bankrolls.

What have been the effects, in fact, of the 1974 reforms? The major conclusion of most observers of, and participants in, the Sacramento scene is that, although lobbying continues to be an essential part of the political process, the atmosphere around the state legislature appears to be more businesslike and less social than previously.

In sum, the Political Reform Act thus far has had a visible impact on the political atmosphere in Sacramento, but its effects on honesty in government and on making public officials more accountable to the general public are hard to assess. Sacramento is a less frivolous city than it used to be. Business has dropped off at a number of well-known eateries, and legislators are caucusing more among themselves. Yet the lobbying arena is still active, even if the lobbying now has to take place more in the open. Although many lobbyists and some legislators prefer the good old days, most of them have shown resourcefulness in adapting to the law.

SELECTED REFERENCES

Alchorn, Faith, "Donors Seek Biggest Bang for Their Political Bucks," *Los Angeles Times,* Orange County edition, May 22, 1988.

Bathen, Sigrid, "Lawyer-Lobbyists Become Big Fish in Capitol Pond," *California Journal,* February 1990.

Borland, John, "Third House Rising", *California Journal,* February 1996.

Cook, Gale, "The New Persuaders," *Golden State Report,* November 1987.

Napolitan, Joseph, *The Election Game and How to Win It,* 2d ed., New York: Doubleday, 1972.

Nollinger, Mark, "The New Crusaders," *California Journal,* January 1993.

Payne, J. Gregory, and C. Ratzan Scott, "The Race Issue," *California Journal,* June 1986.

Price, Charles, "Advocacy in the Age of Term Limits," *California Journal,* November 1993.

Roll, Charles W. Jr., and Albert H. Cantril, *Polls: Their Use and Misuse in Politics,* New York: Basic Books, 1980.

Sabato, Larry, *The Rise of Political Consultants,* New York: Basic Books, 1982.

4

Voters, Nominations, and Elections

The most fundamental question of government is: Who should rule? Although it is generally assumed that in the United States the people rule—that is, we adhere to the principle of popular sovereignty—the U.S. Constitution contains no specific provision guaranteeing the citizen the right to vote or to run for office. Until the 1950s, who could vote had been left up to the states themselves, with the exception that the right of citizens to vote should not be "denied or abridged . . . on account of race, color, or previous condition of servitude" (Fifteenth Amendment) or "on account of sex" (Nineteenth Amendment). However, state governments denied or abridged the right to vote for other reasons.[1] In 17 states the citizen had to be literate (defined differently by the various states), and all states held to a minimum voting age requirement. Some states allowed a person to vote after he or she had lived in the state only six months, and others demanded two years. To vote on certain kinds of issues, such as approving bonds, a half-dozen states have required that the citizen be a property owner.

The provisions in the U.S. Constitution that provide for the popular election of senators and representatives go no further than to require that a state allow the same people to vote for members of Congress as it allows to vote for members of the "most numerous branch of the State legislature." If California's constitution had allowed only dog owners to vote for members of the assembly, it could have established the same requirement for voting in congressional elections.

However, in the past 45 years a far-reaching change has taken place with respect to the legal and constitutional basis of suffrage. Whether by legislation or constitutional amendment, the right to vote has been greatly expanded. Major laws adopted by Congress include the Voting Rights Act of 1965 and its amendments and various civil rights acts, particularly the one adopted in 1964. The age requirement, first established at 18 by the Voting Rights Acts of 1970, was later embedded in the Constitution with adoption of the Twenty-sixth Amendment. Residency requirements have been limited to 30 days by the Supreme Court. The Twenty-fourth

---

[1]The Fourteenth Amendment stipulates that the number of a state's representatives in Congress shall be reduced if the state denies the right to vote to any 21-year-old citizen "except for participation in rebellion, or other crime," but this rule has not been invoked.

Amendment outlawed poll taxes, enfranchising many poor people. In fact, today states have little control over suffrage and not much more over elections.

It has been assumed that the question of who may hold *national* elective office—that is, the presidency, vice-presidency and congressional seats—was established by the Constitution and that states could not add any further qualifications. That assumption came under challenge when first Colorado and later other states (including California) voted to establish term limits for their elected representatives in Washington, D.C. Ultimately the U.S. Supreme Court ruled term limits on Congress are unconstitutional.

WHO MAY VOTE?

In November 1972 the voters of California revised Article II of the state constitution to conform to the new provisions of the Twenty-sixth Amendment to the Constitution, the Voting Rights Act of Congress, and court decisions. Article II accords the right to vote in all California elections to any person who meets the following qualifications:

1. *Citizenship.* A voter must be a citizen of the United States. If the voter is not a natural-born American, he or she must have received naturalization papers before registering to vote.

2. *Residence.* The new Article II gives the legislature authority to set the residence requirements for voting. However, the California Supreme Court declared that, under the equal protection clause in both the U.S. and California constitutions, the state cannot require a citizen to live in the state more than 30 days before being allowed to vote. The legislature then enacted a law that conformed to this decision. Therefore, the present legal requirement is that a voter must live in California, his or her own county, and election precinct only 30 days before the election. The state legislature may reduce this requirement even more if it sees fit.[2]

Voters may vote in advance (in person or by mail), provided they have filed an application for an absentee ballot with the county elections official at least seven days before the election.

Before 1976 voters were supposed to have a valid reason (illness, a handicap, living ten or more miles from the polling place, other commitments) for not being able to go to the polls on election day and thus needing to vote by absentee ballot. Under current law any registered voter can request to vote absentee, even one who will mark the ballot in the privacy of his or her own home next door to the polling place. Critics of this procedure argue that it makes it possible for candidates to make campaign pitches in the home and walk out with a vote in his or her pocket.

Absentee ballots were a major factor in the outcome of the Bradley-Deukmejian election for governor in 1982. The state Republican party sent letters to every

---

[2]In California counties, a citizen is allowed to vote for president in the November general election even if he or she has been a resident of this state less than the 30 days. The citizen must have been eligible to vote in his or her former state and must appear in person at the office of the county clerk or registrar of voters at least seven days before the election. The citizen is permitted to vote only for the office of president and must formally register to vote in any subsequent elections.

Republican household enclosing an application for an absentee ballot and urging a vote for Deukmejian. This effort contributed to the total of 302,000 votes for Deukmejian out of a total of 505,000 absentees—a sufficient margin to overcome the 19,000-vote margin cast for Bradley at the ballot box. And in 1983 San Francisco Mayor Dianne Feinstein made use of the absentee ballot process to defeat a recall election. Use of the absentee ballot has increased greatly in recent years as both major political parties have urged their members to employ it. In 1984 just 6.5 percent of votes cast were absentee; in the early 1990s it had reached roughly one-fifth.

3. *Age.* The minimum age for voting throughout the United States is 18. There is no *maximum age.* A centenarian who can get to the polls in person or who can fill out the application for an absentee ballot can continue to vote as he or she has for the last 80 years.

4. *Special Requirements.* Article II of the California constitution states the legislature "shall provide that no severely mentally deficient person, insane person, person convicted of an infamous crime, no person convicted of embezzlement or misappropriation of public funds, shall exercise the privilege of an elector in this state." Just what an "infamous crime" is or how severe the mental deficiency had to be was left to the voters, who approved Proposition 10 in 1974. That proposition amended Article II, denying the vote to persons "while mentally incompetent or imprisoned or on parole for the conviction of a felony." When someone has finished his or her sentence and has completed the parole period the right to vote is restored.

Before November 1972, Article II required a voter to be able to read the state constitution in the English language and to write his or her name. This was eliminated in the revised version of the Article; furthermore, the Congressional Voting Rights Act of 1970 abolished the literacy qualification throughout the country.

5. *Registration.* A citizen who satisfies all of the qualifications listed cannot merely walk up to the polls on election day and expect to be handed a ballot. To exercise suffrage privileges a citizen must be already registered as a qualified voter with the chief elections administrator of his or her own county. (In most counties this is a duty of the county clerk, but in the counties of Los Angeles, San Francisco, San Diego, San Bernardino, Orange, and Santa Clara the elections official is the registrar of voters.) A person may register at any time except during the 29 days immediately preceding any election. For example, if a prospective new voter fails to register by the end of the thirtieth day preceding the June primary, that voter forfeits any chance of voting in that election and must wait until after balloting day to register for the coming November election. In most counties advance warning of the closing of registration is given by local newspapers and by deputies with the authority to process registrants, sitting at tables placed in front of post offices and supermarkets.

In 1975 the legislature voted to permit registration by mail. California's secretary of state prepared an application form to be uniform throughout the state. Now all that a potential voter has to do is to fill out the form and mail it (postage free) to the county clerk or registrar of voters, who then mails the applicant a card that says he or she is now an officially registered voter. These application forms are made available to political parties or other organizations seeking to get people registered and are kept on hand at many of the state's public offices.

Registration in California is "permanent"; that is, once a citizen is registered, he or she may continue to vote in succeeding elections without reregistering, providing the citizen does not (a) change legal residence to another county, (b) change name,

(c) become ineligible because of insanity or serving a sentence for a felony, or (d) change party affiliation.

At the time of registration each voter is asked to indicate the party with which the voter chooses to be affiliated. This answer is indicated on the registration affidavit, and he or she becomes eligible to vote in that party's primary elections. If the voter "declines to state" party preference, he or she may not vote in any partisan primary and on primary election days is handed ballots only for those officers elected on a nonpartisan basis.

While efforts to get people registered historically have been seen as the responsibility of the parties, special-interest group organizations, and public interest groups such as the League of Women Voters, a state law adopted in 1976 requires local governments to take action to ensure that eligible residents are registered "at the highest possible level." Just how extensive those efforts needed to be became the issue in a suit brought by Common Cause and the American Civil Liberties Union, among others, in 1988. Citing differences in the percentages of those registered in high- and low-income areas of Los Angeles County, they argued that county officials were not doing enough to encourage low-income and minority citizens to register. Although a "voter outreach" program had been created involving bilingual registrars, with a 24-hour "hot line" to help people register at 3,500 locations throughout the county, a superior court judge ruled that these steps were insufficient to meet the intent of the law. The California supreme court disagreed, however, and the lower court order was voided. In 1993, a new federal law, the "motor voter law," was passed requiring states to provide opportunities for residents to register to vote when applying for or renewing a driver's license. Proponents touted the likelihood of greater participation in elections while critics pointed to the cost (between $2 million and $5 million a year in California), inconvenience (longer lines at the Department of Motor Vehicles), and an equal likelihood that those so unmotivated to register they had to be collared at the DMV would not vote anyway.

VOTER PARTICIPATION

Despite extensive efforts to make both registering and voting easier and in the face of expanded "outreach" programs, many Californians, like other Americans, do not vote. Typically, of those who are qualified, *fewer than three out of four bother to register and, of those, 75 percent or less go to the polls.*

In the 1996 presidential election some 65.53 percent of those registered (or, if all those who could have voted if registered are counted, just 52.56 percent) voted. In "off-year" (nonpresidential) elections such as that in 1994 even fewer vote. That year only 60.45 percent of registered persons voted (46.48 percent of the eligibles). Turnout at primary elections is even worse. In the 1996 primary only 41.88 percent of the registered voters (or 31.47 percent of all potential voters) went to the polls. The special election in November 1993 drew just 36.37 percent or an abysmally low 24.74 percent of the eligibles, this despite such presumably "hot" issues on the ballot as school vouchers and a sales tax increase.

Why is there so little interest in exercising a right that men and women around the world fight and die to secure? With respect to primaries in presidential election years, many people are discouraged by the fact that decisions on selecting the parties' standard bearers have been reached before Californians have an opportunity to express their preferences. Since the presidential contest is the most visible and glamorous, many are turned off when it becomes apparent that their votes cannot influence the outcome. Then there are those who, in any election, either distrust all politicians ("they're all the same—crooks") or see no differences among candidates; if there are none, why bother? Still others vote only when they are angry, and when they see things going fairly well they tend to stay at home. Finally, there are some, especially in the lower socioeconomic categories, who have in effect "opted out" of the system in the belief that the system does not work—at least for them. For the nonvoter, all those millions spent on television, radio, campaign brochures, and the like are a waste of money; they simply are not paying attention. If the turnouts at national and statewide elections are for many people scandalously low, participation in local contests for seats on a city council, board of supervisors, or school board often falls below 25 percent of even registered voters.

WHO MAY RUN FOR OFFICE?

Eligibility

The 1964 court ruling in the case of Pierre Salinger, President Kennedy's press secretary who had only shortly before the primary moved to California, shattered the notion that a person is *in*eligible for election to any office for which he or she is not qualified to vote. Specific eligibility requirements are found in the U.S. Constitution for federal offices; in the state constitution and statutes for state senators, members of the assembly, judges of the state courts, county committeepersons, and officers in general law counties and cities; and in local charters for many officers in "home-rule" cities and counties.

California's elected executive officers must be voters and must have resided in the state five years previous to their election. Members of the Board of Equalization, the state's major tax agency, must in addition have resided in their own districts for one year. State senators and assembly members must be voters, and residents of the state for three years and of their district for one year. A ruling of the state supreme court in 1975 held that the residency requirement for candidates seeking local office must be limited to a maximum of 30 days.

Getting on the Ballot

Any individual who meets the minimum legal qualification for any of the offices listed,[3] or any one of the many other local offices, may have his or her name appear on the ballot at primary election day if at least 60 days before the election the individual files a declaration of candidacy with the county clerk or in municipal elections with

---

[3]Except justices of the state supreme court and the district courts of appeal, where the only names appearing on the ballot are those of incumbents whose terms have expired or nominees of the governor in cases in which the incumbent is not running for reelection.

the city clerk. The number of sponsors' signatures required varies for different offices but is nominal.

To appear on the primary election ballot of a given party as a candidate for the U.S. Senate or any state executive office, a petition bearing 65 signatures (of registered voters belonging to the party within the constituency of the office sought) must be filed. Aspirants for the U.S. House of Representatives or for the state senate or assembly are required to file a petition carrying at least 40 signatures. At one time a filing fee was also required of all candidates except those running for party county central committees. However, that practice was declared in violation of the Fourteenth Amendment to the federal Constitution by the U.S. Supreme Court. State law now permits waiving of the fee with the collection of additional signatures on nominating petitions.

In 1975 the state supreme court declared the alphabetical listing of candidates on an election ballot unconstitutional. At the same time the court struck down the automatic listing of an incumbent's name at the head of the ballot. As a result, the names of candidates for state and local offices now appear on the basis of a randomized alphabet determined by a public drawing managed by the office of the secretary of state.

A candidate may not run as an independent in the partisan primaries. All contestants must themselves be registered members of a political party. Getting on the ballot in California is simple and relatively inexpensive; getting *elected* is something else!

PRIMARY ELECTIONS: *THE BLANKET PRIMARY*

The *direct primary* was instituted in California and some other states to give the average voters a say in *nominating* the candidates who will represent their party in the coming general election. It is called "direct" because previously nomination had been indirect—that is, by conventions of party members led by party officials—and the average voters had to take the candidates the party "machine" gave them. Until 1996 it was a "partisan" primary in that only voters registered in the party could participate in it; it was "closed" to all others.

The voters changed that at the March 1996 primary when they overwhelmingly approved Proposition 198, which mandates the use of the "blanket primary". This system, employed by fewer than five states in the country, provides the maximum flexibility to voters. All the candidates of all eligible parties for all the offices to be elected are to be found on a single ballot. All registered voters, Republicans, Democrats, and third party members, as well as independents, receive the same ballot. They may choose which party primary they wish to vote in for each of the offices being contested. Thus a Democrat may elect to vote in the Republican primary for governor, the Democratic primary for controller, the Reform primary for United States Senate, and so on. In arguing for this change, proponents stated it was likely to lead to victory for more moderate candidates whose appeal transcended party lines. (One of the proponents was moderate Republican Tom Campbell, who had lost out to conservative Bruce Herschensohn in the Republican U.S. Senate primary in 1994.) Opponents took the position that it made no sense to allow Republicans a role in the selection of Democratic candidates and vice versa and the procedure could only further weaken

California's already weak political parties. Candidates, they argued, would be even more likely to campaign, not as party members but as individuals, much as they had in the era of cross-filing (see below).

California's direct primary historically has been held on the first Tuesday following the first Monday in June. However, as noted in Chapter 3, legislative action was taken in 1993 to move the primary in 1996 to the last Tuesday in March to enhance the state's influence in the selection of presidential candidates. As we have seen, the experiment did not work and sentiment exists for returning to the June primary for the next presidential contest in 2000 (it was to be in June in nonpresidential years such as 1998 in any event).

The ballot is "longest" in gubernatorial election years (1994, 1998, 2002, and so on) when all state executive offices are open for nomination, as well as all assembly and U.S. House of Representative seats, half the state senate seats, county committee posts, and numerous local offices. The state executive officers serve four-year terms and are not elected in presidential election years (1996, 2000, 2004, and so on).

One of the Progressive reforms (see Chapter 2) designed to weaken political parties was cross-filing. This system allowed a candidate to run not just for his or her own party's nomination but for the nominations of other parties as well. Voters were still restricted to voting in the party in which they were registered but candidates could—and did—file for both (or all) party nominations. If successful, the general election became a formality.

For 40 years it was the political way of life in California for aspirants to state and national office to cross-file. In a majority of the primary contests throughout the state one candidate would capture both major party nominations. For example, in the 1940–52 period 84 percent of the state senate races and 72 percent of the assembly races were decided in the primaries.[4] Among those who used the cross-filing system to secure the nominations of both parties were Governor Earl Warren and U.S. Senator William Knowland.

Led by the League of Woman Voters, a campaign to abolish cross-filing, described by one political scientist as the greatest barrier to party responsibility yet devised, ultimately succeeded in 1958, though efforts to modify it had been made. In 1954 the party affiliations of the candidates were included on the ballot for the first time. Abbreviations were used (Rep. for Republican, Dem. for Democrat, Proh. for Prohibition) and cross-filing victories dropped dramatically. Today the only way a candidate can duplicate the cross-filing victories of the past is through a write-in campaign. Though eliminated over 35 years ago, its heritage lives on in the present focus on the characteristics of the individual rather than party label that typifies the campaigns of today.

The Presidential Primary

Voters in the direct primary in presidential election years are given the opportunity to select California's delegates to the national nominating convention of the parties. California is among the great majority of states that have taken the selection of national convention delegates away from the party committees or state party conventions.

---

[4]Joseph P. Harris, *California Politics* (Stanford: Stanford University Press, 1955), p. 42.

California's convention delegates for each party, varying each convention year according to formulas set by the national parties (in 1996, there were 424 Democratic delegates and 165 Republicans—each with one vote), were selected as a group rather than individually. A Democratic voter, for example, chose among slates of Democrats seeking to be delegates.

In 1972, through a revision of Article II of the state constitution, California voters adopted the "Oregon Type" of presidential primary effective for the 1976 elections. Instead of the presidential candidates having to take the initiative in getting their names on the California ballot, it is now the responsibility of California's secretary of state, who must keep abreast of any political gossip and place on the presidential primary ballot the names of all persons who are "recognized candidates throughout the nation or throughout California for the office of President of the United States." Any candidate whom the secretary of state chooses not to recognize may still get on the ballot by circulating petitions among supporters in California. Furthermore, a person whose name the secretary of state has chosen to put on the ballot may withdraw by filing an affidavit that he or she is not a candidate.

The Democratic Party added further confusion. Its 1972 national convention voted to prohibit winner-take-all primaries. These were primaries in which the candidate with the most votes, even if fewer than half, won all the delegates to the convention. Until then both parties employed this system. The state's Republican Party still does and in so doing hoped to enhance the importance of its primary for 1996. California Democrats have tried several versions of proportional representation. One was winner-take-all by congressional district, but that proved unsatisfactory in that the proportion of the overall popular vote failed to mirror the proportion of delegates won. Currently voters vote directly for the candidates and the number of delegates is determined by the proportion of the popular vote each candidate receives in that district. If there are ten delegates to be chosen and three candidates split the popular vote 40–20–40, the delegates would be apportioned 4–2–4. There is, however, a "threshold" that any candidate must achieve: only those with at least 15 percent of the popular vote in a district can receive delegates.

Although both parties seek to make their delegations broadly representative, the Democrats require that there be an equal number of men and women on each state's delegation. They also mandate that there be Hispanics, blacks, and Asians in proportion to their presence in the party's membership. If the results of a primary cause any group to be underrepresented, the district delegates must fill 41 so-called at-large and 31 alternate slots in ways that will correct the imbalance.

The Nonpartisan "Primary"

One state executive officer—the superintendent of public instruction—superior, municipal, and justice court judges, and county elective officers are *elected* at the June primary elections.[5] They appear on the ballot without any party affiliation and may be voted upon by *all* registered voters. The candidate who receives a majority of the votes

---

[5]The special provision for the appointment and election of supreme court and district courts of appeal judges is discussed under the court system in Chapter 8.

for one of these nonpartisan offices is declared elected. If no candidate receives a majority, a runoff is held at the coming November election between the two candidates with the highest number of votes.

Many California voters do not declare their affiliation with any of the legally recognized political parties in this state; at the time of registration they either "decline to state" their party preference or indicate membership in one of the small, unofficial parties. In 1998 for the first time these Californians will be able to vote for candidates for partisan office in the June primary, as well as for candidates for nonpartisan office (as they have in the past). Figures compiled by the office of the secretary of state show that the number of persons declining to state a party affiliation more than tripled between 1976 and 1996, from 490,000 to 1.77 million or just over 11 percent of those registered. Young people in particular show a tendency to register as independents, perhaps out of a sense of disenchantment with political parties.

Municipal officers are elected on a nonpartisan basis. Some municipalities hold their elections on the second Tuesday in March or the second Tuesday in April whereas others combine their elections with the statewide June primary or the November general election.

THE NOVEMBER GENERAL ELECTION

The final election for partisan offices and those nonpartisan offices for which runoffs are necessary, as well as the vote on most state and county ballot propositions, is held in every even-numbered year on the first Tuesday after the first Monday in November. All registered voters are eligible to vote and receive the same ballots regardless of their party affiliation.

Presidential Election Years

The ballot is slightly different in alternating general election years. In every presidential election year no state executive offices are filled, but California's presidential electors are chosen.[6] Each party's list of presidential electors is selected at its state convention in its fall meeting preceding the general election. The names of each party's presidential electors do not appear on the general election ballot, however. The ballot contains only the names of the national party candidates for president and vice-president, as shown in Figure 4.1. The votes cast for president and vice president are officially counted as votes for the bloc of presidential electors of each party. The electors of the party whose candidates receive the highest vote are declared elected, and they all meet in Sacramento on the first Monday after the second Wednesday in December (as required by an act of Congress) to cast California's entire electoral vote for their party's two candidates. The California law is explicit in binding the electors to vote for only the official candidates of their party. However, this has never been enforced, because a federal law permits an elector to vote for a candidate of any party.

---

[6]The number of each state's presidential electors is the same as its total representation in the U.S. Congress (California: 52 representatives and 2 senators).

CALIFORNIA'S BALLOT FORM

"Long" Ballot

A *long ballot* is one that gives voters many things to decide. A state like California—in which there are ten state executives to be elected besides the governor, as well as judges and local government officials, and a host of ballot propositions, initiatives, bond issues, and charter amendments to be approved—may be said to have a very long ballot. Voters in an average precinct who take their suffrage privilege seriously would be obliged to punch over 100 holes or mark that many crosses in the primary and general elections! The voters complain of the ballot's length but are reluctant to part with their privilege of choice among a multitude of officers and ballot propositions.

"Office Bloc"

The California ballot is divided by office rather than by political party as in some states. Under the heading "Governor," for example, are listed all candidates for that office from all qualified parties. With the office-bloc, in contrast to the party-column, form there is no time saved by voting a straight party ticket. Advocates of tighter party discipline are dissatisfied with the present California ballot; some have urged the institution of the straight-ticket option, in which one punch or one cross placed at the head of a party column is counted as a vote for all candidates of that party.

THE ADMINISTRATION OF ELECTIONS

Election Officials

The chief elections officer of the state for the various elections is the secretary of state, and copies of nomination and election petitions must be filed with this officer. The secretary of state also has the major responsibility for ballot specifications and arrangements and certifies and publishes the final vote count. However, the actual preparation of election ballots, selection of voting sites, and counting of votes are the responsibility of the county clerk or the registrar of voters in each county. The county board of supervisors appoints the board of election officials who are the precinct election workers seen at polling places on election day. In municipal elections the city council appoints these workers.

General Procedures

Voting precincts of an estimated 200–600 voters each are established by the county election officials and are consolidated for local elections. Within each precinct a polling place is selected and polling booths are erected. The polling place may be in almost any convenient building: a private home, a school, the lobby of an apartment house, or a garage, but not a liquor store or bar. The polls are open from 7 A.M. to 8 P.M. in most counties. As soon as the polls have closed, the precinct boards begin to count the votes (called the first "canvass") in the presence of all bystanders. This is usually done at the polling establishments, but provision may be made by county officials for a central

1 | OFFICIAL BALLOT/BOLETA OFICIAL
CONSOLIDATED GENERAL ELECTION/ELECCION GENERAL CONSOLIDADA
November 5, 1996, Fresno County, Condado de Fresno, 5 de Noviembre de 1996

PRESIDENT AND VICE PRESIDENT   Vote for One Party

PRESIDENTE Y VICEPRESIDENTE   Vote por Un Partido

ROSS PEROT for President/por Presidente JAMES CAMPBELL for Vice President/por Vicepresidente	Reform Reforma	4 ▶
HOWARD PHILLIPS for President/por Presidente HERBERT W. TITUS for Vice President/por Vicepresidente	American Independent Americano Independiente	7 ▶
HARRY BROWNE for President/por Presidente JO JORGENSEN for Vice President/por Vicepresidente	Libertarian Libertario	10 ▶
JOHN HAGELIN for President/por Presidente MIKE TOMPKINS for Vice President/por Vicepresidente	Natural Law Natural Ley	13 ▶
RALPH NADER for President/por Presidente WINONA LADUKE for Vice President/por Vicepresidente	Green Verde	16 ▶
MARSHA FEINLAND for President/por Presidente KATE MC CLATCHY for Vice President/por Vicepresidente	Peace And Freedom Paz Y Libertad	19 ▶
BOB DOLE for President/por Presidente JACK KEMP for Vice President/por Vicepresidente	Republican Republicano	22 ▶
BILL CLINTON for President/por Presidente AL GORE for Vice President/por Vicepresidente	Democratic Democratico	25 ▶

Figure 4.1   Ballot for California General Election, 1996

(Dennis Renault, *Sacramento Bee)*

counting. The second "canvass" takes place when county officials—again in public—add together the returns of the individual precincts. The county sends copies of all returns to the secretary of state and stores all ballots for six months, after which time they are destroyed.

Automatic voting machines, at which voters pull a lever to indicate their choice, are being used in a few California counties, including San Francisco. In some counties voting is still done by the old-style rubber stamp on paper ballots, which are counted by hand, but in the majority of counties, including Los Angeles, the voters mark their ballots by some kind of stylus or marking device, and the ballots are then counted by electronic machines.

For many years all elections in California were conducted in English; it was against the law for any election official to speak anything but English in a polling place. This prohibition was repealed in 1973 by the California legislature. Then Congress in the Federal Voting Rights Act of 1975 provided that in any state or local subdivision where a significant number of citizens belonged to a non-English-language minority, election materials were to be published in the language of the minority as well as in English. When this law was applied to California, it meant that sample ballots, voters' pamphlets, and instructions at the polling place had to be available in Spanish in 38 counties and in Chinese in San Francisco County. In 1984 California voters approved an initiative that requests a change in federal law so that ballots and official voting materials need to be printed in English only. This was followed in 1986 with overwhelming adoption of a proposition making English California's "official" language.

Special Protections

California's election laws have numerous provisions designed to ensure fair play and guard against fraud. Each detail, from the opening and inspecting of the empty ballot box on election morning to the defacing and destruction of unused and voided ballots, is carefully outlined in the 11,700 sections of the Elections Code. In the case of most offices, election officials must count write-in votes for actual persons. Ballots cast for Mickey Mouse or Superman are ignored. No one may speak to a voter within 100 feet of a polling place about his or her vote. Employers who distribute political propaganda with the paychecks of their employees are guilty of a misdemeanor. Voting is secret, behind curtains, but a voter may not remain in a polling booth longer than ten minutes. All business concerns, according to law, must give their employees sufficient time to vote on election day. There are provisions for challenging voters at the polls who are suspected of fraudulent voting and for challenging counts and demanding recounts. Penalties are stiff for voter intimidation or inducements in the form of money, property, or employment.

CAMPAIGNS

The process of running for office in California is expensive and arduous. In this age of advertising message overload, simply getting the voters' attention with a candidate or an argument in support of an issue is a major accomplishment. Sustaining such attention and building a favorable voter response to a candidacy or a particular ballot proposition, in the face of opposing candidates and arguments on issues, is a task that has come to require highly specialized skills in itself—the skills of public relations professionals. Few candidates themselves possess the skills, money, or time to manage all of the tasks involved, and so in modern times a new breed of political professional has emerged to take on these duties: the campaign manager. Especially for campaigns in statewide elections, a campaign manager has become virtually indispensable, and campaign management has come to involve so many specialized subtasks that usually entire firms are hired by major candidates and by interest groups for and against ballot measures.

Campaign Management Firms

For the most part, campaigns prior to World War II were run by party leaders or by the candidates themselves who conducted them largely by "feel," a sense of what worked, what appealed to the voters. As dramatically portrayed in such motion pictures as *The Candidate* and *Power*, that is no longer the case. The rise of political consultants began in California in 1933 when the husband and wife team of Whitaker and Baxter formed the first campaign management firm. It is not surprising that what has since become a national phenomenon began here. The state's weak political parties meant that many of the traditional means of conducting campaigns were not available. The lack of patronage with its accompanying stimulus to party loyalty was one factor. Patronage elsewhere provided a ready army of campaign workers on whom candidates could depend, but the Progressive reforms of the early twentieth century had virtually eliminated it in California. The prohibition against party endorsements in primary elections and in all nonpartisan races left official party organizations out of the process. Cross-filing had a similar effect even in partisan contests (see page 66).

Ballot propositions, often involving important public issues, were proposed and opposed usually with little or no reference to party. With parties to a considerable degree foreclosed by law from their traditional roles, campaign management firms took on many of the functions that parties performed elsewhere. Even the size of the state played a role. With a rapidly growing population, campaigns necessarily and increasingly came to depend on newspapers and later radio and television to reach the voters. The expertise needed was provided by these firms. Some might even argue that Californians' penchant for being entertained, arising from the influence of Hollywood and the television industry, enhanced the opportunities for campaign management firms with their emphasis on dramatic, attention-getting political messages. Whatever the reasons, they have come to play an extremely important role in any statewide race as well as many city and county campaigns.

Darry Sragow and Clinton Reilly, Sal Russo and Eileen Padberg are hardly household names, but their organizations and others like them have a great deal to say about the style and substance of campaigns in California. What the public learns about candidates and issues is heavily influenced by how they decide campaigns should be conducted. Their decisions, in turn, are based on what they believe will help most in ensuring that their client, the candidate, wins. That means using public opinion polling.

Polling

Even those who pay little attention to politics know about polls. They measure public attitudes and opinions on a wide variety of questions. Which candidate is ahead? What do people think about the death penalty or higher taxes? What few realize is that what they see in the newspapers or hear about on radio or television is only the tip of a very large iceberg. Most polls are intended solely for the eyes of those who pay for them. How effective is a series of beer commercials? What image do people have of a particular industry? What do they think of a candidate's character? Ability? No major national or large statewide campaign is without the services of a professional polling organization. One nationally prominent campaign manager, Joseph Napolitan, has said: "I personally would no more try to run a campaign without adequate polls than I would try to sail the Atlantic without a compass."

Polls are generally conducted by telephone, with the interviewer following a carefully prepared script. Questions are framed in as neutral a way as possible to avoid bias. Those asking the questions are trained to use vocal intonations that do not invite a particular response. "Do you (really) think this is a good idea?" Use of a word or tone implying skepticism may well result in skewed results, making the poll worthless. In a survey of general opinion, a proper sample must be used. Percentages of the overall population, male and female, by income and education levels, ethnicity, religion, and the like are reflected in the sample of people interviewed.

Polls serve several functions. A *benchmark poll* is taken before the campaign begins. It may be designed to identify those issues of most interest to the voters because that will vary from place to place and race to race. Getting and keeping the voter's attention requires a focus on what he or she is interested in. Another function of such a poll may be to identify the candidate's strengths and weaknesses, the strengths to be emphasized in the campaign, the weaknesses countered. If a candidate is seen as uncaring or abrasive, television commercials may show him or her sitting with—and smiling at—a group of the elderly, for example.

A rather different kind of poll involves what are called *focus groups*. A small number of people representative of the group the candidate hopes to influence views a television commercial before it airs. Is the message clear? Is the announcer believable? Do the pictures help or hinder the message? In the past commercials have been drastically altered and even dropped altogether after measuring the reactions of such focus groups.

While national polling organizations such as Gallup and Harris conduct opinion surveys in California, several state-based polls have earned the respect of professionals. The California Poll, under the leadership of Mervin Field since its inception over 45 years ago, is considered by many to be the best. The *Los Angeles Times* also gets high marks for its polling.

Television

The importance of television in waging a statewide or regional campaign cannot be overemphasized. Virtually every home has one or more sets; most of us watch what is on them several hours a day. When we add the fact that up to 70 percent of the public gets all or most of its news from television, the formula for success seems apparent: Be seen on "the tube" as much and as favorably as possible.

The staple of television advertising is the 30-second commercial. It is long enough to get the candidate's name, the office being contested, and a slogan included, but not so long that "channel surfing" sets in. With so little time, commercials are carefully crafted to ensure maximum impact. That, more often than not, means the use of "visuals" to enhance the image of the person running. The candidate sits in a classroom smiling at—and being smiled at by—a group of children, properly balanced by sex and ethnicity. He obviously loves kids and wants the best possible education for them. The classroom has a prominently displayed American flag, and on the blackboard there may be some arithmetic problems, the scene symbolizing patriotism and an endorsement of "basic" education. In agricultural areas a farmer with a red tractor

(Courtesy World West Features)

substitutes for the children and classroom, but there is a similar message: The candidate knows and supports agriculture. With name identification so important in local contests, the 30-second commercial can make the candidate seem familiar to the voters. A catchy slogan ("She gets things done") or Deukmejian's in 1986 ("Great Governor, Great State") is likely to stick in the viewer's mind when going to the polls.

The subject matter of a television commercial is influenced by those benchmark polls at the beginning of a campaign. How it is presented may be changed after review by a focus group. Then the question becomes when to air it. This decision is the province of the "media buyers." Not all commercials "sell" equally well in all time slots. Some are designed to appeal primarily to a sports-oriented audience and may be shown during football games. Others target those who watch soap operas. Older citizens, blue-collar workers, ethnic minorities—all are "targets" of specially created commercials.

Not all the focus on television rests with commercials, however. While commercials can be effective, coverage obtained on local newscasts has several advantages, not the least of which is credibility. The viewer is likely to assume that if a reporter from Channel XYZ thinks a candidate is worth covering, he or she must have a genuine chance of winning. In one notable case, a candidate ran a commercial in which he was interviewed by several "reporters" (really actors) just to create this impression. A second advantage is of course cost. Compared with a single local television commercial in Los Angeles next to *Seinfeld*, which can run well as much as $50,000, such free coverage is a bargain. Attractive as it is, however, there are some disadvantages. When the candidate buys commercial time, he or she is sure of being seen. When "free" time is given, the candidate may be preempted by a major international incident or even a particularly spectacular fire or traffic accident. And to get the station news editor's attention often means setting up "photo opportunities": Situations in which the candidate can be filmed in colorful and telegenic settings such as visiting a hospital and chatting with patients to underscore support for health insurance or backpacking in the Sierra Nevadas to demonstrate a commitment to wilderness preservation.

Radio Comes Back

The use of radio in campaigns declined precipitously in the late 1950s with the advent of television, but in recent years it has made a comeback and now forms an integral part of most well-developed strategies. Several factors have made radio attractive in the 1980s and 1990s. One is cost. Preparing a radio commercial is much less expensive than preparing and running one for television. When buying time on television, a campaign pays for the entire market served. If running for Congress or the state legislature in San Francisco or San Diego or Los Angeles, that means paying to reach a large majority of viewers who cannot vote for the candidate in any event. They live outside the district. Because of its low cost, radio makes this financially bearable. Another advantage is a greater ability to "target" particular audiences. While television viewers tend to change channels fairly frequently in search of their favorite programs, radio listeners are much more likely to be loyal to one or two stations. What kinds of people listen to which stations is well documented through periodic surveys, though often common sense is an adequate guide. If the music featured is of the "oldies but goodies" variety, a particular type of person is likely to be tuned in. The same is true of rock 'n roll, classical, country-western, and so on. Spanish-language stations are an obvious example, and talk radio has its own clientele. For each a different type of message can be prepared, keyed to that audience's interests. Radio has yet another advantage: The content of what is being communicated is better remembered than on television. And with low cost a 60-second commercial, allowing more to be said, becomes feasible.

Radio is present almost everywhere. Most homes have several—in the family room, the kitchen, the bedrooms. Portables are carried to sporting events, parks, and beaches. Most cars have one, and for those caught up in urban rush hour traffic, radio is an ever-present companion, a companion through which the campaign message can be delivered.

Direct Mail

Of all the means of communicating with the electorate, direct mail may have made the greatest advances in recent years. Mailing campaign brochures ensures hitting the targeted audience—and only that audience—every time. These mailings are carefully designed for maximum positive effect. They are usually colorful in order to attract attention, they make extensive use of pictures showing the candidate with members of the target group, they employ a good deal of what is called "white space" which contains no printing, thus reducing the amount of reading required, and they prominently display the name of the person running on both front and back so that even if the brochure is tossed away immediately the name will be remembered.

The first uses of direct mail employed a single brochure sent to all voters. Today, different mailers are sent to different groups. A student of voting age may receive a mailer specifically created to appeal to student concerns, whereas other brochures, quite different in focus, will go to union members or those who rent apartments. Clinton Reilly, the prominent San Francisco political consultant, described one contest in which 33 different mailers were employed in a single campaign. By using computer-generated mailing lists based on 160 categories, it is possible to identify all single women living in apartments in the Richmond area and send them a brochure designed to appeal specifically to them. Or the prospective audience can be gays with college degrees living in condominiums in Laguna Beach.

Particularly helpful in this process is a system first developed in 1978 called PRIZM. The underlying assumption of the PRIZM system is that people with similar interests tend to live in "clusters." By identifying what kinds of people live where, it is possible to develop campaign messages for those living in such clusters. A few of the many categories used in the system include: "furs and station wagons" (well-educated, affluent, mobile professionals with teenage children living in the suburbs); "shotguns and pickups" (small-town, outdoors-loving, blue-collar workers with school-age children); "Bohemian mix" (integrated singles neighborhoods with generally well-fixed residents, heavy with academics, writers, and artists); and "Hispanic mix" (urban, densely populated bilingual Latino neighborhoods with large families of small children and a high percentage of new immigrants). Knowing that central Los Angeles is high in Hispanic mix or that many communities in the Central Valley have concentrations of those in the shotguns and pickups category makes targeting, especially through television which is less selective than radio or direct mail, more effective.

Print Media

Long a favorite means of reaching the voter, newspapers have been considered less important as the role of electronic media has grown. As noted earlier, most of us get most of our news from television; even those who read the papers tend to turn to the sports or entertainment sections, bypassing any "hard" news about politics. Newspapers continue to play a significant role, however. Opinion leaders are more likely to depend on them since coverage of issues is given in some depth, whereas television, with its time limitations, tends toward what CBS news anchor Dan Rather has called "headline reading." One study pointed out that the entire script of a half-hour national newscast can be printed on two-thirds of the front page of the *New York Times*. Therefore, the opinions of those more likely to influence others are affected by newspaper coverage.

Newspaper endorsements are still sought, especially in races in which the candidates are not well known or, as in most local elections, the cue of party label is absent. The influence of such publications as the *Los Angeles Times,* the Sacramento, Modesto, and Fresno *Bees,* the *San Diego Union,* the *Orange County Register,* and the *San Francisco Chronicle* on such races is considerable. Organizational endorsements are also valued. Police and fire associations; ethnic groups such as the National Association for the Advancement of Colored People (NAACP) and the Mexican-American Political Association (MAPA); professional and economic organizations such as the California State Employees Association (CSEA), California Teachers Association (CTA), and the California Farm Bureau Federation; and environmentalist groups such as the Sierra Club regularly urge their members to support candidates for office. Traditional newspaper advertisements featuring slogans and candidate positions are generally less effective than advertisements listing support for a candidate from several major groups. For voters who know little about the qualifications and positions of the contestants, such endorsements provide a handy guide when voting.

The Dark Side

American politics has long had its perversions. Mudslinging was not invented in the mid-twentieth century. Modern means of communication have simply made it more evident and, it must be added, more sophisticated. Negative campaigning, which emphasizes the faults of the opponent rather than one's own virtues, is not necessarily "dirty." Condemning a policy position or vote cast is part of the give and take of politics, though some believe that so much negative campaigning may help to account for declining voter participation.

Critics of modern campaigning point to two major areas of concern: the tendency toward oversimplification and an increasing use of the half-truth or outright lie in the scramble for votes. The first criticism arises from the impact of television with its focus on short, snappy "bites." A serious address on tax policy may be summarized in a single sentence alleging a "taxpayer ripoff," ignoring the careful analysis that led to it. Speechwriters know this and include such "bites" in their scripts to secure time on television newscasts. The more outrageous and simplistic the statement, the better the chance it will make it on the air.

The second point made by critics centers on what most consider "dirty" politics. Direct mail has been used to make slashing attacks on opponents, attacks that may have no basis in fact. An example is a mailer sent out just before the June 1982 primary. In a hotly contested race to gain the Democratic nomination in a Southern California congressional district composed largely of Hispanics, the mailer sent by one candidate accused his opponent of not being married to the woman with whom he had lived for over 25 years. Among Hispanics with their strong sense of family, this was a devastating charge—and one that was totally false. Sent over the last weekend before the election, it caused what had been a fairly large lead virtually to disappear, though the victim of this smear did manage to pull out a narrow victory. In the June 1988 Democratic primary, incumbent Assemblyman Gerald Eaves' opponent sent a mailer claiming he had the endorsement of Senator Edward Kennedy (D–Mass.). There had been no such endorsement.

Other instances involve deliberate misrepresentation, though not lying. Another 1982 mailer asserted that an opponent was "facing voter fraud, tax fraud, conspiracy and perjury charges." Only by reading the fine print inside was it possible to determine that these "charges" were not being levied by some government agency but by the candidate's opponent, the one sending the mailer. A variation of misleading advertising surfaced in another 1988 primary campaign when one candidate had bumper stickers printed featuring the Reverend Jesse Jackson's name on top with the local state senator's name below. Jackson had not endorsed the senator's bid for reelection, but the apparent tie to Jackson was thought likely to help in a heavily black portion of the district. The senator won.

In 1990 Kathleen Brown's campaign ran a television advertisement that asserted the Republican incumbent State Treasurer Thomas Hayes had lost the state $84 million in bad junk bond investments when the purchases had been made by Hayes's predecessor, Jesse Unruh. During the 1994 senate contest Michael Huffington's campaign ran an advertisement on television that claimed Dianne Feinstein was single-handedly responsible for passage of President Clinton's budget. In fact, she cast one of 51 votes for it and was no more responsible for its approval than the other 50 individuals who voted aye (including Vice President Gore who cast the tie-breaking vote). The "truth boxes" found in some newspapers that analyze television commercials for the accuracy of their assertions are useful antidotes when hyperbole or distortion goes too far.

Controls on Campaign Contributions and Spending

California has strict laws requiring detailed disclosure of money received and spent by candidates for state and local office, by committees acting on their behalf, and by committees supporting or opposing ballot propositions. The purpose of these laws, according to the Political Reform Act of 1974, is to assure "that the voters may be fully informed and improper practices may be inhibited." The Reform Act, a legislative initiative passed by California voters during the height of national furor over the Watergate scandals, also attempted to put limits on campaign expenditures under the premise that "state and local government should serve all citizens equally without regard to their wealth."[7]

California is easily the most expensive state in which to run for office. The number of people to be reached, their great mobility, and the geographic extent of the state all combine to make the use of television, radio, and direct mail virtually mandatory in statewide contests and in many regional and municipal campaigns as well. All this costs a great deal, and these costs have been increasing at a rate many find alarming. Statewide campaigns are of course the most expensive, at least when there is some possibility that either of the major contenders might win. In the general election campaign of 1990, Pete Wilson spent approximately $25 million and Dianne Feinstein close to $20 million. In 1958 the total cost of all the campaigns for the state legislature (80 assembly seats and 20 state senate seats) was $1.3 million. In 1984 that figure had grown to just over $30 million. In the 1995–96 campign cycle the total broke through the $100 million mark for the first time with $121.7 million spent on the one hundred legislative contests, 38 percent more than the previous

---

[7]*Political Reform Act of 1974* (Sacramento: State Printing Office, 1974), p. 5.

record. The average cost of an assembly race climbed to $864,665, up from $599,631 in 1993–94, while the average expenditures in a senate contest rose from $1.4 million to $1.7 million. And in most cases "money talked." In 90 percent of the contests the candidate with the most money won, with the beneficiaries largely incumbents who enjoyed an average 5–1 advantage in contributions and won 58 out of 60 of these races. In part this increase was due to more open seats (term limits leading a number of incumbents to seek other positions) and more competitive seats following the court-ordered redistricting of 1991.

Those spending records created serious concern on the part of the public that political action committees and well-financed interest groups were dictating government policy. The extent of this concern was indicated in the results of a *Los Angeles Times* exit poll conducted during the 1988 primary elections. When asked whether they agreed with the statement that "campaign contributions from special interest groups are corrupting the state legislature," an overwhelming 86 percent of these voters said they did.[8]

Many legislators had grown weary of having to spend so much time on fundraising and were also sensitive to the bad press they had received because of it. For several years, California Common Cause and the League of Women Voters have been pressing for reforms to curb the influence of big money in elections, including the financing of campaigns. A 1983 California law allows individuals to contribute to the party of their choice with a nondeductible donation at the time they pay their income taxes. However, this has proved an inadequate incentive. As a result, several bills have been introduced in the legislature—all unsuccessful—to allow donations to political parties to be deducted from taxes and for such funds to be given to candidates on a matching basis.

Public concern with what was perceived to be too great an influence by special interests on elections and policymaking led to approval of two propositions in the June 1988 primary designed to curb campaign contributions. The details of these two measures need not be elaborated on here since a series of court decisions effectively emasculated both. In the past when two propositions on the same subject had been approved by the voters at the same election, the one with the larger number of "yes" votes prevailed *to the extent of any conflict,* but both propositions could be implemented when there was no conflict. Since Proposition 68 included partial public financing of campaigns and Proposition 73, the one with the greater number of votes, prohibited public financing, none could be provided. However, the state supreme court ruled it would no longer allow a "melding" of two initiatives and held Proposition 68 invalid in its entirety. Later most of Proposition 73 was declared unconstitutional (the courts holding that by having fund-raising limited to calendar years and tying those efforts to how much any source could contribute both gave an unfair advantage to incumbents and violated the First Amendment guarantee of freedom of speech). Common Cause, an original sponsor of Proposition 68, asked the court to reinstate it since Proposition 73 no longer stood in its way. By a 4–3 vote, a badly divided court refused to do so on the grounds that a *portion* of Proposition 73

---

[8]*Los Angeles Times,* June 9, 1988.

remained in place (a ban on taxpayer-financed legislative newsletters that were thinly veiled campaign pieces). Critics of the majority complained that only a minor part of Proposition 73 was left and should not be permitted to stand in the way of the substantial and needed reform contained in Proposition 68. The majority disagreed, leaving the voters who had approved two reform measures frustrated and any meaningful reform dead for the time being. Ironically, the ban that remained in Proposition 73 proved almost totally ineffective. Using a variety of loopholes (no use of "I" but on the legislator's stationery with his or her name on the letterhead, for example, or generating many pieces in lots of 200 which is allowed) thousands of such pieces of mail were sent. Three legislators mailed over 600,000 pieces in a period extending from January 1995 to August 1996.

In 1996 the voters approved Proposition 208, another attempt at campaign finance reform. It sets voluntary limits on spending that vary with the office sought. For example, a candidate could spend up to $150,000 running for the assembly in the primary and up to $200,000 in the general election. Gubernatorial candidates are limited to $6 million in the primary and $8 million in the general. (It is worth noting for comparison purposes that in 1994 Pete Wilson and Kathleen Brown spent just about twice what Proposition 208 now allows, $31.5 million.) Together with spending limits, voluntary contribution limits were established. These vary, depending on the office, from $250 for legislative and local offices to $500 for statewide contests. No contributions in contests involving up to one million residents may be accepted more than six months before the primary or general election. For larger constituencies the limit was set at one year.

The candidates may reject spending limits but should they accept them, the limits on contributions are doubled, from $250 from an individual to $500. And a statement in support of their candidacy will be placed in the ballot pamphlet at taxpayer expense while those who do not accept limits can have such a statement included but at their expense. Also prohibited: contributions from lobbyists and transfer of funds from one campaign to another (a practice pioneered by former assembly speaker Willie Brown and used extensively in recent years by legislative leaders).

An issue not addressed by Proposition 208 is the extent to which office holders and candidates receive contributions from outside their districts. The competing measure at the 1996 election, Proposition 212, would have limited "outside" contributions to 25 percent of the total raised. This was included because of the developing trend of obtaining most campaign contributions from beyond district lines. One study, released in September 1996, found that 80 percent of all campaign funds for the state senate and assembly had been raised from individuals and groups outside the incumbent's home district. This raised in the minds of those backing 212 a question as to who, exactly, was being represented.

SELECTED REFERENCES

Borland, John, "Let the Games Begin," *California Journal,* November 1996.
"Campaigning in California," 7th ed., *California Journal,* Sacramento: California Journal Press, no date.
Collet, Chris, "Bye-bye, GOP, Ta-ta, Dems," *California Journal,* November 1993.

Cook, Gale, "Mail Order Voters Tip the Balance in Close Elections," *California Journal*, February 1991.

Costantini, Ed, and Charles Dannehi, "Safeseat," *California Journal*, November 1991.

Guber, Susan, *How to Win Your 1st Election*, Del Rey Beach, FL: St. Lucie's Press, 1997.

Haynes, Jim, "FPPC's Model Campaign Code Fails to Stop Mudslinging," *California Journal*, August 1983.

Jones, Bill, "Statement of Vote, March 26, 1996 primary," Sacramento, 1996.

————, "Statement of Vote, November 5, 1996 general election," Sacamento, 1996.

Trent, Judith, and Robert V. Friedenberg, *Political Campaign Communication*, New York; Praeger, 1983.

Zeigler, Richard, "Few Citizens Make Decisions for Everyone," *California Journal*, November 1990.

Chapter 5

Referendum, Initiative, and Recall: Democracy Through Petition

Proposition 13, the Jarvis-Gann initiative passed in 1978 limiting property taxes, brought nationwide attention to the importance of the petition process for direct democracy in California. Under this procedure the people themselves make their own laws rather than relying solely on legislative bodies for the formulation of public policy. Furthermore, by means of the recall petition voters may remove from office any elected official before the expiration of the term. For nearly 90 years Californians have been making major governmental decisions at almost every election.

Popular petition for legislation and the recall of elected officials, along with the direct primary and cross-filing, were part of the reform program sponsored by the Progressives to rid the state of control by political bosses and the railroad machine. In California the movement was championed by the Direct Legislation League, headed by the prominent Los Angeles physician John Randolph Haynes. At the instigation of Haynes and his associates, petition devices were adopted in several cities, including Los Angeles and San Francisco, from 1902 to 1910. The election campaign of the Progressives in 1910 contained the promise to institute a statewide initiative and referendum system. Upon election Governor Hiram Johnson sponsored a series of constitutional amendments that, when approved by the voters in 1911, extended the initiative, referendum, and recall to the state and to local governments that had not yet adopted the system. California is now among 21 states where both initiative and referendum may be employed on a statewide basis. Only 15 states, including California, allow for the recall of both state and local elected officials.[1] Most of the states authorizing these forms of direct democracy are located west of the Mississippi River. Referendum and initiative measures may be presented at primary and general elections and at special elections called by the governor. Recalls are voted upon at special elections.

---

[1] *The Book of the States, 1992–93* (Lexington, KY: Council of State Governments, 1993).

REFERENDUM BY PETITION

Referendum by petition is used to prevent laws already passed by the legislature and signed by the governor (or passed over the governor's veto) from going into effect. This should not be confused with the so-called compulsory referendum, whereby constitutional amendments and bond issues passed by the legislature must always be approved by the people in order to become law. Referendum by petition is a popular device for *interrupting* the normal legislative process. Any law passed by the legislature may be held up on referendum, "except urgency statutes, statutes calling elections, and statutes providing for tax levies or appropriations for usual current expenses of the State."[2]

Procedure

To prevent a statute from taking effect, a petition bearing the signatures of registered voters amounting to at least 5 percent of the vote cast for governor in the last election must be filed with the secretary of state. The filing must take place within a 90-day period after the enactment of the bill at a regular session or 91 days after a special session. If the petition qualifies, the act to which it refers is not enforced until the next election when the people have a chance to accept or to reject it.

Before each election voters receive in the mail, along with their sample ballot, a booklet containing all of the ballot propositions with arguments pro and con. These arguments are written by legislators or citizens whom the presiding officer of the senate or assembly has designated as a legitimate spokesperson for each side. At the polls a majority of "yes" votes allows the measure to become law; a majority of "no" votes defeats the measure.

Extent Used

During the first 30 years of its use in California, the popular referendum was applied to 34 legislative acts. Twenty-one of them were voted down by the people. During the next 40 years and until 1982 only one referendum proposition appeared on the ballot: a legislative act that exempted nonprofit private and religious schools from the property tax was held up by a referendum petition only to be approved by the voters at the 1952 election. In 1982 Republicans registered their protest of the Democrat-controlled Reapportionment Act of 1980 by placing three referendum measures on the June 1982 ballot. All three were approved by the voters, and thus the Democratic reapportionment plans for congressional, state senate, and state assembly districts were invalidated. In the same election, another referendum measure that would authorize a peripheral canal across the Sacramento–San Joaquin delta was disapproved by the voters.

The short time limit given referendum petition circulation before a legislative statute goes into operation has made the referendum much more difficult to qualify than an initiative. Thus those who disagree with legislative policy find the direct initiative a more suitable and feasible means to employ.

---

[2]Constitution of the State of California, Article II, section 9.

DIRECT INITIATIVE

Through the direct-initiative method, groups of people (often organized interest groups) originate and pass laws and constitutional amendments without recourse to the legislature. No subjects are exempted from the direct initiative. The only constitutional restriction is that a given initiative proposal must deal with only one main subject.[3] The governor may not veto an initiative measure.

Procedure

The sponsors of a direct initiative may draft their proposal as either a statute or a constitutional amendment. However, under the 1966 revision of the state constitution the petition for a constitutional amendment must be signed by a number of registered voters equal to at least 8 percent of the vote cast for all candidates for governor in the last gubernatorial election; the required number of signatures for a statutory initiative, on the other hand, is 5 percent of the total votes in the last gubernatorial election. (In 1996, the number of signatures required to qualify a constitutional amendment was 693,230 and for a statutory initiatitve it was 433,269.) Despite this fact, more direct initiatives have been constitutional amendments than statutes, because constitutional amendments, once enacted, are more difficult to amend or repeal, since they require a two-thirds majority vote of both houses of the legislature and a subsequent majority vote of the electorate for any constitutional change. A statutory initiative may be amended or repealed by a *simple* majority vote of the legislature and an approval by the electors unless the statutory initiative permits amendment or repeal without their approval.

The draft of a proposed initiative is sent to the secretary of state for recording and is then referred to the attorney general, who must approve the official title and add a brief description of the initiative. A maximum of 150 days is allowed for sponsors to secure the required number of signatures. Once the necessary signatures are secured, the petition is transmitted to the secretary of state for final verification of the signatures and placement on the ballot.

The title of the initiative measure, its summary, which is prepared by the legislative analyst, its complete text, and its arguments pro and con appear in the ballot booklet sent to all registered voters in advance of the election. If the measure receives a majority affirmative vote, it becomes law. A law thus passed may not be amended or repealed by the legislature (unless so provided in the measure) without approval by the voters. In the event that conflicting initiative measures appear on the same ballot and are passed, the one receiving the highest vote becomes law.

Extent Used

During the first four decades of initiative activity (1912–1950) some 40–70 initiative petitions were circulated in every ten-year period, slightly more than half of them qualified for the ballot, and about one-third were approved by the voters. In the 1950s

---

[3]A motion to disqualify the Jarvis-Gann initiative on the basis that it covered more than one subject was denied by the courts.

and 1960s only 55 initiatives were proposed, with 21 qualifying for the ballot, and only 5 were approved. However, beginning in 1970 California experienced a tremendous increase in the use of the initiative, since numerous ballot measures have been proposed by elected officials, special-interest groups, citizen organizations, and citizens with pet projects trying to reform government and the way of life. The peak for initiatives up until now came in 1988 and 1990 when 12 and 13 appeared on the respective November ballots. Up through the 1996 election, over 550 initiatives had appeared on the ballot in California with about one-fourth approved by the voters. However, that very flood of initiatives may have turned voters off and in 1992 only seven were submitted to them and just three were approved. None appeared on the June 1994 ballot and only five were voted on at the general election the following November. A new "flood" accured at the November 1996 election when a dozen initiatives were voted on. Half were approved by the voters. And new uses continue to be found. San Francisco voters faced an extremely lengthy ballot for the November special election in 1993, including Proposition BB, which asked approval for a police officer to carry a ventriloquist's dummy with him while on patrol. The dummy won.

Initiatives have covered an extremely wide range of subjects over the years. One early use dealt with Prohibition. More recently there have been initiatives concerning possession and use of marijuana, limitations on affirmative action, extension of the death penalty, gun control, clear-cutting of forests, taxes on tobacco products, English as the state's official language, physician-assisted death, and term limits for elected officials, to mention only a few of the controversial propositions.

INITIATIVE AND REFERENDUM IN COUNTIES AND CITIES

Procedure

As already noted, the initiative and referendum as petition devices were adopted by cities before they were instituted by the state and included in the state constitution. As revised in 1966, the state constitution now provides that "initiative and referendum powers may be exercised by the electors of each city or county under procedures that the legislature shall provide." This section does not affect a city having a charter.[4] Under present legislative requirements most cities and counties are prevented by state law from requiring more than 15 percent of their electors' signatures to qualify an initiative or more than 10 percent to qualify a referendum. The usual practice is for local governments to require signatures equal to 10 percent of the vote in the last general election for initiative petitions. The time allowed for securing signatures is longer than that for statewide petitions. Completed local petitions may be presented to city councils and county boards of supervisors for their action. If the proposal is approved, a direct vote of the electors is not necessary. Many of the noncontroversial measures are adopted in this manner. In most jurisdictions financial matters and public works are not subject to popular petition.

---

[4]Constitution of the State of California, Article II, section 11.

Extent Used

The referendum and initiative have been more frequently used on a statewide basis than locally. On the local level they have been used more often in the more populous cities and counties. The rule at work seems to be that there is less need for direct legislation when government is close to the people.

Subjects put before local voters by petitioners have included police officers' and fire-fighters' salaries and pensions, garbage and refuse collections, and regulation of liquor establishments and dance halls. Many local referenda and initiatives are in charter cities and counties where charter revisions require voter approval. A local referendum that received nationwide attention, and on which much money and wrath were spent, concerned a contract between the Los Angeles (formerly Brooklyn) Dodgers and the city of Los Angeles to sell public land to the baseball club for the construction of a stadium. Backers of the referendum charged that the city council had no right to grant land that was planned for a public park and public housing to a private corporation. Opponents of the referendum claimed that a vote against the contract was a vote against the Dodgers and against major league baseball in Los Angeles. The Dodger fans thought they had won when the contract was approved by the voters in June 1958, but a superior court judge ruled that the contract violated the city charter. Outraged Dodger fans appealed this decision to the state supreme court. Finally, in January 1959 the supreme court in a unanimous decision upheld the original contract with the Dodgers as approved by the voters.

EVALUATION OF THE INITIATIVE AND REFERENDUM

California's experience with direct-legislation devices, especially in recent years, has highlighted many features unforeseen by the Progressives who championed the 1911 constitutional amendments. Much could not be foreseen, since the "great game of politics" has been transformed dramatically since the days of Hiram Johnson and the Lincoln-Roosevelt league. Thus some of the criticisms against the initiative and referendum are new and cannot be dismissed by reference to the standard theories of democratic government and popular sovereignty. Other criticisms, however, are perennial, recurring each time the matter comes up for discussion. Yet a balanced evaluation must grant the possibility that even the old criticisms may assume a new validity with changing conditions. The arguments, pro and con, are discussed in the following areas of concern.

Voter Confusion

A long list of complicated fiscal, administrative, and technical matters frequently confronts voters as ballot initiatives. Many do not have the time, the training, or the inclination to cast informed votes on such issues as judicial procedures, insurance practices, and reapportionment of legislative districts, or attempt to understand the intricacies of environmental protection, all of which have appeared on the California ballot. To add to the confusion, there has been an expanded use of what are termed

"The woods are full of 'em." (Bastion, *San Francisco Chronicle*)

"counter-initiatives" in recent years. A proposition dealing with a subject such as campaign finance reform is placed on the ballot. A second proposition dealing with that subject is put on the same ballot, typically, though not always, with the intent of confusing the voters, who, in their confusion, vote "no" on both. Intended or not, that was the effect in 1992 on propositions dealing with an increase in liquor taxes and protection of the state's forests when all the propositions dealing with these subjects were defeated.

The voter pamphlet (occasionally more like a book) the voters receive in the mail before each election can help, but it is often written in legalese and its very size, with many pages devoted to the texts of the propositions in small print, is daunting. For the November 1990 election, voters were asked to read 222 pages of material before casting their ballots! The arguments given are so at odds with one another (at times from highly respected experts on *both* sides) and are at times so guilty of hyperbole the voters are turned off. Thirty-second television commercials proclaim a great future or an unprecedented disaster, this on the same proposition. The 1986 toxic waste disposal proposition, Proposition 65, was going to clean up the environment and make it safe or it would drive farmers out of business. In 1996, proponents of Proposition 215, which attempted to legalize the medicinal use of marijuana, argued its usefulness in relieving suffering from AIDS, radiation treatments for cancer, and the pressure on the eye from glaucoma. Opponents claimed it was a back door attempt to legalize general use of the drug and would lead to greater use of hard drugs such as cocaine and heroin.

In rebuttal to the argument that citizens are asked to vote on measures that are too complicated for them to be able to evaluate wisely, it is contended that the experience is good for them: It contributes to their civic education. In answer to the charge that in initiative and referendum campaigns voters are made captives of the public relations consultants hired by pressure groups, it can be observed that misleading advertising is not a problem exclusive to the area of direct legislation. Although in recent years the public relations people are frequently found in the coaching box during political campaigns, the basic question is really how to secure an enlightened public opinion in this age of mass communications.

Often voters *do* appear to discriminate between proposals on the same subject, as they did in 1988 when they approved one of five propositions dealing with automobile insurance on the same ballot. In 1996 two initiatives dealing with campaign finance reform were voted on; one lost while the other won handily.

In recent years voter cynicism concerning this procedure may have been given a booster shot by repeated court interventions into propositions approved by the electorate. Proposition 103 guaranteed a 20 percent reduction in auto insurance; the courts held insurance companies had a right to receive a fair return on their investment, nullifying the guarantee. In 1994 Californians overwhelmingly approved Proposition 187 denying a variety of services to illegal immigrants. Suits immediately tied that measure up in court for years. Two years later the voters saw three measures they passed, Proposition 208 on campaign finance reform, Proposition 209 limiting state affirmative action programs, and the aforementioned Proposition 215, challenged and effectively barred from implementation by court action. Those bringing suit noted, however, that no law, approved by no matter how large a majority, can be allowed to stand if in violation of basic constitutional principles. At issue in these instances was what were these principles and how are they to be interpreted?

High Costs

Perhaps the most severe criticism of the initiative and referendum is that the expense of petition circulation and ballot proposition campaigns discourages all except highly organized special-interest groups from using them. In 1994 it took 384,974 signatures to qualify a direct initiative and referendum and 615,958 to qualify an initiative constitutional amendment. With the state's continued growth, these requirements almost certainly will increase. With the big numbers involved these days a new industry has developed: Companies that specialize in circulating petitions to get propositions on the ballot. Paid by the signature (from 65 cents to as much as $6 each though usually around $1.50 apiece), they will work for any cause and may even carry petitions for opposing interests. They focus on malls, markets, racetracks, anywhere people move slowly, and usually have little understanding of the issues they are pushing. If it takes too long to explain, profits go down. The average cost of qualifying an initiative runs around $700,000.

Then comes the campaign. Costs are enormous in a state as large—and as media-conscious—as California. Television is crucial in many cases, radio and direct mail important in virtually all successful efforts (see Chapter 4). Millions are spent to convince or dissuade the voters by using 30-second television spots focused on imagery and slogans. The height of prolific spending occurred in 1988 when there were five initiatives on the November ballot dealing with auto insurance. After years of deadlock in Sacramento and facing heightened public concerns over rapidly rising auto insurance premiums, the insurance industry qualified three propositions, a fourth was backed by the trial lawyers, while a fifth supported by consumer advocate Ralph Nader also made it. One report showed that the insurance industry interests spent a total of $63.8 million to promote its three separate losing initiatives and to defeat the other two. The Trial Lawyers Association spent an estimated $17.2 million to sell its own proposition and defeat the insurance industry's proposals and that backed by Nader. In the end the only one to gain voter approval was Nader's Proposition 103, which had virtually no special-interest support and had just $2.9 million spent in its support.

Money does not always win elections, as is shown by the success of Proposition 103. However, one estimate from California Common Cause is that in the contests with a substantial difference in the amounts spent, in roughly 90 percent of such cases the side with the bigger checkbook has won. That usually means special interests have put a great deal of money into the electoral pot. Examples of campaigns that resulted in losses for the underfinanced side include an antismoking initiative in 1980 (Proposition 10), a gun-control measure in 1982 (Proposition 15), and the school voucher initiative in the special election in 1993 (Proposition 174).

Radical and Irresponsible Legislation

There is the possibility that an initiative or referendum measure will be hastily prepared with more emotion than reason in order to take advantage of a given situation. Sponsors representing narrow interests promote their own causes without regard for the general welfare of the public. With a well-organized and effective campaign a proposal could be approved by a majority of the voters, and once the legislation was passed, the sponsors would have no more responsibility for the political and social consequences of their proposal, for it would now become the duty of the legislature, the governor, and the courts to enforce and implement the initiative or referendum. Critics of direct legislation point out that under these conditions the very fabric of legislative processes and representative government is being threatened.

Supporters of the initiative and referendum respond by emphasizing that the purpose of direct legislation is to act as a check on the legislature, not to replace representative government. Public and special-interest groups employ the initiative and referendum to raise important issues after failing to receive satisfaction from the legislature. People go through this difficult process because they feel the legislature has not done its job.

As far as the criticism relating to radical and hastily drawn proposals is concerned, it can be shown that very few measures of this type have been successful. Proposals for the single tax, for instance, have been turned down six times by the voters. An initiative making radical changes and providing for unreasonably large pension payments, although originally approved under the McLain plan in 1948, was repealed by a subsequent initiative and voted down by the electorate. In fact, the voting record of the public stands up well. The California voters have approved only about one-third of the measures submitted through the petition process. Among those that have been accepted are some highly regarded public policies such as the merit system for government employees, a centralized executive budget, state financial support of elementary and secondary schools, and coastline conservation. Were it left to the legislature, these reforms might never have come about.

Proposals for Reform

Today Hiram Johnson would not recognize the system he proposed in 1911 as a means of breaking the special-interest influence on the state's legislative process. Largely because of the large amounts of money necessary to qualify and to secure a favorable vote for the initiative, the will of special interests has most frequently prevailed.

Scholars and representatives of public-interest groups such as Common Cause have suggested several reforms to restore the process to its original intent. Among the ideas are: limiting the number of initiatives on any one ballot, limiting the subjects that can be addressed, increasing the number of signatures required on petitions, and limiting those paid to circulate petitions. A state commission in 1994 proposed extending the period for circulating petitions from 150 to 180 days to give volunteer-based efforts (as opposed to paid efforts by professionals) a more level playing field. The commission also suggested listing in the ballot pamphlet and on the ballot the names of the five biggest contributors to a campaign to increase voter awareness.

One reform was undertaken by the California State Supreme Court in 1991. The justices invoked a constitutional requirement that holds initiatives must deal with one subject, not a variety of them. Proposition 105, known as the "truth in advertising" initiative, was approved by the voters in 1990 but the court ruled that while all its provisions dealt with informing the public (publishing the health and safety records of nursing homes, warnings on products that should not be poured down the drain, requiring companies to say whether they had investments in South Africa, etc.), the scope of the proposition was so broad virtually anything could be included, ". . . essentially obliterating the constitutional requirement."

One of the most prominent and controversial proposals as advanced by the League of Women Voters would allow initiatives to go straight to the legislature for vote instead of to the ballot. If the legislature approved, and upon signature by the governor, the measure would become law, eliminating the need for a costly and time-consuming campaign. However, if the legislature added amendments that the backers did not like, or if the legislature refused to approve the initiative, it would be referred to the electorate for vote. This process, known as the "indirect initiative," was on California's books between 1912 and 1966.

RECALL

By means of the recall, voters in California may remove from office any *elected* state official before the expiration of his or her term. A proposition approved by the voters in 1974 provided that all elected state and local officials are subject to recall at any time after their election. In contrast to an impeached official (for whom a misdemeanor is the required indictment for removal), the recalled official need not have violated any law.

Signatures Required

To recall an official elected by the entire state, the petition must be signed by registered voters equal to at least 12 percent of the total vote cast in the last election for the office involved. The petition must also contain signatures of voters in at least five counties equal to not less than one percent of the vote cast for the office in each of these counties.

If the recall involves state officials elected by districts (members of the legislature, district courts of appeal judges, and members of the Board of Equalization), the petition must contain signatures of voters in the district equal to at least 20 percent of the vote cast for the office in the last election. Because of the large number of signatures required for a recall of state officials, this process is rarely used.

Procedure

The procedure for circulating the recall petition and verifying the signatures is the same as that for referendum and initiative petitions, except that proponents have a 160-day time limit for filing signed petitions. The recall petition must contain a statement of grounds for removal, but since there is no requirement for specific charges, the petition may, in fact, say no more than "we don't like the way the official is performing." Upon certification of the petition by the secretary of state, the governor is required to call an election to take place within 180 days from the date of qualification.

Candidates who want to replace the official to be recalled are required to file a petition 25 days before the election, signed by at least 1 percent of the vote cast for that office at the last election.

If the recall fails, the state reimburses the incumbent for election expenses incurred, and another recall election of this individual may not be initiated until six months after the election.

Extent Used

No recall of a statewide officer has actually been on the ballot in many years, mainly because of the large number of signatures necessary to qualify the petition. Among those who have been subject to recall petitions are Governor Ronald Reagan (1967, 1968, 1972), Governor "Jerry" Brown (1979, 1980), Chief Justice Rose Bird (1981, 1982), and Governor Pete Wilson (1991, 1992). None of these petitions secured the necessary signatures to qualify for the ballot. Recall efforts brought against state legislators have proven almost as futile. The most recent cases involved the unsuccessful attempt to remove state senator David Roberti (see page 93) and in May 1995 the first successful effort in 81 years when voters ousted Republican assemblyman Paul Horcher—he had voted to keep Willie Brown as speaker, a heresy his constituents could not forgive.

Recall of Local Officials

As with direct legislation, local governments may set their own recall procedures under general requirements of the state legislature. Local governments are prohibited from requiring petition signatures equal to more than 25 percent of the vote cast in the previous election for the office involved. The number varies depending on whether the recall is for a county office, city council, or a school or special district office. If enough signatures are secured, an election is called and a ballot prepared asking, "Shall (name of official) be removed from the office of (title)?" A majority of "yes" votes removes the public official from office. Most local jurisdictions allow voters to select a successor by plurality vote from a list of persons who have qualified to run if the recall succeeds. A state law prohibits a recalled official from being a candidate to succeed himself. In addition, the state legislature has ruled that in city recall elections voters may not simultaneously choose a successor—either the city council appoints a successor or the voters choose one at a later election.

Local recall attempts have taken place frequently in California. They have focused on judges ("soft" on crime, enforcing school busing), city council members, county supervisors, and those serving on local school boards.

A well-publicized example was the effort in 1983 to recall the then mayor of San Francisco, Dianne Feinstein. A white supremacist group, the White Panthers, started the petition drive, citing Feinstein's sponsorship of a city ordinance banning handgun ownership. Other groups joined in, including gay rights groups, which sought to oust her for her veto of "domestic partners" legislation that would have given official recognition to homosexual and other unmarried couples. The mayor's supporters pointed to her record on crime and a budget surplus and the recall failed by a 6–1 margin. Another well-publicized effort was directed against State Senator David Roberti in 1994, only months before term limits were to force him out of the senate in any event. Mounted by gun owners opposed to his long-running efforts on behalf of gun control (he was the author of the ban on semiautomatic weapons passed by the legislature in 1989), Roberti easily survived the recall attempt.

Evaluation of Recall

The generally accepted purpose of the recall is to give the voters a chance to remove from office elected officials who have demonstrated incompetence and corruption but who are not necessarily guilty of criminal action. (When criminal action is involved, the impeachment process may be used.) A brief examination of the issues that have caused recall elections will reveal how well the purpose of the recall in California has been accomplished.

Most of the recall petitions cite causes that are related to corruption, misbehavior, or ineffective administration on the part of elected officials. Charges of bribery, graft, and improper personal conduct are common. Many recalls list unsatisfactory personnel relations as the reason for removing elected officials. For instance, the firing of a city manager or a police chief may cause enough unfavorable public reaction to bring about a recall of members of the city council.

However, some recall movements take place because of the alleged unresponsiveness of the official or officials involved. The charges may be the result of a dispute over a single major policy between the elected officials and some of their constituents. Those who sponsor the recall might even be those who had opposed the incumbent in the previous election. This particular type of recall raises some serious questions, since it may be true that the public good may require leaders who adopt unpopular policies—policies that may be beneficial in future months or even years.

It may be argued that voters should employ regular elections, not the recall, to decide policy issues. If the time between elections is too long, the initiative or referendum is available. The threat of removal at any time may make elected public officials reluctant to alienate political factions or organized interests, and a sacrifice of the public good might be the result.

Despite the controversy over the proper use of the recall, there is every indication that it will continue to be popular, particularly with local governments in California.

SELECTED REFERENCES

California Commission on Campaign Financing, *Democracy by Initiative: Shaping California's Fourth Branch of Government,* Los Angeles: Center for Responsive Government, 1992.

Citizen's Commission on Ballot Initiatives, "Report and Recommendations on the Statewide Initiative Process," Sacramento: State of California, 1994.

Dubois, Philip L., and Floyd F. Feeny, *Improving the California Initiative Process: Options for Change,* Berkeley: University of California, 1992.

Jeffe, Sherry Bebitch, "Risk Wary Voters Look for Security in a 'No' Vote," *Los Angeles Times,* November 7, 1993.

Lee, Eugene, "California," in David Butler and A. Ranney, eds., *Referendums: A Comparative Study of Theory and Practice,* Washington, D.C.: American Enterprise Institute for Public Policy Research, 1978.

Magleby, David, *Direct Legislation: Voting on Ballot Propositions in the United States,* Baltimore: Johns Hopkins University Press, 1984.

Naisbitt, John, *Megatrends,* New York: Warner Books, 1992.

Price, Charles, "Initiative Reform," *California Journal,* April 1994.

Price, Charles, and Robert Watson, "Initiatives: Too Much of a Good Thing?" in Thomas Hoeber and Larry Gertson, Sacramento: *California Government and Politics Annual,* 1993.

Scott, Steve, "Ballot Bulge," *California Journal,* July 1996.

Chapter 6

The Legislature

The California legislature plays a vital role in the government and politics of the state. Its members, as lawmakers, represent local views at the state level and are constantly engaged in mediating conflicts and reconciling pressures from competing special-interest groups. It is important to understand how well these lawmakers represent and carry out the will of the citizens of California.

COMPOSITION AND STRUCTURE

Similar to the Congress of the United States and to the legislatures of all states in the Union but one, California has a *bicameral* (two-house) legislature. At the 1849 convention the proposal for a two-house legislature was passed unanimously and without debate. The more numerous house was named the "assembly"; the less numerous house was named the "senate."

Before 1926 representation in both houses was based on population. In that year a constitutional amendment instituting the "federal plan" was approved by the voters. This plan retained population as the basis of representation in the assembly and provided for geographical-area representation in the senate. However, the "federal plan" was replaced in 1966 under the Reapportionment Act of 1965, which returned to population as the basis for representation by districts in both houses (see Figures 6.1 and 6.2).

Apportionment of Assembly Seats

The assembly has 80 members—somewhat fewer than the lower house in most state legislatures. According to the California constitution, assembly members are to be elected from districts "as nearly equal in population as may be." To paraphrase the old saw, all assembly districts are created equal, but some are more equal than others. Unequal districts come about naturally through population growth and shifts between the reapportionment the legislature made after each ten-year census.

Apportionment of Senate Seats

California's second constitution (1879) set the number of state senate seats at 40, and the size has not been changed since. The difficulty under the "federal plan" was how to divide 40 senators equally among the state's 58 counties. It was decided that county

Figure 6.1 State assembly districts. (Map provided by *California Journal*)

lines should be the basis of division and that no county could have more than one senatorial district. However, it was further provided that a senatorial district could cover as many as three sparsely populated counties. As a result of apportionment by the legislature in accord with this formula, the majority of counties had one senator each representing them in Sacramento, but some counties were represented by only one-third of a senator. While some counties, such as Mono and Alpine, were represented by one-third of a senator, those really shortchanged lived in the most populous

Figure 6.2   State senate districts. (Map provided by *California Journal*)

counties. Some 60 percent of the people resided in four counties (San Francisco, Alameda, Los Angeles, and San Diego) and were represented by just four senators. The rest of the counties with 40 percent of the population elected the other 36. The senator from Los Angeles County represented 6.5 million people; the senator from District 28 (Inyo, Mono, and Alpine counties) represented fewer than 15,000—a ratio of about 440 to 1! This imbalance had the dubious honor of being more severe than that of any upper house in the United States.

REAPPORTIONMENT—CONTROVERSIES AND PLANS

The U.S. Supreme Court and Reapportionment

The move for California senate reapportionment was given tremendous impetus by the U.S. Supreme Court in the decision of *Baker v. Carr* (1962), in which the court declared that state legislative reapportionment was within the purview of the federal courts.

On June 15, 1964, the U.S. Supreme Court, in a historic decision (*Reynolds v. Sims*) involving six different suits in six states, held that the districts in *both* houses of state legislatures must be "substantially equal" in population. The court said that there was no valid analogy between state legislatures and the federal Congress in which the Senate is based not on population but on two members for each state. The specific provision in the Constitution for the Senate, the court said, resulted from a compromise among the sovereign states that formed the Union. But counties and other subdivisions of the state have never been sovereign, and states are subject to the Constitution's overriding requirement of equality.

The decision cited the Fourteenth Amendment of the Constitution, which provided that "no state shall . . . deny to any person within its jurisdiction the equal protection of the laws." Chief Justice Earl Warren, a former governor of California, said "legislators represent people, not trees or acres. "Legislators are elected by voters, not farms or cities or economic interests."[1] The chief justice specifically said that both houses of a bicameral legislature must be based on population. To apply the rule to only one house, he said, would permit a minority veto in the other and thus stalemate or frustrate the will of the majority.

State Battles over Reapportionment

The reapportionment of 1966 dramatically changed politics in California. The balance between north and south was upset as at one stroke both houses of the legislature became dominated by Southern California. If the Supreme Court order was based on principle (one person, one vote), the result nonetheless was to have major political consequences.

Of course reapportionment itself is almost always political; it must be inasmuch as those drawing the lines are, in most cases, politicians. Controversy has surrounded every reapportionment effort in recent years, beginning with the deadlock that developed between a Democratic legislature and then-Governor Ronald Reagan following the 1970 census. The legislature refused to bend but was unable to overturn Governor Reagan's vetoes of plans he believed unfair to Republicans. The impasse was broken only when the state supreme court appointed three retired judges as special "masters" to create the new legislative and congressional districts. Instead of making districts that were "safe" for this or that party or incumbent, the masters, employing computer technology, redistricted using criteria foreign to most partisan plans: compactness,

---

[1] *New York Times,* June 16, 1964.

ACTUAL DISTRICTS DRAWN UP BY CALIFORNIA
LEGISLATURE IN 1982

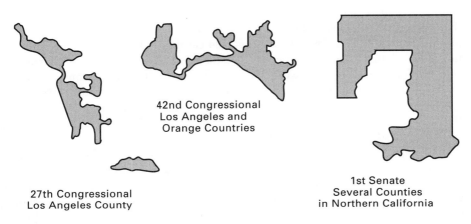

**42nd Congressional
Los Angeles and
Orange Countries**

**27th Congressional
Los Angeles County**

**1st Senate
Several Counties
in Northern California**

Figure 6.3   Actual districts drawn up by California Legislature in 1982.

community of interest, and of course population equality. Two assembly seats were "nested" in each senate district. The result was districts that were more competitive, as shifts in party control of legislative seats over the next several elections showed. Reinforcing the 1966 change, the north-south balance now had the eight southern counties with 23 senate seats and 48 in the assembly.

New battles arose following the 1980 census. The legislature, still solidly in Democratic control, approved congressional and state legislative district lines that had in large measure been drafted by Congressman Philip Burton (D–San Francisco). Though the Democrats held a slim 22–21 edge in California's congressional delegation following the 1980 election, Burton's plan was designed to ensure a 28–17 majority following the 1982 elections and through the remainder of the decade. Republicans found themselves gerrymandered out of their districts or, in several instances, lumped together in the same district, ensuring that one of them would not survive. The Burton plans (he termed them "my contribution to modern art" for the sometimes weird shapes the districts took) was signed into law by Governor Jerry Brown. The fight was not over, however. Republicans, using the referendum by petition procedure, got all three plans on the June 1982 ballot and all three were rejected by the voters.

Republicans joined with the public-interest group Common Cause to place on the ballot the following November a proposal to take reapportionment away from the legislature and place it in the hands of an independent commission of ten members, four appointed by the courts and three by each of the major parties. Having expressed their unhappiness with the way the legislature had redistricted, many expected the proposal to pass, but it did not. Poorly funded, the proponents may have lost out because of voter confusion or a desire not to add another government commission.

A second plan, dubbed "Burton II," was unveiled and found by most to be at least as biased as the Burton I plan had been. It was signed into law by Governor Brown on his last day in office. Republicans were once again "outraged" and sought to place another initiative before the voters, the so-called Sebastiani initiative, named for its principal author, Assemblyman Don Sebastiani. It secured over 700,000 signatures, considerably more than the number required to qualify it for the ballot. The sympathetic new governor, George Deukmejian, was asked to call a special election so that new districts could be in place before the 1984 elections. He announced his intention to do just that when the Democrats took the question to the courts. In a remarkable decision, the state supreme court held the Sebastiani initiative unconstitutional on the grounds that reapportionment could take place only once every ten years. The fact reapportionment had already occurred twice seemingly escaped the attention of the majority.

Undaunted, the Republicans, under the leadership of Governor Deukmejian, drafted a new initiative to create a nonpartisan commission of retired superior court judges to undertake redistricting in the future. The criteria to be employed mirrored those in the Common Cause/Republican proposal of 1982. Districts should be compact, equal in population, reflect communities of interest, and so on. After a long and, on the side of the opponents, very costly campaign, the proposal was defeated by a ten-point margin. The loss was due in part to the vigorous opposition of the Democratic Party, which spent heavily to defeat the measure in a campaign that featured Hollywood celebrities urging voters not to let politicians draw election lines, an interesting message since the proposal was to take that power *away* from the politicians in Sacramento.

Having lost at the polls, the Republicans decided to challenge the Democratic reapportionment in the courts. They were encouraged by a decision of the U.S. Supreme Court relating to an Indiana case in 1986 stating that a legal action against a political gerrymander existed where an electoral system had been arranged in a manner that degraded a voter's or a group of voters' influence on the political process as a whole. California Republicans maintained that in the outcome of three elections (1982, 1984, and 1986) the proportion of 40 percent of congressional seats they had won was well below the 45–50 percent of the popular votes the GOP had received.

In 1987, however, a specially empaneled federal court decided (*Badham v. Eu*) by a 2-to-1 margin against the Republican challenge, maintaining that, inasmuch as the GOP had won the gubernatorial election, a U.S. Senate seat, and 40 percent of the House of Representatives seats, it had not been excluded from the political process. It now appeared that any new reapportionment plan would be determined by the state legislature elected in 1990—the time of the next decennial census.

A replay of the 1970–1972 scenario took place when newly elected Republican Governor Pete Wilson vetoed redistricting plans forwarded to him by the Democrat-controlled legislature. (The main reason he received such strong support from the Republican right was to prevent the party from being "Burtonized" again.) Once again the Democrats could not override the governor's vetoes and the matter went to the state supreme court. Masters were appointed and in due course districts that lacked any similarity to "modern art" emerged. The masters returned to the practice of "nesting" two assembly seats in each senate district, generally thought to be less confusing to voters. The most significant change from the Burton districts, however, lay in their relatively more competitive character. This led Republicans—and indeed most impar-

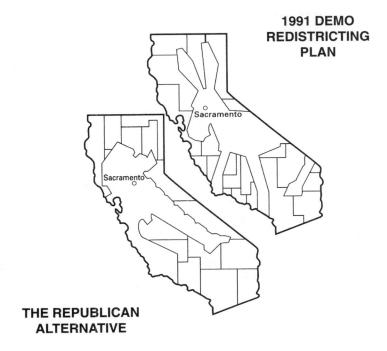

1991 DEMO REDISTRICTING PLAN

THE REPUBLICAN ALTERNATIVE

("Every Ten Years." Dennis Renault, *Sacramento Bee*)

tial observers—to forecast major Republican gains in the November 1992 elections. As we saw in Chapter 3, that did not happen. The other significant change, and this one *did* happen, was in the creation of a number of districts designed to elect minorities, especially Hispanics.

QUALIFICATIONS, TERMS, AND COMPENSATION

To be eligible for election to the state legislature an individual must be 18 years old, a U.S. citizen, a resident of the state for three years, and a resident of the district for one year previous to election.

Members of the assembly have terms of two years, whereas state senators serve for four years with half of the membership elected every two years to provide continuity. A large proportion of the members are reelected for more than one term, and there is no restriction on the number of terms an individual legislator may serve. The longer term for senators has tended to make this office more attractive than that of a member of the assembly, who must conduct a campaign every two years.

Before 1966, when California had a part-time legislature, members' annual salaries were set at $6,000. When the constitution was revised in that year providing for a full-time legislature, the annual salary was raised to $16,000 and the legislature was allowed to set the amount of its own salaries with a limitation of no more than a 5 percent increase each year.

Legislative salaries are now set by an independent commission created following approval of Proposition 112 in 1990. Under the proposition the power to raise their own salaries was taken from the legislature (something they wanted, given the unpopularity of such raises with the public) and given to the California Citizens Compensation Commission. Its first meetings resulted in an increase in legislative salaries from $40,816 to $52,500. Another change, illustrated by the foregoing, was the lifting of a 5 percent cap on annual salary increases adopted years before. The Commission dramatically increased legislative salaries in 1994, arguing that with term limits the job had to be made more attractive to those who could take a mid-career sabbatical as lawmakers. The Commission settled on $72,000 as appropriate, a 37 percent increase. The commission voted to increase legislative salaries an additional 5 percent to $75,000 in 1995 and an additional 4 percent in 1997 to $78,624. In addition to their salaries, legislators receive a per diem (per day) tax-free allowance to cover living expenses while away from their homes ($105 a day in 1998 or an average of $22,000 a year). Other perquisites include the use of a state-owned car with a credit card for free gas and oil and maintenance of the leased car; a telephone credit card for official calls; and a generous retirement plan valued at twice that of other state employees. One source of supplementing their incomes was taken away by Proposition 112. Previously, many legislators pocketed thousands of dollars in speaking fees known as *honoraria*. There were occasions when little was done for the $2,000 or $3,000 check and often there was at least the appearance of conflict interest. That practice was eliminated by the proposition.

MEMBERS OF THE LEGISLATURE

Traditionally, there has been a preponderance of attorneys and businesspeople as members of the California legislature. These occupations lend themselves well to the legislative schedules and sessions, because they allow persons to take leave and to be absent from their offices or places of business for a period without any sacrifice; in fact, such governmental experience may enhance their regular positions and interests. Most state legislators have had previous experience in government by serving at the state, county, or city level before their election. A notable development in recent years has been the increase in the number of former staff members elected to the legislature. These former staffers run as "insiders," people knowledgeable about the politics of Sacramento. There has also been an increase in the number of women, blacks, and Hispanics elected, the last, especially, aided by redistricting.

Because of the change in annual sessions and the accompanying increase in salaries, the California legislature has now become more a "professional legislature," in which members serve on a full-time basis and look on their job as a profession in itself. This is in contrast with most state legislatures, "citizen legislatures," where members serve only part-time and have other full-time jobs.

Legislative Officers

In the Senate   The lieutenant governor of the state is the president of the senate and presides over senate sessions but may not introduce a bill or vote on a measure except in the case of a tie vote. The senators elect a president pro tempore (or "pro tem") from their membership to preside over the senate when the lieutenant governor is absent. The president pro tem is regarded as the most important official of the senate, serving as chairperson of the powerful rules committee. Under the constitution the president pro tem becomes the acting governor when both the governor and the lieutenant governor are out of the state. In 1968 when both Governor Reagan and Lieutenant Governor Robert Finch were in Florida attending the Republican convention, Senator Hugh Burns, president pro tem, successfully invoked this power and adjourned the legislature despite the opposition of Assembly Speaker Jesse Unruh. Nonmembers are elected by the senate to serve as secretary, sergeant-at-arms, chief clerk, and chaplain.

In the Assembly   A member of the assembly, the speaker, who functions as the presiding officer, is elected by the members of the house and retains all voting and debating rights. As the most powerful member of the state legislature, the speaker appoints all committee chairpersons and selects nearly all committee members (except those on the Rules Committee). The speaker also designates his or her choices for assembly majority party positions including the majority party leader, the caucus chairperson, the speaker pro tem, and party whips. In addition, the speaker has the power to make the bill referrals to committees and is also in charge of the assignment of legislative offices and the allocation of office staff for all members of the assembly. (This was not true during the period of turbulence in 1995 when Democrats and Republicans were either evenly split or where defections by one or two Republicans led to a temporary arrangement under which committee chairmanships were evenly divided between the parties and the speaker's powers were significantly reduced.)

In recent times the speaker has come to be seen as second only to the governor in power, though the influence of term limits makes it unlikely any subsequent speaker will ever achieve the power of some past occupants of that office. As an elected office, the speakership is controlled by the majority party. A number of strong speakers have occupied the office over the years. Probably the most respected was Jesse Unruh, famous for his statement that "money is the mother's milk of politics." However, the most powerful may well have been Willie Brown, a master political tactician and fervent party man. Indeed, the longer his tenure in office the more partisan the temper of the assembly became. This was not entirely Brown's fault, as more conservative Republicans came to win elections and posed a blunt challenge to his role. Brown survived several rebellions, both by Republicans and by conservative Democrats such as the "Gang of Five," and served nearly 15 years as speaker until, facing term limits, he ran successfully for mayor of San Francisco.

Other Officers

A speaker pro tempore, also elected from the assembly, presides in the absence of the speaker. Nonmember officers include the chief clerk, the sergeant-at-arms, the minutes clerk, and the chaplain.

Serving Both Houses

Three major officers serve both houses of the legislature: the legislative analyst, the legislative counsel, and the state auditor (formerly auditor general). The legislative analyst, as the chief fiscal adviser to the legislature, provides an analysis of the annual governor's budget, as well as a review of any bill that has a fiscal implication. The detailed study of the budget becomes the basis for legislative hearings on the fiscal program of the state government. The legislative counsel is the legislature's legal specialist and expert on drafting bills. This official prepares or assists in preparing measures for legislators and also writes digests of bills for use by the legislature. The function of the state auditor is to keep close scrutiny over the financial management of state agencies and to keep the legislature advised of ways and means to secure more efficient and economic operation of the state government. All three officials are appointed by, and are responsible to, the legislature. Their services are very significant to the legislative process.

The Committee System

The committee system in the California legislature is a vital part of the legislative process and organization. Each house maintains its own set of standing committees to handle bills dealing with basic and general subjects such as agriculture, education, finance, local government, and resources.[2] Senate and assembly subcommittees and select committees are created from time to time to consider special subjects as they arise and need attention. The California legislature also has established several joint committees made up of an equal number of members from each house to work on continuing matters such as audit, budget, and rules during the session, throughout recesses, and after adjournment. Generally, each senator serves on four committees, and the average member of the assembly is assigned to three committees.

Committees vary in size from 5 to 21 and are made up of both Democrats and Republicans in varying proportions. Assignments to committees are not made on the basis of seniority, as is true in the U.S. Congress, and it is even possible, though rare, to have a committee chaired by a member of the minority party.

Party Organization in the Legislature

California's atmosphere of nonpartisanship (or *bipartisanship*, as state legislators prefer to call it) used to prevail at the state capitol. "The words 'Democrat' and 'Republican' are not often heard on the floor of the houses," reported the secretary of

---

[2]There were 23 standing committees of the senate and 25 standing committees of the assembly in the 1994–1995 legislature.

the senate in 1957, "and when they are heard it is frequently in some friendly or humorous connection."[3] Since the Democrats assumed control of the administration and the legislature in 1959 party alignments have become increasingly more marked.

There has been much more partisanship exhibited in the assembly than in the state senate. Cooperation between Democratic leaders and Republican leaders, especially during the tenures of David Roberti, the Democratic leader of the senate, and Republican leader Ken Maddy, was reasonably frequent. Compromises leading to bipartisan votes were not unusual. As already noted, however, the assembly has been far more partisan with party lines in general holding firm. The caucus system (meetings of all members of the party in the legislature to decide positions to be taken and strategies to be used) is used extensively by both parties.

SESSIONS

Several state legislatures are in session for only short periods during the year, and generally the length of the session is limited by law. Some 15 states convene only once every two years for legislative sessions. (California had this arrangement from 1862 to 1946.) These practices are in contrast with the U.S. Congress, which convenes in early January and usually does not adjourn until late in the summer or early in the fall, when it deems it has finished its annual business. Until California changed its plan for legislative sessions with constitutional revision in 1966, New York was the only state having annual year-long legislative sessions.

Today, sessions of the legislature begin on the first Monday in December of even-numbered years and must close no later than November 30 of the following even-numbered year. Thus sessions are not annual but biannual, that is, bills can be carried over from one even-numbered year through the next.

Extraordinary (Special) Sessions

The legislature can be called into extraordinary session by the governor at *any* time between regular sessions or even concurrently with regular sessions. To call an extraordinary session, the governor issues a proclamation stating the purpose of the session and listing the subject to be considered. On such occasions the legislature has power to legislate only on subjects specified in the proclamation. The governor thus has a tighter control over legislation in extraordinary sessions than in regular sessions. The governor's power to call extraordinary sessions can also be used as a threat to encourage the legislature to act on certain measures deemed important by the governor.

The legislature has frequently been called into special session over the years. The record was set by Governor Culbert Olson, who called five such sessions in 1940. Some topics covered in the years since include medical malpractice, prisons, and earthquake relief.

---

[3]Joseph A. Beek, *The California Legislature* (Sacramento: State Printing Office, 1957), p. 152.

LEGISLATIVE REORGANIZATION

The state legislature became a full-time body in 1966 with voter approval of Proposition 1A. A second ballot measure, Proposition 4, was approved in 1972, changing the legislative calendar from one-year to two-year sessions.

Bills may be introduced in either the first or the second year, and bills introduced in the first year are automatically carried over to the second, except in the case of bills that have not been passed by their house of origin by January 30 of the second year. No bill may be passed by either house on or after September 1 of the even-numbered year, except statutes calling elections, providing tax levies, or appropriations; "urgency measures"; and bills passed over the governor's veto. The legislature may not present any bill to the governor after November 15 of the second year. Most newly enacted statutes go into effect after January 1 but only after 90 days have passed since enactment; otherwise they do not go into effect, in the absence of an urgency clause, until the next January 1.

In many respects, this plan resembles the system now used in the U.S. Congress.

LEGISLATIVE ACTION

The legislature may take action in any of three basic ways: It may express an opinion; it may pass a law; or it may refer a measure to the voters for approval, which is required with bond issues and constitutional amendments.

Resolutions are used for expressions of opinion by one or both houses of the legislature. *House resolutions* are made by one house only and may pertain to any matter. *Joint resolutions* are expressions by both houses relating only to national government matters. They are usually expressions of approval or disapproval by the California legislature of legislation pending in Congress. *Concurrent resolutions* are used for all other matters on which both houses wish to express an opinion or must act jointly, as for adjournment or recess or to commend individuals for public service.

Constitutional amendments and bond issues are treated as regular bills but are submitted to the voters for final adoption or rejection at the following general election instead of being sent to the governor for signing.

How A Bill Becomes a Law

1. Introduction   The act of introducing a bill consists of a legislator submitting a signed copy to the clerk of the house to which the legislator belongs. Although all bills must be formally introduced by members of the legislature, most of them originate in government agencies, the office of the governor, or with pressure groups. In fact, more often than not the legislator acts merely as an intermediary for other interested parties. After submission of the signed copy, the bill is numbered, given its "first reading," and assigned to an appropriate committee. (Committee assignment is the responsibility of the speaker in the assembly and the committee on rules in the senate.)

2. Consideration by Committee   The fate of most bills is determined by the committee to which they are assigned. Public hearings are scheduled for important legislation, and anyone wanting to testify is usually given an opportunity to appear.

A state assembly committee meeting. (Courtesy Sirlin Studios)

The state senate in session. (Courtesy Sirlin Studios)

Committees have the authority to subpoena witnesses and documentary evidence related to their investigations. (Failure to honor a subpoena is grounds for legal prosecution.) A committee may dispose of a bill in any of the following ways: (a) table it, that is, postpone action indefinitely; (b) report it out (back to the whole house) without recommendation; or (c) report it out with the recommendation "do pass," either in its original form or as amended by the committee. Many bills (more than half in the assembly) are never reported out of committee—they are *pigeonholed,* to use the legislative vernacular. However, a bill can be forced out of committee by a majority vote of all members in the house concerned, but this process is rarely used. Usually, the house follows the committee's recommendations.

3. Consideration on the Floor   After the bill has been reported from committee it is given a "second reading," at which time committee amendments and amendments from the floor are adopted. It is then reprinted with the amendments for the "third reading," which opens floor debate. Debate may be closed and the question brought to a vote in each house by a majority vote, so there can be no minority "filibusters" in the California legislature. A bill may be passed with or without amendments, referred back to committee, or rejected. The final vote on passage of a bill is by roll call—the vote of each member placed in the record—in each house. The senate retains the traditional oral roll call, the clerk droning out the name of every member. The assembly uses an instantaneous electric recording device that simultaneously flashes all votes on a scoreboard in view of everyone as members press the "yes" or "no" buttons at their desks. It takes 41 votes in the assembly to pass an ordinary bill and 21 in the senate (a majority of the total membership of each house). To pass a constitutional amendment, an urgency measure, or a budget bill, or to override a governor's veto, 54 assembly votes and 27 senate votes (a two-thirds majority of each house) are required. Once a bill is passed by either house, it is signed by the presiding officer and sent to the other house for consideration. Final passage by the legislature requires approval by both houses.

4. Referral to Conference Committee   If the second house to consider a bill passes it with amendments and the originating house refuses to concur in these amendments, a conference among selected members of both houses is called to iron out the differences. The conference committee is composed of three members of the assembly appointed by the speaker and three senators appointed by the committee on rules. Two of the members from each house must be from the majority that voted to pass the bill and one from the minority. If the report of the conference committee is not accepted by both houses, another conference committee is convened, but there can be no more than three such committees for one bill. The conference committee is extremely powerful and influential, since practically every major piece of legislation is referred to this committee. In turn, the report of these six legislators is generally approved by the two houses and then becomes law. It is interesting to note that for many years conference committee meetings were closed; it was not until 1974 that they were ordered open to the public.

5. For Approval by Governor   After an agreed-upon version of a bill has been passed by both houses, it is technically referred to as a legislative act. If it is signed by the governor, it will go into effect the following January 1, providing 90 days have passed since signing.[4] If the governor fails to sign the bill within 12 days after receiving it and the legislature is still in session, the bill becomes a law without the governor's signature. A bill passed within the last 12 days of a general session will become law unless the governor vetoes it within 30 days after the end of the session.

6. Overriding the Governor's Veto   A bill returned to the legislature by the governor with his or her objections can be passed and become law over these objections only by a vote of two-thirds of the elected members of each house. If the legislature is unable to obtain such a vote against the governor's action, the bill fails to become a law. A special five-day veto session of the legislature, called for the purpose of considering and possibly overriding the governor's vetoes as established by the 1966 constitutional revision, was eliminated by Proposition 4 in 1972. No governor's veto was overridden by the legislature from 1946 until 1974, when a Reagan veto was overruled (for a full discussion of the veto power, refer to Chapter 7).

Amount of Legislation

Over 4,000 bills are now introduced at each session of the legislature. The number any one legislator may introduce is now limited to 40 for a member of the assembly and 65 for a senator. About one-third of them are almost immediately abandoned and never receive serious consideration by the committees or on the floor of the legislature. Most of them have been introduced by legislators to satisfy their constituents, and the authors themselves have little enthusiasm or hope for passage. Another one-third of the measures introduced are killed either by the committee or on the floor of the assembly or the senate, or are vetoed by the governor. Thus in recent years about 1,100–1,400 bills have finally become law during each legislative session.

Unfortunately, a large number of bills do not reach the senate and assembly floors until the last moments of the closing session of the legislature. In spite of the reorganization, which placed the legislature on a full-time basis, lawmakers allow bills to proceed through committee earlier in the session but then fail to seek the required final votes on the floor until the last days of session, when the press of time might thwart organized opposition. The result is a huge backlog of bills that await action. In the 1987 session, for instance, there were about 400 measures still pending when the legislature began its last week of sessions. After the end-of-session frenzy, some 120 bills simply died on the senate and assembly floors. There was nothing necessarily wrong with them; lawmakers simply ran out of time.

Media Coverage

Though news coverage of the legislature is not good (there is no television station from outside Sacramento with a crew permanently assigned to that "beat"), some television stations do carry CAL-SPAN, the state equivalent of the national network covering Congress, C-SPAN. It carries legislative debates and committee hearings to a

---

[4]If an urgency clause has been attached to the bill and two-thirds of the members of each house have approved its passage, it becomes a law as soon as the governor signs it.

potential audience of some two million in the state. In general, however, media coverage of what goes on in Sacramento tends to be very limited unless there are dramatic or scandalous developments. A survey by the Annenberg School of Communications at the University of Southern California in 1989 found local television and radio newscasts devoted approximately 2 percent of air time to Sacramento government and politics.

EVALUATING THE CALIFORNIA LEGISLATURE

In the 1960s and 1970s the California legislature experienced many major reforms. During this period the time limits on sessions were removed, legislators were given more adequate compensation, more effective regulations on lobbyists and conflicts of interest were passed, and the principle of "one person-one vote" was applied in the reapportionment of the senate, which improved the pattern of representation. A strong system of standing committees was given well-defined jurisdiction, and the number of joint committees was increased, thus facilitating more cooperation between the two houses.

As a result of these changes, California's legislature has been considered one of the best in the nation. Historically, California's legislature has been in the forefront of such reforms as openness of meetings, regulation of lobbyists, disclosure of campaign contributions and spending, and conflict-of-interest laws. However, in recent years there has been increasing concern about special-interest influence and the inability of the legislature to act on major issues when faced with intense lobbying by major campaign contributors. Enter the initiative process.

When the legislature failed to act on a plan to safeguard the state's coastline, voters approved Proposition 20 in 1972, establishing the California Coastal Commission. When the legislature balked at campaign reform, the voters approved the Political Reform Act of 1974. Probably the best-known instance was passage of Proposition 13 in 1978 limiting property taxes, action taken by the voters when the legislature and governor seemed unable to act (see Chapter 10). In 1988, faced with inaction on escalating automobile insurance rates, they approved Proposition 103 in an attempt to roll back those rates. The message has been clear: If the legislature will not or cannot act, the people will.

Current Criticisms

In recent years the great reputation of the legislature has suffered a number of blows. Increased partisanship, especially in the assembly, led to a phenomenon known as legislative gridlock. That gridlock was enhanced by increasingly powerful special interests that exercised an effective veto power over legislation they opposed. The aforementioned auto insurance crisis, which involved the insurance industry, the trial lawyers and the medical profession, each able to block the proposals of the others, is an example. A poll taken in 1988 during this crisis found 86 percent of Californians agreeing with the statement that "campaign contributions by special interests are corrupting the state legislature." Then there was the partisan struggle between the Democratically controlled legislature and successive Republican governors. All this

(Dennis Renault, *Sacramento Bee*)

led to impasse and alienated a public fed up with an apparently powerless government in Sacramento.

On top of everything else came the disclosures that some members of the legislature had been caught, on videotape in some instances, with their hands in the political cookie jar. Payoffs had been made by Federal Bureau of Investigation agents to legislators and their aides to gain approval of a bill giving a fictitious shrimp-packing company financial aid. The investigation, known popularly as "the F.B.I. 'sting'" operation, led to the conviction of three state senators, one member of the assembly, several staff members, and a prominent lobbyist, and indictment of several others who played the political game in Sacramento.

This again brought to the forefront the fact that legislators, facing the need to raise large amounts of cash for their reelection campaigns, had increasingly turned to special interests for funds. As discussed in Chapter 4, spending on legislative races has escalated in recent years, reaching over $120 million in 1996.

As noted earlier, one effort to improve the image of the legislature with the public came with passage of Proposition 112 in 1990. Abolition of honoraria, limits on the value of gifts that could be received, and prohibitions against former legislators from lobbying their ex-colleagues for one year after leaving office—all this was to improve the appearance of integrity in Sacramento.

Term Limits

All this apparently was not enough because the voters approved the more draconian of two versions of term limits, Proposition 140, the following November. Members of the assembly are limited to three 2-year terms, state senators and statewide elected officials to two 4-year terms.

Those favoring term limits pointed to the long tenure of a great number of elected officials, many protected by gerrymandered districts from which they could not be dislodged. They asserted an elitist attitude by those holding secure seats and a lack of responsiveness to voter concerns. There was no other way of "cleaning house" they said. And there were too many politicians with no experience in the "real world." As one wag put it, "[he] never held a job in a place without a dome." Term limits would ensure there would be open seats on a regular basis and that would mean more competitive elections.

Opponents argued you should not throw the baby out with the bathwater (all legislators, good and bad, would be removed) and that the voters could always remove a legislator at election time. They also expressed concern that, by mandating a revolving door of "citizen legislators," the voters would be ensuring inexperienced lawmakers who might well be overmatched by lobbyists and bureaucrats with much greater experience and expertise. Many agreed with the argument that the complexity of issues before the legislature meant that staff—with long experience unmatched by elected members—would become more important and more influential.

These arguments proved ineffective and Proposition 140 passed easily. Members of the legislature took their case all the way to the U.S. Supreme Court, but were told the states had the right to determine the conditions for state office. The impact was quickly felt. The decision left many legislators both bitter and casting about for ways of extending their lives in government. Some retired, but many opted to run for other offices. Members of the assembly looked to the state senate, Congress, or local government while state elected officials in some cases sought to shift to other state offices, for example, Treasurer Kathleen Brown's run for the governorship in 1994.

A federal court judge ruled in 1997 that the lifetime ban on running for a legislative office once the limit had been reached was unconstitutional. She held that this both denied the voters an opportunity to vote for experienced legislators and violated the rights of lawmakers to reenter politics by running for their old seats. The ruling left open the possibility that a new limit without the lifetime ban provision, one that would require a member who reached the limit to sit out a term but then be allowed to run for his or her old seat, would be found constitutional. The judge said her decision would not go into effect until the federal court of appeals ruled on it. However, it seemed clear this question ultimately would be decided by the U.S. Supreme Court.

Entering the 1997 legislative session, there were no members of the assembly who had served more than four years. Yet the composition of that body had changed relatively little from the days when there were no term limits. Those members who formerly had been involved in politics numbered 51 in 1988; that declined only slightly to 49 in 1997. There were 15 lawyers in the assembly in 1988; 14 held seats in 1997. And fund-raising was just as prevalent a preoccupation under term limits as it had been before.

SELECTED REFERENCES

Bell, Charles, and Charles Price, "20 Years of a Full-Time Legislature," *California Journal*, January 1987.

Block, A. G., "'Nesting' in the Assembly Does Not Refer to a Comfort Zone," *California Journal*, July 1993.

Cain, Bruce, "Redistricting: Public Policy or Just Politics," in John J. Kirlin and Jeffrey I. Chapman, eds., *California Policy Choices*, Vol. 6, Los Angeles: University of Southern California School of Public Administration, 1990.

California Political Almanac, Sacramento: California Journal Press, annual.

Driscoll, James, *California Legislature*, Sacramento: State Printing Office, 1978.

Endicott, William, "Limit on Terms Makes its Mark," *Sacramento Bee*, July 17, 1993.

Fairbanks, Robert, "Reapportionment, 1982," *California Journal*, March 1983.

Gunnison, Robert B., "In Sacramento, Term limits Have Handed Staff New Clout," *San Francisco Chronicle*, January 5, 1997.

Grumm, John G., "The Effects of Legislative Structure on Legislative Performance," in Richard I. Hofferbert and I. Sharkanski, eds., *State and Urban Politics*, Boston: Little, Brown, 1971.

Hyink, Bernard, "The California Legislature Looks at the State Constitution," *Western Political Quarterly*, March 1962.

Jeffe, Sherry Bebitch, "Can a Speaker Make Policy and Still Hold Power?" *California Journal*, May 1987.

————, "Have the Voters Created Their Own Dream Legislature?" *Los Angeles Times*, December 1, 1996.

Legislative Analyst, *California Legislative Interim Committee and Reports*, Sacramento: State Printing Office, biennial.

Price, Charles and Helen Neves, "Term Limits: California's Gift (?) to the Nation," *California Journal*, December 1991.

Vanz, Max, "Assembly Profile little Changed by Term Limits," *Los Angeles Times*, December 2, 1996

Chapter 7

The Executive and the Administration

The governor is the most visible political personality in California, and almost every resident knows the names Ronald Reagan, Jerry Brown, George Deukmejian, and Pete Wilson. Californians expect the governor to provide the same type of executive and administrative leadership for the state as the president of the United States provides for the nation. Yet unlike the federal government, but like most state governments, California's government has several elected executive officials. In addition to the governor, there are 11 state executives—lieutenant governor, attorney general, secretary of state, controller, treasurer, superintendent of public instruction, insurance commissioner, and four members of the Board of Equalization—all elected directly by the people (see Figure 7.1). The voters have, with some regularity, elected governors of one party and lieutenant governors or attorneys general of another. In 1990 Democrat Leo McCarthy was elected to a third term as lieutenant governor serving with his second Republican governor (Deukmejian and Wilson). Republican Mike Curb was elected to that same position along with Democratic Governor Jerry Brown. And in 1994 the voters chose Democrat Gray Davis to serve as second to Republican Pete Wilson. As can be seen in Figure 7.2, the same pattern has been typical of the attorney general's position. Originated to prevent excessive concentration of power in the hands of one person, this arrangement has contributed to a divided administrative structure.

This "plural executive" system contrasts with the national government, in which the president and vice-president are always of the same party and the president has the power to appoint and remove the major executive officers. Although the power of the governor has been augmented by the establishment of the executive budget and the item veto (see below), the dominant fact is that the 11 executive officers mentioned are not dependent on the governor for their jobs.

THE GOVERNOR

As the state's chief executive, the governor has the responsibility of carrying out the laws enacted by the legislature and those initiated by the people. This broad executive power, plus other constitutionally delegated powers, makes the governor the most important public official in the state.

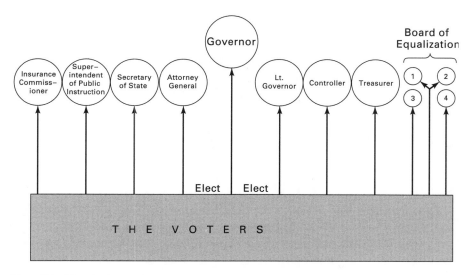

Figure 7.1   The plural executive

Major Powers

A governor's ability to *direct* public policy depends on using the constants and variables attached to California governorship. The constants are the constitutional powers inherent in the position. The variables are the governor's administrative and political leadership in exercising these powers. These constant and variable powers, when used strategically or aggressively, can have a significant impact on public policy.

The Executive Budget   Probably the most important grant of authority to the governor is in the constitutional amendment of 1922, which placed the duty of originating the annual state budget in the governor's office. Whereas formerly each department and agency submitted its own request for funds to the legislature, under the present system all request for appropriations must be channeled through the governor. The aim was to eliminate piecemeal and happenstance financial legislation and to diminish the interplay of politics among the legislature, individual departments, and pressure groups.

The governor has the final responsibility for preparing and submitting to the legislature an annual budget containing most of anticipated state income and expenditures. Under the constitution the revenues must be sufficient to support the proposed budget, and if they are not, the governor must recommend tax changes. The technical and detailed work of reviewing and making budget estimates for the various departments, holding hearings, and composing the budget documents is the task of the Department of Finance, which is directly responsible to the governor. After the governor has approved the budget document, the governor submits it to the legislature with a message outlining and defending the year's financial program. Until the

Term of Office	Governor	Lt. Governor	Attorney General	Secretary of State	Controller	Treasurer
1955–1959	Goodwin J. Knight	Harold J. Powers	Edmund G. Brown	Frank M. Jordan	Robert C. Kirkwood	Charles G. Johnson (A. Ronald Button 1956–59)*
1959–1967	Edmund G. Brown	Glenn M. Anderson	Stanley Mosk (Thomas Lynch 1964)*	Frank M. Jordan	Alan Cranston	Bert A. Betts
1967–1971	Ronald Reagan	Robert Finch (Ed Reinecke 1969–)*	Thomas Lynch	Frank M. Jordan	Houston Flournoy	Ivy Baker Priest
1971–1975	Ronald Reagan	Ed Reinecke	Evelle Younger	Edmund G. Brown, Jr.	Houston Flournoy	Ivy Baker Priest
1975–1979	Edmund G. Brown, Jr.	Mervyn Dymally	Evelle Younger	March Fong	Kenneth Cory	Jesse Unruh
1979–1983	Edmund G. Brown, Jr.	Mike Curb	George Deukmejian	March Fong Eu	Kenneth Cory	Jesse Unruh
1983–1987	George Deukmejian	Leo McCarthy	John Van de Kamp	March Fong Eu	Kenneth Cory	Jesse Unruh
1987–1991	George Deukmejian	Leo McCarthy	John Van de Kamp	March Fong Eu	Gray Davis	Jesse Unruh (1987) Thomas Hayes*
1991–1995	Pete Wilson	Leo McCarthy	Dan Lungren	March Fong Eu	Gray Davis	Kathleen Brown
1995–1999	Pete Wilson	Gray Davis	Dan Lungren	Bill Jones	Kathleen Connell	Matt Fong

*Served out the unexpired term of the elected officer.

Republican   Democratic

Figure 7.2 Elected state officers, 1955–1999

budget has been passed, the legislature may not take up any other appropriation measures except those for operational expenses of the legislature itself, unless the governor specially requests an emergency bill.

The governor is in a strong position when dealing with the state's financial programs, though of course the legislature plays a major role. The two-thirds requirement for approval of the budget may force concessions from the governor or be used by the governor if his or her party is in the minority to gain concessions from the opposition.

The Veto   The governor can also influence legislation through the exercise of, or the threat of exercising, the veto. The governor has two classes of veto: the *general veto* for rejecting an entire bill and the *item veto* for rejecting only portions of bills.

1. *The general veto.* The governor may disapprove a bill within 12 days after receiving it by sending it back to the legislature. The vetoed bill is usually accompanied by a written statement from the governor indicating any objections. A vetoed bill can be passed over the governor's objections only by a two-thirds vote of the elected members of both houses.[1] If the governor neither signs nor formally rejects a bill within 12 days of receiving it, as long as the legislature has not yet adjourned, the bill becomes law without the governor's signature. Until Proposition 6 was passed in 1966, if the legislature adjourned before the 12-day period had expired, the governor was allowed 30 days after adjournment in which to sign the bill. If after the 30-day period the bill remained unsigned, it was considered a *pocket veto*, and there was no possibility for the legislature to override the veto.

An examination of the veto records of the last five governors shows they were not reluctant to use this power. Edmund "Pat" Brown vetoed 6 percent of legislative bills presented to him and Edmund "Jerry" Brown turned down 7 percent. Both were Democrats. The rate for Republican governors Ronald Reagan and George Deukmejian was about 12 percent. Such a differential can be explained by the fact that for most of the time involved the state legislature was under the control of the Democrats with whom these men more often disagreed. Pete Wilson entered office striking a conciliatory tone toward the Democratically controlled legislature, but soon found himself at loggerheads with its leadership. He vetoed 17 percent of the bills placed on his desk in his first term.

2. *The item veto.* California's governor, like the chief executives of four-fifths of the states, may reject individual items in any appropriations bill.[2] California's governor may either *strike out* an item completely or *reduce* it but may make *no increases* in expenditures. The legislature has the same power to override an item veto as a general veto. However, it rarely uses this device, almost always allowing a bill that has received an item veto to take effect.

The purpose of the item veto, instituted along with the executive budget in 1922, was to strengthen the governor's hand in the formulation of the state's fiscal program.

---

[1]The California legislature rarely has been successful in overriding a governor's veto. For the first time since 1946, both houses in 1974 secured the necessary two-thirds vote to override Governor Reagan's veto of a bill relating to closure of state hospitals. Although Governor Jerry Brown was overridden eight times in 1979, all but one of the bills involved a conflict over employee salaries.

[2]A few states go even further and allow their governors to apply the item veto to all legislation.

Whereas previously the governor had either to accept a bill or to reject it *in toto*—thus encouraging legislators to add unrelated "riders" to the budget bill or other vital legislation—the governor may now reject only those provisions that are found to be objectionable, while retaining the basic measure.

Initially, the item veto was not used often by California governors. However, more recent governors, including Ronald Reagan, Jerry Brown, George Deukmejian, and Pete Wilson, have frequently "blue penciled" certain items involving appropriations by decreasing the amount or eliminating the item entirely.

Recommending Legislation   Although the governor may not formally introduce a bill to the legislature, many proposals for legislative action emanate from the governor's office. The constitution requires the governor to send a message to the legislature at the beginning of every regular session describing the condition of the state and recommending action on specific matters. It matters not whether the State of the State message is long or short (Jerry Brown's state addresses lasted less than ten minutes); it receives a good deal of public attention and becomes the keystone of the governor's policy for the ensuing year. Like the State of the Union message of the president of the United States, it receives serious consideration by the legislature.

Every governor builds a legislative program around a series of specific proposals, which are drafted into measures for introduction into either the assembly or the senate. The governor's office makes an agreement with a legislator, who is generally a political ally and colleague of the governor, to introduce these bills. Such agreements are frequent and come as a result of the governor's political influence. Throughout the course of the legislative session the governor normally sends numerous informed messages on various matters encouraging the passage of legislation that he or she favors. In February 1979 Jerry Brown became the first governor ever to testify before a legislative committee when he appeared before the Assembly Ways and Means Committee in support of a proposal to convene a national constitutional convention to write an amendment requiring a balanced federal budget. The threat of the governor's veto and the ability to call extraordinary sessions give weight to the governor's recommendations, but their success or failure depends on his or her political influence with the members of the legislature and an ability to win their support.

Calling Special Sessions   The state constitution provides that "on extraordinary occasions the governor by proclamation may convene the legislature in special session. When so convened it has power to legislate only on subjects specified in the proclamation but may provide for expenses and other matters incidental to the session" (Article IV, section 3b). Governors have used this device frequently. They may, and often do, call these extraordinary sessions to meet at the same time the legislature is sitting in regular session, and on these occasions the results are sometimes truly extraordinary.[3] The effect of the governor's power to call sessions and to specify their business is readily seen: Senate and assembly leaders know they cannot ignore a governor's legislative program.

---

[3]See discussion of *extraordinary sessions* in Chapter 6, p. 115.

Appointing State Officers   Although the governor's power of appointment is limited by the plural executive system, which provides for the direct election of many important officials, and by the large state civil service program, it is nonetheless a substantial power. California's governor appoints most of the top administrative officials, including the director of finance, the secretaries of the five major administrative agencies (business, transportation, and housing; health and welfare; resources; state and consumer services; youth and adult correctional), and most of the department heads. Two departments are headed by elective officials: the department of justice, which is directed by the state attorney general, and the department of education, whose head is the superintendent of public instruction.[4]

The governor also appoints members of the several independent boards and commissions, such as the Public Utilities Commission, the Transportation Commission, the Agricultural Relations Board, the Post-Secondary Educational Commission, and the Fair Political Practices Commission, many of whom have terms overlapping the governor's four-year term; thus any one governor may not have the opportunity of making all board and commission appointments.

The governor's appointments to these high offices are subject to review and approval by the state senate, and the law requires the secretary of state to post notices of vacancies in appointed positions. The many interest groups are active in proposing candidates for the governor's approval and appointment.

The governor is given a free hand to appoint members of his or her cabinet. This group of 10 to 12 individuals comprises the governor's administration, a legislative secretary, and an appointments secretary, all of whom serve at the pleasure of the governor.

Another facet of the governor's appointment power is the responsibility for filling any unexpired terms (because of resignation, disability, death, or conviction of crime) of certain elected officials: U.S. senators, state executive officers, and judges of the state courts.[5] Filling vacancies on the court bench has become a frequently exercised and important duty.

When a judicial office becomes vacant or when the legislature establishes a new superior or municipal judgeship, the governor is authorized to make a new appointment. The governor's appointments to the state supreme court and the courts of appeal are subject to review by the Commission on Judicial Appointments, consisting of the chief justice of the state supreme court, the state attorney general, and a judge of the state court of appeals. One of the most controversial appointments in recent years was that of Rose Bird to chief justice of the state supreme court by Governor Edmund Brown, Jr., in 1977. The first woman to be appointed to this post, she had no previous experience as a judge, and this caused considerable opposition

---

[4]A constitutional amendment to have the superintendent appointed by the state board of education (rather than elected) failed to pass in the November 1958 election. An attempt to change the method of selection, which would allow the legislature to determine how the superintendent should be chosen, was defeated in the 1968 proposal to revise Article IX of the state constitution.

[5]When vacancies occur in many other elective offices, as in the state senate and assembly, the governor issues writs for special elections. In any office in which there is no provision for filling a vacancy, the governor has general constitutional authority to make an appointment.

from the legal profession and the California State Bar Association (see Chapter 8 for further discussion of Rose Bird). The governor appoints nearly 2,000 members of the nearly 300 regulatory boards and commissions in the state. Thirty-nine regulate various professions. Some are prominent, such as the franchise tax board which deals with state taxes, while others are less visible such as those dealing with optometry or auctioneering.

Power as Political Leader   Occupancy of the office itself brings to the governor, whether the person be a strong or a weak leader, a position of political prominence second to none in the state. The governor is looked on as the titular leader of his or her party, often becoming its favorite candidate at the presidential nominating convention; with the increased electoral weight of California, the governor is automatically regarded as a presidential possibility. The position's prestige and its resultant influence over public opinion may be used—if a governor is so inclined—as a whip to corral would-be mavericks in the party or in the state government. Such influence can be exerted through informal conferences, breakfasts, press conferences, and phone calls.

Other Powers

The governorship carries with it many other responsibilities in addition to the major powers already discussed. Many of them are the traditional duties of any governmental chief executive in the United States, whether it be president, governor, or mayor.

Commander in Chief of the State Militia   Whenever police officers of the state, counties, or cities are unable to handle emergency situations such as fires, earthquakes, or floods, or to quell civil disturbances such as riots, insurrections, or strikes, the governor may call out the state militia. The militia—now integrated with California's National Guard units—is a standby military reserve composed primarily of men who have served in the nation's military forces. Although the governor may order the militia to act at his or her own discretion, the governor rarely ever calls on it except on request from a local law-enforcement official.[6] The actual administration of the militia is delegated to the adjutant general of the California National Guard, an appointee of the governor, subject to presidential approval.

Executive Clemency   Except in the case of impeachment, the governor has power to grant pardons, reprieves, and commutations of sentence to individuals convicted of any felony. The difficult nature of such decisions and the large number of requests place a heavy strain on the chief executive. "I'd bleed from every pore each time I went over a case," recalled Goodwin Knight.

> You realize that all you have to do is scratch your name on a piece of paper—you do it as governor about 20 times a day anyhow—and a man can live. A flick of the wrist and I can let him breathe, I'd tell myself. And if you did

---

[6]Occasionally, the Guard may be called into national action; for example, in 1950 California's 40th Division was sent to Korea. The National Guard was also called to quell the Watts riot in 1965 and again for the Rodney King riots in 1992.

not many people would know. . . . Executive clemency appeals are strenuous and the toughest thing a governor has to face. The evening before the day of execution isn't pleasant.[7]

The burden is eased somewhat by two agencies—the Adult Authority and the Board of Trustees of the California Institution for Women—which act in an advisory capacity to the governor. Yet all final decisions are the governor's alone and not subject to overrule; however, the governor may not pardon a person twice convicted of felonies without the recommendation of the state supreme court.

Ceremonial Functions   Representing the state at all sorts of public functions demands a great deal of time and effort. The governor must host visiting dignitaries, deliver dedicatory addresses, proclaim a multitude of special "days" and "weeks," cut ribbons at the opening of new freeways, ride in parades, drink the first glass of orange juice at the Orange Show, and sample the first date at the Indio Date Festival. Although some governors may find, and have found, such activities to be not unpleasant, these ceremonial functions all too often prevent a chief executive from attending to the pressing business awaiting her or him in Sacramento.

Qualifications, Term, Succession, and Salary

To be elected governor of California a person must be a voter who has been both a U.S. citizen and a resident of California for five years preceding election. The governor is elected for a term of four years, beginning with the first Monday after January 1 following election.

Before 1967 the constitution contained a detailed list of succession to the office of governor in case the governor is unable to complete the four-year term. The 1966 constitutional revision provides that the lieutenant governor succeeds to the office, but further successors are to be designated by the legislature through statutes. Constitutional revision also authorized the California Supreme Court to determine when the governor is unable to carry out his or her duties and should be removed from office.

California paid its governor the same yearly salary, $49,100, for 20 years until 1987. The governors of 38 smaller states were paid more, and all ten of the state executive officers have received more—their annual salary level in 1983 was $63,628. The governor's salary now is set by the California Citizens Compensation Commission, which raised it to $126,000 a year effective the end of 1995. The person holding the office also enjoys a number of "perks," including the services of a limousine and driver, money to cover expenses for having to maintain two residences, and a liberal travel allowance. There is, in addition, an expense account for running the governor's office.

Who Becomes Governor?

Most of California's governors have been about 50 years old at the time of inauguration and have brought with them previous experience in state government. With the exceptions of Hiram Johnson, a noted criminal lawyer from San Francisco, and

---

[7] *Sacramento Bee*, June 11, 1959, Sec. A.

Ronald Reagan, a motion picture and television actor, all of California's chief executives had previously held important public offices in the state. The attorney general's office has become increasingly regarded as a steppingstone to the governorship (as it indeed served for Earl Warren, Edmund Brown, Sr., and George Deukmejian). Lieutenant governors have succeeded to the office of governor in seven instances because of the death or resignation of the incumbent, the most recent being Goodwin Knight's assumption of the office upon the appointment of Earl Warren to the U.S. Supreme Court in 1953.

Wilson as Governor

Even those who oppose him might concede Pete Wilson's timing in becoming governor was not very good. He entered office just as the national recession was beginning. The Cold War was winding down and major cuts in defense contracts meant more belt-tightening lay ahead. Welfare rolls were growing rapidly just as revenues were dropping. On top of all that, Mother Nature appeared to have it in for him. The ongoing drought (broken only by the rains in the winter of 1992–1993) was joined by a disastrous freeze in 1991 that crippled a good deal of the state's agriculture. Brush fires swept much of the southland in 1993, including the posh Malibu and Laguna Beach areas. The capper came with the highly destructive (and expensive) Northridge earthquake in January 1994. All this and a flood of illegal immigrants that was running up bills the state had to pay (for education, emergency medical care, prisons, and the like).

Wilson entered office proclaiming his desire to support programs that would be preventive in nature. Rather than lock people up, the emphasis would be on crime prevention. Rather than pay out more and more to welfare recipients, enact programs that would help them get off the welfare rolls. He supported funds for family planning and prenatal care. For these and other ideas he was welcomed by members of both political parties in Sacramento.

The honeymoon proved short, however. The tough economic times precluded expenditures for many of the programs Wilson had urged be adopted. From a preventive stance he moved toward cutting back many programs that were costing the state increasing amounts of money. A favorite target was welfare; he made several efforts (including an initiative in 1992) to reduce payments by as much as 25 percent. His original approach was doomed by the rough economic winds that blew through the state. No, his timing might have been better.

However, his ability to overcome these problems in his winning bid for reelection in 1994 immediately led to speculation he might become a candidate for the Republican nomination for president in 1996. The late President Richard Nixon had predicted just that scenario shortly before his death. That is precisely what happened. Though Wilson had promised he would complete his second term and would not seek the presidency in 1996 if reelected, shortly after defeating Kathleen Brown he announced his bid for the White House. That proved very unpopular, even among Republicans, and, stricken with serious voice problems that required weeks of nonspeaking and minor surgery, his campaign never did get off the ground. (A *Los Angeles Times* poll conducted in mid-September 1996 found that only 23 percent of

Governor Pete Wilson. (Courtesy Sirlin Studios)

Californians thought Wilson should be running for president and only 30 percent of Republicans thought he should be.)

THE LIEUTENANT GOVERNOR

The constitutional status of California's lieutenant governor is much like that of the U.S. vice-president—once described by Benjamin Franklin as "His Most Superfluous Majesty." This does not mean that any occupant of either post is doomed to obscurity and political impotency, but there is a built-in anonymity to the office that is difficult to overcome. The lieutenant governor serves as president of the senate but has only a casting vote (one needed to break a tie). He or she becomes acting governor upon any temporary disability of the governor or upon the governor's absence from the state; he or she becomes governor when a vacancy occurs in the office of governor.

The spotlight may fall on a lieutenant governor, however, if the person who is then governor has a flair for travel. The lieutenant governor is "acting governor" when the chief executive is out of the state or physically disabled. This provision was the cause of an interesting controversy involving Mike Curb, a Republican, who had been elected lieutenant governor in 1978 at the same time Jerry Brown, a Democrat, had been reelected governor. Later in 1979 when the governor was out of state, Curb, as "acting governor," appointed a judge to the appellate court. Upon return to California Brown withdrew the appointment and substituted his own. This conflict in action was appealed to the courts for decision. The state supreme court concluded that Curb had the authority to make the appointment, though Brown had the authority to withdraw this particular appointment as it had not yet been confirmed by the Commission on Judicial Appointments.

The California Constitutional Revision Commission suggested that, in order to avoid this kind of political maneuvering, an amendment to the state constitution be approved requiring the governor and lieutenant governor to run as a ticket, as do presidential and vice presidential candidates. The idea was soundly rejected by both the politicians and the public.

By virtue of the office, the lieutenant governor also serves as a member of the State Lands Commission, the University of California Regents, and the board of trustees of the California State Universities and Colleges.

THE ATTORNEY GENERAL

The attorney general is the most important executive officer in the state after the governor. Article V, section 13, of the constitution specifies that among the responsibilities of the attorney general:

> . . . It shall be the duty of the Attorney General to see that the laws of the State are uniformly and adequately enforced. He [or she] shall have direct supervision over such other law. . . . Whenever in the opinion of the Attorney General any law of the State is not being adequately enforced in any county, it shall be the duty of the Attorney General to prosecute any violations of law of which the superior court shall have jurisdiction, and in such cases the Attorney General shall have all the powers of a district attorney. . . .

Although the attorney general has the responsibility for the enforcement of state laws, local law enforcement is generally left to the cities and counties. The attorney general's responsibility for local law enforcement involves her or him directly with the state's difficult crime problems, including narcotics, illegal gambling, and juvenile delinquency. The attorney general heads the Department of Justice and is legal counsel for the state and most state agencies, rendering them legal advice and representing them in court. Another duty is to prepare the titles and summaries of all ballot propositions submitted to the voters in state elections.

Persons who serve in this office are often selected as candidates for governor, as in the case of Earl Warren in 1942, Pat Brown in 1958, Evelle Younger in 1978, and George Deukmejian in 1982.

THE SECRETARY OF STATE

The secretary of state is California's chief clerk and as such has the responsibility of keeping the official record of the acts of the legislature and the executive departments. The secretary of state appoints a keeper of the archives, who maintains the central records depository in which are kept the enrolled copy of the constitution, all acts and resolutions passed by the legislature, the journals of the senate and the assembly, other official deeds, parchments, maps, papers, and the Great Seal of the state.[8]

An especially important function of the secretary of state is the supervision of elections. He or she certifies initiative, referendum, and recall petitions and assigns them places on the ballot (see Chapter 5); publishes official and sample ballots and the voters' preelection booklet; certifies and maintains the records of affidavits of candidacy and campaign finances; and certifies and publishes election results. In much of these elections administration responsibilities, the secretary of state works through and with county election officials.

The secretary of state also processes charters and collects fees for the incorporation of private businesses, counties, and cities.

This office used to attract little interest, and its occupants have exercised few discretionary powers. From 1911 to 1970, except for a brief three and one-half years, Frank C. and Frank M. Jordan (father and son) held this office, and most voters were not aware that these individuals were two different persons. However, when Edmund Brown, Jr., assumed office in 1970, he actively led moves to reform campaign methods and ballot procedures, and this position became a steppingstone to the governor's office. It is interesting to note that Governor Reagan in his State of the State message proposed a constitutional amendment for making the office of secretary of state nonpartisan. He maintained that this officer should be free of conflict of interest in the conduct of elections and in reporting campaign contributions. In 1975 March Fong Eu succeeded Brown in this office and became the first Asian to hold a statewide office in California.

THE CONTROLLER

The state's chief accounting and disbursing officer is the controller, who maintains accounts of all state and local government finances, authorizes withdrawals from the state treasury, and audits all financial claims against the state. This officer also has general responsibility for overseeing the collection of all state taxes, with specific responsibility for the collection of inheritance and gift taxes, the gasoline tax, and the

---

[8]The Great Seal must be affixed to all documents signed by the governor.

motor-vehicle-transportation license tax, the insurance-company tax, and the petroleum gas tax (for an explanation of these and other state taxes see Chapter 10).

The controller is a member of several boards and commissions, including the state Board of Equalization, the Franchise Tax Board, the state Board of Control, the State Lands Commission, and the Water Resources Control Board. The criticism has been leveled that the controller is a member of too many unrelated boards and that his or her efforts are spread too thin.

The office of controller has become one of the most important in the state. The controller's staff includes about 100 tax appraisers who are appointed, thus affording considerable patronage. As the elective state fiscal officer, the controller is a key person in state government. Both Thomas Kuchel and Alan Cranston served in this office before their election to the U.S. Senate in 1954 and 1968, respectively. Houston Flournoy, a candidate for governor in 1974, was state controller from 1966 to 1974. Ken Cory, a former state assemblymember, was elected to a third term as controller in 1982. He decided not to run for a fourth term, and Gray Davis, an assemblymember and former chief of staff for Governor Jerry Brown, was elected to the office in 1986, serving until 1994 when he successfully ran for lieutenant governor and was succeeded by fellow Democrat Kathleen Connell.

THE TREASURER

It is the duty of the state treasurer to provide for the safekeeping of public funds, but this officer is a custodian only, having no authority to issue payment of monies except upon authorization of the controller. The treasurer is required to report periodically to the legislature on the condition of the state treasury.

Elected for four years, the treasurer is also the chief administrative officer for the sale and redemption of state bonds and the investment of surplus state funds under general authorization of the legislature.

Ivy Baker Priest, elected in 1966, became the first woman to occupy this post. She was formerly treasurer of the national government in the Eisenhower administration. Jesse Unruh, former speaker of the state assembly and a candidate for governor in 1970, became state treasurer in 1974. As state treasurer, he was reelected in 1978, 1982, and 1986—the last time without opposition in the primary and in the general election. Unruh expanded the role of the treasurer's office and increased the state's billions of dollars that he invested for it. As noted earlier, in August 1987 he died from cancer.

Governor George Deukmejian appointed Dan Lungren, a Republican U.S. congressional representative from Long Beach, to fill Unruh's position as state treasurer. This appointment was subject to confirmation by the state legislature and the assembly voted 43–32 to confirm the nomination, but the senate voted 21–19 to reject the nomination. After his nomination of Dan Lungren to replace Jesse Unruh failed in the senate, Deukmejian gained approval of state auditor Thomas Hayes, a far less partisan choice, the governor knew it would be hard for the legislature to refuse confirmation of their own auditor general whom they had appointed. He in turn was defeated in 1990 by Kathleen Brown, sister of Jerry and daughter of Pat. Another example of "family ties" followed when Matt Fong, son of March Fong Eu, was elected to this office in 1994.

THE STATE BOARD OF EQUALIZATION

The State Board of Equalization, composed of four members (each elected from one of four districts) and the state controller who serves ex officio, is the state's major tax agency. The four members are all elected on a partisan basis in gubernatorial election years for terms of four years.

The board surveys average levels of property-tax assessment in the 58 counties with a view to equalizing assessments throughout the state, assesses the property of public utilities for purposes of local taxation, and assists local assessors in their duties.

State taxes administered by the board account for more than half of the state's revenue and include sales and use tax, cigarette tax, alcoholic-beverage tax, motor-vehicle-fuel license tax, insurance tax, and state-assessed property tax.

THE SUPERINTENDENT OF PUBLIC INSTRUCTION

The position of the superintendent of public instruction in the state executive hierarchy is a peculiar one because the superintendent is the only state executive officer elected on a nonpartisan ballot. Although elected by the voters every four years, the superintendent is responsible in some respects to the ten-person state Board of Education appointed by the governor and serves as secretary and executive officer of the board. He or she is administrative head of the state Department of Education and in that capacity is expected to execute Board of Education policies.

This led to a major confrontation between a conservative board of education and the more liberal superintendent, Bill Honig. Elected in 1982, Honig campaigned for a return to "traditional" education and an increase in state funding for schools. That eventually brought him into a confrontation with Governor Deukmejian, a controversy that continued when Pete Wilson took over the governor's chair. Wilson's attempt (ultimately unsuccessful) to cut the education budget as a means of dealing with budgetary red ink in the early 1990s led to open warfare between the two.

The conflict with the Board of Education arose out of the belief of board members that Honig was usurping their power to make policy and their control over the Department of Education. Ultimately Honig lost when he was convicted (some felt unfairly) of criminal conflict of interest with respect to his wife's work with the Quality Education Project (QEP). She was president of this nonprofit foundation and a jury found him guilty of illegally approving $337,000 worth of contracts with QEP. The funds went to enhance parent involvement in the schools, a highly commendable objective, but the process by which the funds were received was deemed improper.

The superintendent has general responsibility for administering the state laws relating to public schools in California and appoints the boards and commissions within the Department of Education—two important ones being the curriculum commission and the credentials commission. In addition, the superintendent sits as an ex officio member on the Board of Regents of the University of California and the Board of Trustees of the State Universities and Colleges.

THE INSURANCE COMMISSIONER

The state's voters chose to make the position of insurance commissioner an elective rather than appointive office when they approved Proposition 103 in 1988. Some previous holders of the position had come under fire as being too close to the insurance industry they were to regulate.

Though some provisions of Proposition 103 were modified by the courts, the responsibility of the insurance commissioner to review and approve insurance rate increases has been upheld (though subject to challenge in the courts if the existing rates do not permit a "fair and reasonable return" on the company's investment). The first elected commissioner, John Garamendi, proved an ardent advocate for consumer rights and pressed for rate reform during his four years in office. He chose to seek the Democratic nomination for governor in 1994 and was defeated by Kathleen Brown in the primary.

THE ADMINISTRATIVE BRANCH

A good share of the work of state government is carried on by myriad state agencies, departments, boards, and commissions. Because of its size and scope of power, this collection of governmental units often is considered to be a fourth branch of government and is referred to as the administration or the bureaucracy. The function of this branch of government is to implement and enforce public policy and to perform public services as determined by the legislature and the people of California.

The governor is the manager of this large structure, and all departments are responsible to the governor except two: The Department of Justice reports to the elected attorney general, and the Department of Education is accountable to the elected superintendent of public instruction. The governor is the appointing power of most of the important officers of the administration and thus has some control over policy. However, an increasing number of commissions and boards, such as the Public Utilities Commission, the Fair Political Practices Commission, and the Agricultural Relations Board, have powers established by the legislature or by the direct initiative and thus are independent of the governor. Also, although the governor appoints the members of these governmental bodies, their terms overlap that of the governor, and they are beyond the reach of the appointing power. These independent boards and commissions cover a wide range of important areas of government activities and are involved in policymaking as well as administration.

The governor maintains several "staff" agencies that serve as advisers in different areas of administrative policy. The functions of staff organizations are to plan, advise, observe, and assist the chief executive officer—but not to command. The all-important Department of Finance supervises all financial operations of the administration and recommends fiscal policy to the governor. The other staff offices—the Office of Planning and Research, the Office of Emergency Services, the Department of Personnel Administration, and the Office of Criminal Justice Planning—all serve as advisers to the governor in other specific areas.

Most of the state administration consists of "line" agencies and departments. In contrast with "staff" organizations, "line" agencies have their own authority and power of command in the exercise of their functions. Most of the "line" departments that perform direct services to Californians are now organized into five superagencies: business, transportation, and housing; resources; health and welfare; youth and adult correctional; and state and consumer services. The various departments and offices are grouped on a functional basis with the aim of simplifying governmental procedures. Each superagency is headed by a governor-appointed secretary who is responsible for coordinating the activities of the departments assigned to the agency and for handling communications between the department and the governor's office. Organized within the Department of Consumer Affairs are some 40 boards and commissions with responsibility to license and regulate various professional and occupational activities. Established to protect the consumer, these organizations set competency standards, administer licensing exams, and discipline errant practitioners. A wide range of professions and trades is within the control of such boards and commissions, including medical doctors, attorneys, dentists, osteopaths, accountants, funeral directors, pharmacists, electronic and appliance repair persons, nurses, and physical therapists. The governor appoints both professional and lay members of these boards and commissions.

This plan of organization was initiated by Governor Reagan under the Reorganization Act of 1966, which empowers the governor to shift departments around, subject to legislative veto, within 60 days after the proposal is submitted to the senate and the assembly.

Selected directors of "staff" and "line" agencies including the chief of staff, the director of finance, and the secretaries of the superagencies serve as members of the governor's cabinet. This body acts in an advisory capacity to the governor and serves as a coordinating body to the state administration.

SELECTED REFERENCES

Boyarsky, William, *The Rise of Ronald Reagan*, New York: Random House, 1968.
California Political Almanac, Sacramento: California Journal Press, annual.
Cannon, Lou, *Ronnie to Jesse: A Political Odyssey of Two Political Champions*, Garden City, NY: Doubleday, 1969.
Fairbanks, Robert, "Unruh's Growing Power," *California Journal*, February 1983.
Melendy, H. Brett, and Benjamin F. Gilbert, *The Governors of California: Peter H. Burnett to Edmund G. Brown*, Georgetown, CA: Talisman Press, 1965.
Park, Robert, *Jerry Brown: The Philosopher Prince*, Briarcliff Manor, NY: Stein and Day, 1978.
Quinn, T. Anthony, and Ed Saltzman, *California Public Administration*, Sacramento: California Journal Press, 1982.
Saltzman, Ed, "Judging Jerry," *California Journal*, June 1982.
Skelton, George, "A Split Verdict on Deukmejian's Legacy," *Los Angeles Times*, December 30, 1990.
Zeigler, Richard, "Pete Wilson: Steering Through a Sea of Woes," *California Journal*, April 1992.

Chapter 8

The Judiciary

In the United States the judiciary differs from the other two branches of government, the legislative and the executive, in that the courts do not initiate action but only react when a request for action is brought to them. Before our courts issue a judgment someone from outside the judicial system must file a suit or enter a plea.

Our national courts tend to have more prestige than our state courts. However, some of the most controversial—even lurid—cases are found in state courts. In California in recent years screaming headlines have chronicled the progress and announced the verdicts in such cases as the McMartin school case (alleged child molestation), the Rodney King beating and the Reginald Denny assault cases (the verdict in the first case was the spark that gave rise to the LA riots and the other a result of the riots), the Menendez brothers (shot their parents as they watched television), and the most watched courtroom drama in history, the case of football great O. J. Simpson (accused of killing his former wife and her friend with a knife). The cases that are most likely to affect the average citizen are heard in state courts, from murder to fraud to traffic violations.

The states exercise police power, the power to protect the health, safety, and morals of their citizens. From murder to arson, from fraud to sanitation and traffic violations, the state's jurisdiction over criminal law is very extensive. The same can be said with respect to civil law, where suits for damages, and such matters as divorces, wills, and breach-of-contract suits are taken up in state courts. California's judicial system is the largest in the United States with 194 courts and over 1,550 judges. Over 15 million cases are filed each year, including 5 million dealing with parking violations. The system costs $1.7 billion a year to operate.[1]

ORGANIZATION, JURISDICTION, AND PERSONNEL

California's court system is organized on four levels: (1) municipal courts (sometimes called "inferior" courts); (2) superior courts; (3) district courts of appeal; and (4) the supreme court (see Figure 8.1).

---

[1]Information provided by the Judicial Council of the State of California.

THE SHOW GOES ON...AND ON...AND ON...AND...

(Dennis Renault, *Sacramento Bee*)

The Inferior Courts

There must be at least one municipal court in each county. Until 1995 justice courts served populations of less than 40,000 and municipal courts populations over 40,000. The voters passed Proposition 191 at the November 1994 general election, eliminating justice courts. The action was less drastic than it might seem. Revisions over the years had made the jurisdiction of justice courts, the qualifications of judges to serve on them, and the rules followed by them identical with municipal courts. Proposition 191 transformed justice courts into municipal courts and made justice court judges full-time municipal court judges.

Municipal Courts   Civil suits for damages of less than $25,000 and all nonjuvenile criminal cases of a minor nature (misdemeanors and infractions) carrying penalties not exceeding one year in the county jail or a fine of $1,000 are handled by the municipal courts. It is notable that more than 90 percent of the criminal cases heard in California's municipal courts concern traffic violations. Small-claims cases involving amounts of $5,000 or less are also handled by municipal courts.

The municipal courts also hold preliminary hearings for more serious offenses. When a municipal judge decides there is sufficient evidence to warrant holding a person, the accused individual is bound over to the superior court for trial.

Qualifications   To be eligible for election as a municipal-court judge a person must be a registered voter in his or her own district and must have been a licensed attorney in California for five years.

Election   Municipal court judges are chosen for six-year terms by the people of their respective districts through nonpartisan elections. An incumbent judge may be declared automatically elected without his or her name appearing on the ballot, unless a rival candidate files nomination papers or a specified number of voters sign a petition for a write-in campaign against the incumbent. If there is a contest the names of the candidates appear on the ballot. Vacancies on the municipal-court bench between elections are filled through appointment by the governor. County boards of supervisors fill interim vacancies in justice courts.

The Superior Courts

The superior courts are the general trial courts of the state. Each county has one superior court; however, a court may be authorized by the legislature to establish a number of judgeships. The superior court of Los Angeles, for example, has more than 200 judges, and Alameda, Orange, Santa Clara, and San Francisco have more than 30 each. Each judge conducts a set of trials in his or her own courtroom. In the larger counties the superior court judges select one of their number to be the presiding judge, who has the duty of assigning cases to the individual judges. In very large counties the tendency is to assign particular types of cases, for example, juvenile, domestic relations, probate, and criminal, to judges in specialized divisions of the court.

The superior courts have *original jurisdiction* over (1) all civil cases where the suit is for at least $25,000, and annulment, divorce, and probate of wills cases regardless of the amounts involved; (2) all major criminal cases (felonies) carrying sentences of one year or more in state prison; and (3) all those that involve minors.

Appellate jurisdiction is exercised by the superior courts over all cases originating in the municipal and justice courts. According to a constitutional amendment passed in 1960, the legislature may specify the circumstances and procedures under which a case originating in the inferior courts can be appealed beyond the superior courts to higher state courts.

Qualifications   To be eligible for a superior court judgeship a person must have been a citizen of the United States for five years, a practicing attorney in California for ten years, and a resident of the county for two years.

Election   Superior-court judges are elected in nonpartisan primary elections in the same manner as municipal- and justice-court judges. Most superior-court incumbent judges are reelected automatically, but occasionally, a judge will have a challenger or an incumbent will decide not to run for reelection. Challenges to incumbents in superior-court elections are rare. The low visibility of incumbents, the high cost of campaigning, and the slim chance of winning the election discourage individuals from competing for the office.

The Courts of Appeal

The state courts of appeal are the intermediate layer of tribunals between the superior courts and the supreme court. Three such courts were created by constitutional amendment in 1904, and in 1928 another amendment gave the legislature authority to increase the number of appeals courts as it saw fit. The state is now divided into six districts with one appeals court in each.

The jurisdiction of the district courts is strictly appellate. They review cases already tried in the superior courts and are the review courts for appeals from decisions of quasi-judicial agencies, such as the state industrial accident commission. Some cases appealed from the superior courts go directly to the supreme court for review (see the next section), but many of them wind up on the dockets of a district court of appeal anyway, since the high court may delegate any cases it wishes to them. The supreme court also has the right, however, to assume jurisdiction over any case on a district court's calendar.

The State Supreme Court

The supreme court is the top state court. Its decisions are final and cannot be appealed unless the U.S. Supreme Court finds that a decision has violated the federal Constitution.

There are six associate justices on the supreme court and one chief justice. The chief justice may convene the court at any time. Concurrence of four judges present at the argument is necessary for a judgment.

The jurisdiction of the supreme court is both appellate and original, but deciding appeals from the lower courts constitutes most of its work. Practically all of the cases reaching the court on appeal originate in a superior court, are then appealed to a district court of appeal, and from there are carried to the supreme court. Cases in which the death sentence is imposed may be appealed directly from the superior courts to the supreme court. The supreme court also can order certain unique cases transferred to it from the courts of appeal before hearing. Since the supreme court usually has discretionary jurisdiction, it hears only about 3 percent of the cases submitted to it. For the most part, the court considers only cases involving a public policy.

The supreme court has original jurisdiction to issue writs of mandamus (to compel a public corporation or officer to act in accord with legal obligations), prohibition (to prevent a lower court from exercising jurisdiction over a suit pending before it), and habeas corpus.

Qualifications   To be eligible for a supreme- or appeals-court judgeship a person must meet certain minimal requirements: The person must be a U.S. citizen, a California resident, and a practicing attorney in the state for ten years.

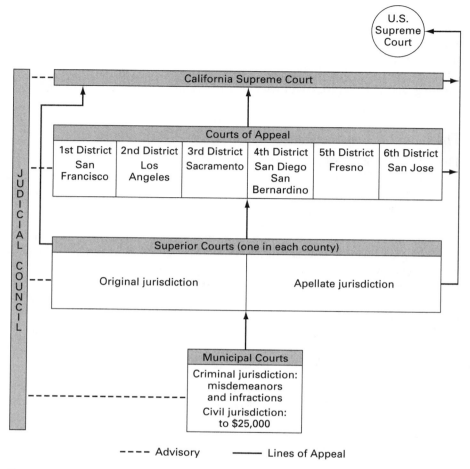

Figure 8.1   Organization of the court system

Election   The present method of electing judges to the state supreme court and the district courts of appeal was instituted by a constitutional amendment in 1934. It put an end to contested elections to all appellate courts in an effort to insulate the judiciary from political pressures. High court justices continue to stand for election after appointment by the governor, but they do not run against anyone.

Supreme- and appeals-court judges serve for staggered terms of 12 years. At the end of the 12-year term, these judges may run for reelection. In this case, only the name of the incumbent, without opponents, appears on the ballot for the judgeship. If the incumbent does not choose to seek another term, the governor appoints an individual who, as nominee, becomes the only person listed on the ballot. The governor also appoints persons to appellate judgeships in cases of the resignation or death of a judge prior to the completion of the term of office. In such cases the appointee

California State Supreme Court. From left to right: Justice Ming Chin, Justice Stanley Mosk, Justice Marvin Baxter, Chief Justice Ronald George, Justice Kathryn Mickle Werdegar, Justice Joyce L. Kennard, and Justice Janice Rogers Brown. (Courtesy California State Supreme Court)

(without opposition) would be subject to confirmation at the next general election and would also be on the ballot at the time of expiration of the particular 12-year term to which the replaced judge had been appointed.

In appointing judges the governor is subject to certain procedures. Before making a nomination, he or she must consult the Commission on Judicial Nominees—a 25-member commission appointed by the Board of Governors of the State Bar of California, a private association of lawyers in California. This commission has 90 days in which to make a recommendation that consists of rating a nominee on a four-point scale: "exceptionally well-qualified," "well-qualified," "qualified," and "not qualified." The governor is not bound by the commission's report, but the commission may make the report public if the governor appoints a candidate it has rated as unqualified. However, another commission—the Commission on Judicial Appointments (consisting of the chief justice of the supreme court, the presiding judge of a district court of appeal, and the state attorney general)—has the authority to approve or reject a governor's appointment to California's appellate or supreme court.

Since the ballot for judges of the appellate courts and supreme courts contains only one name, voters record a "yes" or "no" vote to the question of the reelection of a judge. If a justice seeking reelection receives more "no" votes than "yes" votes, the governor appoints someone else to serve on the court until the next election. Until 1986 all supreme- and appeals-court incumbents or nominees whose names appeared on the ballot had received a majority of "yes" votes. However, on a few occasions campaigns for "no" votes have been launched against certain judges in controversial cases. For example, in 1966 right-wing groups in the state sought to defeat for reelection three of the supreme court justices who had declared Proposition 14 of 1964 (allowing racial discrimination in housing) unconstitutional. By all odds, the most effective campaign was that against Chief Justice Rose Bird in 1986.

THE CASE OF ROSE BIRD

Rose Bird, the first woman to become the chief justice of the California State Supreme Court, also became the first justice under the present form of selection of judges to be voted out of office. In the November election of 1986 she lost reelection to office by a 2–1 margin. At the same time two associate justices of the supreme court, Joseph R. Grodin and Cruz Reynoso—other members of the court's liberal majority—also failed to receive a majority of "yes" votes (though by smaller margins than that of the chief justice) and thus did not retain their positions.

Rose Bird's tenure on the court was marked by controversy. Her unwillingness to approve any of over 50 death sentences in capital cases angered many voters who felt she was substituting her judgment for the law of the state. In many instances the grounds for reversing a death sentence appeared to the public to be stretching credibility. In one notable instance a man shot and killed three persons kneeling before him, having to reload twice, yet Bird with three other justices held there was inadequate evidence of an intent to kill.

Bird was approved by the narrowest margin in history in her first public confirmation vote in 1978 (51.7 percent). There was concern over her youth and lack of legal experience (she had never sat on any bench). Once confirmed Bird became a lightning rod for the public's belief that the courts had grown too concerned with the rights of the accused and too little with the harm done to victims. Had she been simply a justice, that might have proved less true, but her highly visible stance as chief justice focused the public's attention on her and her role in a series of controversial decisions.

Several separate campaign organizations that spent between $8 million and $10 million waged efforts against her reconfirmation in 1986, though it is doubtful they had much effect. Public opinion polls taken before these campaigns got under way indicated the public opposed reconfirmation of Bird by a 2–1 margin. When the votes were tallied election night, Bird was rejected by a 2–1 margin. Both Cruz Reynoso and Joseph Grodin, targeted by anti-Bird campaigns as well, were also voted off the court.

THE LUCAS COURT

Following a series of resignations, only Justice Stanley Mosk, appointed by Governor Edmund G. ("Pat") Brown, remained of the "liberal" court of Rose Bird. Contrary to the expressed fears of Bird supporters, there has not been a rash of attempts to oust other judges and the independence of the courts has not been jeopardized. In fact, the less colorful (some have termed it a "grey flannel court") and less controversial court has seen public attention to its decisions dwindle. For some who would prefer a more pioneering court, that is disappointing. There has been more of an inclination to go along with federal standards rather than raise new state criteria. Where the Bird court appeared to seek out minor mistakes in judicial proceedings as a means of overturning convictions, the Lucas court has adopted the federal standard of "harmless error" under which, if the error had no effect on the outcome, it is ignored. Though the Lucas court has not been a "hanging court," it has been far more willing to uphold lower court convictions than its predecessor. With respect to capital punishment cases, for example, the Bird court overturned 64 of 68 cases reviewed. The rate of convictions upheld by the Lucas court was roughly 85 percent. Finally, it might be noted the Lucas court has not always been quite as predictable as some anticipated. When Dan Lungren was nominated by Governor Deukmejian to be state treasurer, Deukmejian maintained approval was required from only one house of the legislature. Opponents held both houses had to approve. The court sided with the opponents (and, since the senate refused to give its approval, Lungren was blocked from office). Though favorable to business, the court declined businesses' plea to make the "deep pockets" initiative (which banned a process under which those with money paid for damages even if only slightly at fault when others more at fault could not) retroactive. On the other hand, the court sided with the insurance companies when they complained that Proposition 103's requirement that all automobile insurance premiums be cut a minimum of 20 percent denied them a reasonable profit. And, in a blow to conservatives, the Lucas court has consistently held that the state does have to pay for abortions for the poor.

There has been concern that fewer cases are being heard in recent years. That is at least in part due to the flood of death penalty cases inundating the court, and some, most notably Chief Justice Lucas, have argued that such cases, instead of being automatically sent to the supreme court from superior courts, should first be reviewed at the appellate court level.

A major contributor to the court's workload has been multiple appeals (using the writ of habeas corpus, which asks for immediate investigation by the courts as to the propriety of the prisoner being held) that have stretched over many years. Many pointed to the case of Robert Alton Harris, who spent 13 years on death row before his execution. His lawyers forwarded appeal after appeal, each on different grounds (he was the victim of child abuse, he was afflicted with fetal alcohol syndrome, the use of the gas chamber was cruel and unusual punishment, to mention just three), a practice called "piecemeal litigation" that delayed his execution and added to the court's case load.

In 1993, in the case of *In re Clark* (5 Cal. 4th, 750), the court in a 5–2 decision held that virtually all prisoners on death row would be allowed just one petition for a writ of habeas corpus. Additional applications will be rejected unless it can be shown that denying the writ would result in a "substantial miscarriage of justice." Critics stated the ruling created too rigid a standard and would hurt those accused who could not afford experienced trial lawyers.

Chief Justice Lucas resigned in May 1996 and was replaced as chief justice by Associate Justice Ronald George. Diversity appeared the watchword for the new court with three women, two Asians, and a black constituting the new George court. Indeed, there was some concern at the unusually rapid turnover on the court. With the exception of Justice Stanley Mosk, appointed by Governor Pat Brown in 1964, there was an entirely new court in 1996 from that of 1989. Reasons for the changing membership ranged from age through relatively low pay to work overload. However, new justices require time to familiarize themselves with their positions and roles and that can and does slow the judicial process.

The Judicial Council

California is among the three-fourths of the states that have established a judicial council to oversee the entire state court system. Although not a court, the Judicial Council is an integral part of the state's judicial organization and has some authority to make rulings on judicial procedure that have the force of law.

There are 21 members of the council, 15 of whom are drawn from the various levels of the court system. In addition, there are four members of the state bar and one appointee from each house of the legislature.

The chief justice is the presiding officer and, in that capacity, may temporarily reassign judges from courts with low demand to others with high workloads or where there is a vacancy.

The main business of the Judicial Council is to carry on a continuous study of the work of the courts. It publishes biennial reports showing the numbers and kinds of cases handled by the various levels. It recommends and sometimes decrees procedural improvements to the courts. It holds seminars that orient newly appointed judges and that keep them up-to-date on the law. The Judicial Council recommends constitutional and statutory changes to the legislature that would improve the administration of justice. The council appoints an administrative director to implement its decisions.

Compensation of Judges

The salaries for the judges of all state courts are set by the legislature, the judges in each level of court receiving the same salary throughout the state. The justices of the state supreme court and the courts of appeal are paid from the state treasury; the wages of superior court judges are paid partly by the state and partly by the county; and the salaries of municipal-court judges are paid entirely by the county.

The pay of the chief justice in 1996 was $127,104 while that for associate justices was $121,207. Appellate-court judges were paid $113,632, superior-court judges $99,297, and municipal-court judges $90,680. The relative generosity of the legislature in this respect may be due to a belief that at some time in the future lawyer members might have occasion to appear before the court. Or it may simply be a fear of the court's political clout.

Removal of Judges

There are several ways that judges may be removed from office, although they are seldom invoked. First, judges may be recalled by the voters. Second, they may be impeached by the assembly and convicted by a two-thirds vote of the senate. Third, if a court finds them guilty of a felony or any crime involving moral turpitude and if the conviction is upheld by a higher court, the supreme court must dismiss them from office. Finally, on the recommendation of the Commission on Judicial Performance[2] the state supreme court has the power to retire a judge for a disability that interferes with his or her ability to perform and is likely to continue or for willful misconduct (e.g., swearing, sexual harassment, ethnic bias).

The Commission acts to police judicial actions and may impose penalties less than removal from the bench. In several instances judges have been "admonished" for falling asleep during a trial. In another case a judge received the same penalty for improperly disclosing to a friend confidential information from the Department of Motor Vehicles. A more serious penalty, also less than removal, is a censure. A judge in Central California was censured for discussing pending cases with the media in violation of the code of judicial ethics.

A special procedure was created in 1976 by the voters when they amended the state constitution to deal with the supreme court. Upon recommendation of the Commission on Judicial Performance involving censure, removal or forced retirement of a justice shall be determined by a panel of seven chosen by lot from the ranks of the appellate-court judges.

In 1979, the Commission on Judicial Performance made an investigation into the conduct of the state supreme court—the first investigation of its kind in the nation. This action was taken following newspaper allegations that politically sensitive cases had been held up by the court until after the November 1978 general election, in which Chief Justice Bird and three associate justices were candidates for retention. The commission held hearings for nearly five weeks, and detailed accounts of how the state's top judges went about their business became available to the public.

Evidence gathered did not prove the justices guilty of wrongdoing or of intentionally delaying action on politically sensitive cases. However, exposing the many squabbles between the judges did considerable damage to the court's public image.

THE ADMINISTRATION OF JUSTICE

The law enforceable in the state courts is found in the California constitution and in the state's body of statutory law that the legislature has incorporated into a series of codes, such as the *Civil Code,* the *Government Code,* the *Penal Code,* and the *Elections Code.* However, no written law can anticipate every variety of case that may arise. Judges must often rely on English common-law precedent to render a decision; sometimes they have no guide but their own sense of justice. Because of the complexity of the law, its interpretation, and its application to individual cases, detailed rules of procedure are established to protect citizens against arbitrary handling by the state's legal authorities and to ensure all citizens equitable treatment in court.

---

[2]Composition of the Commission on Judical Performance was changed by the voters when they approved Proposition 190 in November 1994. Responding to complaints the Commission was "stacked" in favor of judges, they enlarged the membership from nine to eleven and provided for six public members who are joined by three judges appointed by the supreme court and two members of the state Bar who are appointed by the governor.

Criminal Procedure

A criminal offense is a crime against society. There are three general categories of criminal offense: *felonies,* which are the most serious crimes, such as murder, armed robbery, rape, forgery, and perjury; *misdemeanors,* which are lesser offenses, such as selling liquor to a minor; and *infractions,* which are the least serious violations, such as illegal parking and operating an automobile without proper equipment. Upon conviction of a felony the judge may impose upon the defendant the sentence of one year or more in state prison or a heavy fine or both. In the case of a misdemeanor the penalty may be a term of not more than one year in the county jail or a fine of not more than $1,000 or both. Those guilty of an infraction suffer only a fine.

The general rights of the accused in criminal cases are outlined in Article I of the state constitution. The defendant is guaranteed a preliminary hearing before a magistrate (if accused of a felony), the right to legal counsel, the right to know the charges against him or her, the right of trial by jury, the right to confront witnesses, and the right to summon witnesses on his or her own behalf. These provisions have been elaborated by the courts and the legislature to provide for the following procedures.

In Cases of Felony   (1) At the time of arrest, the accused is "booked" at the police station or the sheriff's office, and the section of the law that allegedly has been violated is listed against this name. (2) The accused is taken before a municipal judge or justice court for a preliminary hearing, whereupon the judge informs the accused of his or her rights under law. If the accused pleads guilty he or she is handed over to the superior court; if the accused pleads not guilty, but the judge believes the evidence is strong enough, he or she is committed to the superior court anyway. Pending further action the accused is held in jail or released on bail. (3) An *information* (accusation) is signed against the accused, usually by the district attorney of the county, or the county's grand jury votes an *indictment.* (4) When the accused appears in superior court he or she pleads either guilty or not guilty. If the plea is the former, the accused is sentenced; if the plea is the latter, a trial is held. The accused may waive jury trial, in which case the judge determines guilt or innocence. If the accused does not waive trial by jury, a panel of potential jury members is called up. Prosecuting and defense attorneys may question the prospective jurors and disqualify those whose impartiality is doubted. Ultimately, a jury of 12, satisfactory to both sides, is sworn in. (5) After hearing witnesses and arguments of attorneys, the jury strives for a unanimous verdict of guilty or not guilty. If unanimity cannot be reached within a reasonable time, the jury is dismissed, and a new trial is ordered. (6) A verdict of not guilty releases the defendant. If the verdict is guilty, the defendant is sentenced by the judge after an interval of a few days to allow for a probation report. During this period the defendant's attorney may make a motion for a new trial or file notice of appeal.

In Cases of Misdemeanors   The procedure usually is simpler for misdemeanors, a less serious type of crime. The accused (or attorney) is required to appear in a municipal court in the county where the offense allegedly occurred. Frequently, those arrested plead guilty. But a defendant may plead not guilty and demand a jury trial or may waive this privilege in favor of a trial by the judge alone. If found guilty, the defendant may be fined or sentenced to the county jail, or both.

In Cases of Infractions   The 1968 legislature made provision for a type of criminal offense less serious than a misdemeanor, namely, the infraction. At first, very few offenses other than illegal parking were so classified. In the decade following, however, the list of infractions expanded enormously, so that today 80 percent of the violations defined in the California Vehicle Code are characterized as infractions. The list includes all speeding violations, for example. Typically, a person who is cited for an infraction does not appear before a judge; instead the person goes to the clerk of a nearby justice or municipal court and pays the ticket. (Technically, the defendant is not paying a fine, only posting bail and then automatically pleading guilty, which forfeits the bail.) However, if the prosecutor or the defendant requests a formal court trial, there is no jury, and the judge makes the decision as to innocence or guilt. In such a case free legal counsel is not guaranteed to the defendant, although he or she may hire a lawyer. If found guilty, the defendant may be fined but not sentenced to jail, unless he or she refuses to pay the fine. In certain counties, traffic violations are heard by special commissioners rather than by a judge.

Plea Bargaining   Important in actual law enforcement is the practice of *plea bargaining*. This occurs when a person is arrested and charged with a relatively serious criminal offense. However, before the case comes to trial the defendant (usually through the defendant's attorney) enters into an agreement with the prosecutor whereby the prosecutor reduces the charge, that is, accuses the defendant of a less serious crime, in return for which the defendant pleads guilty to the lesser offense. Thus a formal trial is avoided with its cost in time and money. Frequently, a felony is reduced to a misdemeanor. For example, if a person is caught throwing clods of dirt at passing automobiles, this individual could be booked on the felony charge of "throwing a missile with intent to do serious bodily harm," but the prosecutor may in return for a guilty plea reduce the charge to the misdemeanor of "throwing a substance at a vehicle." Rigorous advocates of law and order denounce plea bargaining as "coddling the criminals," but law-enforcement agents defend it as the only practical course in view of the crowded dockets of California's courts.

Proposition 8, approved by the voters in 1982, prohibited plea bargaining in any case in which the indictment or information charges any serious felony or any offense of driving while under the influence of alcohol, drugs, narcotics, or any other intoxicating substance, unless there is insufficient evidence to prove the case.

The Grand Jury   Every county in the state has a grand jury whose members are volunteers and serve for one year. Judges provide many nominees to the grand jury pools, though advertisements in the mass media result in others. The requirements to serve are simple: one must be a citizen, live in the county, and possess a sufficient grasp of the English language to be able to participate. Grand juries typically spend much of their time investigating the ways in which county government operates, making suggestions for improvement. In Fresno County, for example, a system under which pay for police and fire personnel was linked to the average salaries of comparable employees in eight other cities was recommended for elimination. (It was later, by public vote.)

Much more dramatic are instances in which a grand jury indicts someone for a criminal offense. This power was enhanced in 1990 with voter approval of Proposition 115. Now indictments no longer need to be followed by another preliminary hearing.

Instead they go directly to trial. That increased the frequency of using grand juries for indictments, up from 20 in 1989 to 540 in 1992. But, placed in perspective, the vast majority of indictments are not through grand juries. In Los Angeles County in 1992 there were 50 grand jury indictments out of 70,000 felony complaints.

One issue that has recently arisen involves this increased use and the composition of grand juries. Because they are volunteers and the work can be long and hard for very little money ($25 a day), those serving tend to be non-Hispanic whites. Many Hispanics cannot afford to serve or have been disqualified as noncitizens or by their statement that they are not fully comfortable with English. However, that results in grand juries that are not reflective of the county population in most cases. Several counties have developed second grand juries, which require service for a few weeks to three months and are drawn from regular jury lists. That is, of course, more expensive.

Civil Procedures

California civil law, like all law based on English jurisprudence, is divided into two broad categories—cases at law and cases in equity. Cases *at law* generally include all suits brought by one party to collect money from another party for debts owed or for damages already done. Cases *in equity* are usually to prevent harm, especially irreparable damage. Equity also involves annulments and divorces (where often the harm already has been done), the administration of trusts, cancellation of fraudulent contracts, and various judicial writs and most injunctions.[3] A voter who feels that he or she has been deprived of his or her rights, for example, files an equity suit against the appropriate elections official.

In Cases at Law   The procedure for cases at law (provided they are for more than $5,000 in damages) is briefly as follows. (1) The plaintiff (or attorney) files suit against the defendant, stating the amount of money that is expected to be collected and the reasons for the claim. (2) The defendant, after having been notified of the suit, has any one of three options: not to contest the suit and allow the plaintiff to win by default; to settle the dispute with the plaintiff out of court; or to contest the matter, in which case the defendant's attorney files a formal answer to the charges and sometimes a countersuit. (3) Both parties appear in court and decide whether or not to waive a jury trial. If either party wants a jury trial, members are selected and sworn in (12 jurors unless both parties agree to fewer). (4) After witnesses are heard and arguments are given, the jury deliberates. The jury must decide whether the defendant is liable as charged and also to what amount the defendant is liable. (If a jury has been waived the judge makes these decisions.) Three-fourths of the jurors must agree in order to deliver a verdict.

Cases under $5,000 are classified as *small claims* and are handled by a simplified procedure. There are no attorneys or juries. The plaintiff merely appears at a municipal court (some larger municipal courts have special small-claims divisions) and files a complaint with a nominal filing fee. The defendant is summoned to appear, whereupon the judge hears both parties and renders a decision. If the decision is against

---

[3]A well-known example of an *injunction* (in equity) is a court's order to a labor union to prevent a strike.

the plaintiff, there is no further recourse under state law, but if the judge decides against the defendant, the defendant may petition for another hearing in a superior court. The popular syndicated television program *The People's Court* is an example of a small claims court in action.

In Cases in Equity   There are no jury trials in cases in equity. All issues of law and fact are determined by the judge. A few start in municipal courts, but most are handled by superior-court judges. When a case involves a highly important matter, for example, in the attempt of one local government to compel another local government to fulfill a contract, the state supreme court may assume original jurisdiction.

The basic steps in equity procedure are as follows. (1) The plaintiff or attorney files a petition to the court requesting a specific action in equity, such as an injunction for a divorce. (2) The defendant is notified of the charges in the petition and is asked to appear in court to show good reason why the petition should not be granted. The defendant or attorney thereupon files a formal answer. (3) In open court before the judge both sides present their arguments. (4) The judge renders a decision, which may be appealed by either party to a higher court.

IMPROVING THE ADMINISTRATION OF JUSTICE

Eliminating Unnecessary Delays

"Justice delayed is justice denied" is a long-held belief. In California's courts the denial has been prevalent. Civil cases in particular have seen delays of as much as seven years and typically of three to four years. In recognition of this sorry state of affairs, the state legislature in 1990 passed the Trial Court Delay Reduction Act. Under the old procedures different aspects of a complex case were heard before different judges. Now the same judge hears all aspects of civil cases from the filing of the complaint through pretrial motions to the trial itself. Judges have set strict deadlines and have the power to impose sanctions on lawyers who attempt delaying tactics. The impact has been impressive, at least in many courts. The new rules have encouraged more out-of-court settlements, relieving court congestion. For example, approximately 5 percent of cases filed in 1992 in Orange County actually went to trial. And the waiting period dropped from three to five years before the act to an average of 17 months in 1993.

Other proposals have been put forth to relieve court congestion. Some have urged that minor traffic violations be handled by the Department of Motor Vehicles. Others have suggested increased use of mediation and arbitration procedures as a means of cutting court caseloads. Another recommendation was turned down by the voters in 1988 when they rejected a (possibly flawed) no-fault auto insurance system that would have radically reduced the number of civil lawsuits in the courts. Medical malpractice cases might be handled by a special commission rather than the courts, a means of reducing court overload and at the same time cutting medical costs. Proposition 115, passed in 1990, allows judges—rather than lawyers—to question prospective jurors as a means of expediting the selection process. In view of the fact that a large volume of cases in the criminal courts deal

Caucus. (Courtesy World West Features)

Selecting Well-Qualified Judges

with narcotics and alcohol addicts, it has been said these are, in many cases, medical problems and should be dealt with by special tribunals.

Although for the most part California citizens have been satisfied with the quality of the state judicial personnel, there has been some criticism of selecting judges on the basis of their political appeal. Some go so far as to criticize the whole system of popular election of judges. It has been suggested that judges be appointed by the governor with the consent of the state senate (similar to the national pattern). Others have proposed that the state supreme court (whether elected by the people or appointed by the governor) should appoint all lower-court judges. The Judicial Council has proposed a "merit plan" of selecting judges; that is, when the governor appoints a judge to fill any vacancy the governor selects a name from a list submitted by a nominating commission that consists of an equal number of judges, lawyers, and laypersons.

Others maintain that the method of selecting judges is adequate but that some of our most qualified lawyers do not seek judgeships because the salaries are lower than the income they receive from private practice. More security of tenure has also been advocated as a means of attracting better judges, the possibility of the recall being cited as a major deterrent (see discussion of the recall in Chapter 5).

Reforming the Jury System

There is no significant movement to do away with the jury system, since it is generally regarded as a deeply rooted and valuable heritage of American jurisprudence. Yet thoughtful observers are aware of its imperfections. A person's peers are not always the best judges and often not the most objective. Jurors frequently confuse questions of moral right or wrong (which they are not expected to answer) with questions of legal fact, and when penalties are severe they will at times hesitate to convict in the face of overwhelming evidence.

Most suggestions are for improving the system rather than for tearing it down. Higher compensation and fewer exemptions from serving for professional persons would increase quality. One proposal would reduce the size of juries. In the case of *Williams v. Florida* (1971) the federal Supreme Court held that the U.S. Constitution permitted a state to decrease the number of jurors to six. California, so far, has retained the 12-member jury in criminal cases, although the state constitution does permit fewer jurors in a trial for a misdemeanor, provided both parties agree. It has been proposed that less than a unanimous vote, such as three-fourths, be required for conviction in any criminal case, except when the death penalty is involved. The state constitution also allows a jury of fewer than 12 persons in civil suits (subject to agreement by the plaintiff and the defendant), and furthermore only a three-fourths majority is necessary for a civil verdict. A committee of the Bar Association has suggested that an eight-member jury be made standard for all civil trials, with six votes being required for a verdict.[4] Since 1982, eight-member juries have been authorized for civil cases heard in municipal courts.

Merging the Courts

In each county there are now two layers of trial courts: the inferior courts (municipal) and the superior courts. Both levels are often involved in handling the same case. A person charged with a felony is arraigned in the inferior court and then tried in the superior court. Proposals to merge the two tiers of courts into one have been made by various interested parties, including the Los Angeles County grand jury. In 1982 the legislature submitted a constitutional amendment, Proposition 10, to the voters in the November general election that would have permitted the legislature to authorize a county to unify municipal and justice courts within the superior court upon approval by a majority vote of county electors. A unified superior court would have original jurisdiction in all matters currently falling under the jurisdiction of superior, municipal, and justice courts and all municipal- and justice-court judges would become superior-courts judges. Proponents, including the County Supervisors Association of California, the California Trial Lawyers Association, and the California

---

[4]Pat B. Anderson, "Bar Suggests Ways to Cut Court Costs," *Los Angeles Times*, July 2, 1978.

Taxpayers Association, contended that unification of the courts would eliminate much of the duplication and delay that presently cause severe congestion of cases in the lower courts. The principal argument against the proposal was the increased cost resulting from the higher salaries that would have to be paid to the more than 500 municipal- and justice-court judges who would automatically secure the rank of superior-court judges. Proposition 10 was defeated at the polls by a 2–1 margin.

Reducing the High Cost of Justice

The right to a fair trial in court is one of our most treasured civil liberties, but it can be a very expensive privilege. Lawyers' fees are not low, nor is the cost of printing the record for an appeal to a higher court. Consequently, many persons do not have the money to avail themselves of their constitutional rights. Various attempts are being made to correct this inequity. In criminal proceedings, for example, indigents are furnished the services of a public defender or of a private attorney assigned by the court. In civil matters county legal-aid societies and the California Rural Legal Assistance agency, financed by the national government, offer assistance to people with low incomes. It has been pointed out that these efforts still are not sufficient; public defenders are often overworked, and the private attorney appointed by the court to represent the indigent often is not as experienced as the high-priced lawyer a rich opponent has hired. There is pressure to increase the appropriations for the public defenders' offices.

GETTING TOUGH ON CRIME

The voters have long favored a "get tough" approach to crime and criminals. In 1982 they adopted the Victim's Bill of Rights (Proposition 8), which includes restitution for the victim or victim's family by the felon and secures the right of that family to appear and testify at parole hearings, limits plea bargaining in serious felony and drunk driving cases, and lengthens a variety of sentences. In their approval in 1990 of Proposition 115 voters once again acted to toughen the criminal-justice system. This multifaceted initiative put into the state constitution the following, among other things, in addition to the aspects already referred to earlier: an expanded list of "special circumstances" (allowing imposition of the death penalty) to include killing a witness; a provision allowing minors 16 and 17 years old to be tried as adults and, if convicted of first degree murder with special circumstances, to be punished by life in prison without possibility of parole; permitting the introduction of hearsay evidence at preliminary hearings if given by trained and experienced officers; and establishing the crime of torture, which carries with it life imprisonment without possibility of parole. The move toward a "three strikes and you're out" initiative in 1994 simply continued this "get tough" policy of California's citizens (see Chapter 12).

SELECTED REFERENCES

Adams, G. Dennis, Thomas A. Ault, and Alden J. Fulkerson, "Proposition 10: Court Unification Arguments," *Los Angeles Daily Law Journal,* October 25, 1982.

Allen, Nancy, "Have Grand Juries Outlived Their Usefulness?" *California Journal,* August 1986.

Barbieri, Richard, "Law-and-Order Court Shows No Sign of Softening," *The Recorder,* December 29, 1993.

Blume, William W., "California Courts in Historical Perspective," *Hastings Law Journal,* November 1970.

Cochran, Dena, "A Victim's Bill of Rights or a Lawyer's Employment Act?" *California Journal,* April 1982.

Egelko, Robert, "The Supreme Court's Revolving Door," in Thomas R. Hoeber and Charles M. Price, eds., *California Government and Politics Annual, 1993–94,* Sacramento: California Journal Press, 1993.

———, "A Low Profile Court," *California Journal,* June 1994.

———, "End of the Lucas Era," *California Journal,* July 1996.

Judicial Council of California, *Annual Reports,* Sacramento: State Printing Office, annual.

Kang, K. Connie, "Brown's Crusading Court," *California Journal,* September 1962.

Maharaj, Davan, "Civil Justice Is Speedier in Courts These Days," *Los Angeles Times,* October 26, 1993.

McMillan, Penelope, "Grand Juries' Racial Makeup Under Challenge," *Los Angeles Times,* October 12, 1993.

Stoltz, Preble, *Judging Judges,* Glencoe, IL: Free Press, 1973.

Local Government in California

Although local governments are not mentioned in the U.S. Constitution, they play the most immediate role in the lives of citizens. A wide variety of public services, including the protection of life and property, the promotion of health and welfare, the provision of public education, and other essentials of everyday life such as roads and removal of trash, are performed by counties, cities, special districts, and school districts. As agencies of the state governments, there are more than 80,000 local governments in the United States and some 7,000 are organized in California. A substantial part of all Californians' annual tax payments—some of which are collected by the national government—finds its way back to them in the form of locally performed services.

RELATION OF THE LOCAL UNITS TO THE STATE GOVERNMENT

All local governments in California, although they possess varying degrees of autonomy, are creatures and agents of the state. Their functions, powers, and structure are determined by the state constitution and by statutes of the state legislature, and they have no authority other than that granted by the state.

Constitutional Provisions

The inherent right of the state legislature to create local governments, define their powers, and prescribe their structure is recognized in Article XI of the state constitution. However, the legislature does not have a free hand in the discharge of these functions. The constitution permits counties and cities to frame their own charters and outlines in detail what provisions these charters must contain. Important financial relations between local governments and the state are also immune from legislative tampering—the most important being the distribution of motor vehicle tax funds and the constitution-set floor for funding per student of state money to local school districts. The direct relation between local law-enforcement officers and the attorney general also would require constitutional amendment to be altered.

State-Local Relationships

Some administrative departments of the state government have established close relations with local government units, not so much because of a provision in the state constitution as because of the mutual advantages to be gained through practical, day-to-day cooperation. Local sheriffs' offices and police departments, for example, file copies of fingerprints and reports of crimes with the Bureau of Criminal Identification in the state Department of Justice, and the bureau in turn makes available to the local agencies a fund of information and expert analysis possible only in a centralized criminal information agency. The area of social welfare provides another illustration of coordinated effort between levels of government. The state director of social welfare and staff makes rules for the administration and distribution of public assistance monies. However, individuals desiring aid must apply at their county welfare department, and it is the local agency that gives them that check.

THE COUNTY

The county is the local subdivision through which the state performs many of its most important functions: maintenance of public health programs, public relief administration, law enforcement, administration of justice, upkeep of roads, administration of elections, and the maintenance of vital statistics and property records.

In 1850, the California State Legislature created 27 counties, and by 1907 they had been subdivided to make up the present 58. From that time when Imperial County split from Riverside County no new county has been formed. Organizers for a proposed new county must present a petition containing signatures of a sufficient number of the county's registered voters to divide the county. This proposal is reviewed by the state to determine the economic viability of the proposed new county and at the same time to decide whether the division would drastically hurt the remaining county. If approved by the state, final approval requires concurrent voter majorities in both the proposed new county and the remaining territory. In the past 12 years, six of the attempts to form new counties have reached the election stage. In 1978 three areas in Los Angeles County attempted to break away: the Newhall-Saugus area, the Palos Verdes peninsula, and the South Bay area. Other attempts were made in 1982 in Eastern Fresno County, the Lake Tahoe region of eastern El Dorado County in 1984, and recently, in 1988, the northern area of San Bernardino County. All were turned down by the voters.

California's counties vary widely in size, population, and economy. San Bernardino County with 20,164 square miles is larger than any county in the nation, and San Francisco with 46 square miles is among the smallest. Los Angeles County is the most populous—more than 8 million—and Alpine with about 1,300 inhabitants is one of the least populated. Alameda County is one of the most highly industrialized counties in the United States, and Sierra County is one big forest area.

Types of Counties

The General-Law County   Forty-seven of California's counties are organized under general laws enacted by the state legislature. The constitution provides (in Article XI, section 1, b) that:

> The Legislature shall provide for county powers, an elected county sheriff and an elected governing body in each county . . . each governing body shall prescribe by ordinance the compensation of its members, but the ordinance prescribing such compensation shall be subject to referendum. The Legislature or the governing body may provide for other officers whose compensation shall be prescribed by the governing body. The governing body shall provide for the number, compensation, tenure, and appointment of employees.

Successive acts of the legislature have established the present statewide pattern in which the voters in each county elect a board of supervisors, sheriff, district attorney, coroner, assessor, tax collector, treasurer, auditor, county clerk, recorder, public administrator, superintendent of public schools, and judges of the superior, municipal, and justice courts. The voters clearly do not receive a short ballot in county elections. The legislature also requires that the board of supervisors appoint a long list of lesser officers, including a sealer of weights and measures, health officer, civil service commissioner, airport manager, and pound master.

The board of supervisors is the chief legislative and administrative body of the county. It adopts the county budget, enacts special taxes such as the 1 percent sales tax, and in some counties sits as a board of equalization to hear complaints against the property valuations set by the county assessor. (A constitutional amendment adopted in 1966 permits a county board of supervisors to create tax-assessment appeals boards to perform this function.) The board also has the power to enact criminal ordinances, such as prohibitions on gambling, to apply to residents of *un*incorporated areas (not part of cities) within its jurisdiction. It hires and fires county civil service personnel, approves all purchases made by the county, manages all county property, and markets bonds floated by the county and school districts. In election years the board serves as elections commission. Other ex officio roles of the supervisors are to act as board of directors for the county smog control, flood control, and road districts.

Probably the best known of all elected county officers is the sheriff, whose major responsibility is the apprehension of all alleged offenders against the criminal laws of the state and county within the unincorporated areas of the county. Other important officers concerned with law enforcement are the district attorney, who is the county's prosecuting officer in some criminal cases and represents the county in civil cases to which the county is a party, and the coroner, who is responsible for investigating the causes of deaths not attended by a physician, especially those that indicate violence, foul play, or poison.

The most important county officers concerned with finance are the assessor, the tax collector, the auditor, and the treasurer. The assessor, aided by a large staff of deputies, determines the taxable value of real and personal property in the county. The tax collector has a thankless job—mailing out tax bills to each property owner, deeding to the state property on which tax payments are delinquent, and collecting the various business and license fees. The auditor's (in some counties the controller's) duties are comparable to those of the state controller: authorizing all payments of county funds as provided for in the budget. The treasurer is the custodian of the county funds, depositing them in banks and making payments only when presented with warrants signed by the auditor.

Another officer with substantial responsibilities is the county clerk, who is the clerk of the superior court and in most counties the ex officio clerk for the board of supervisors. In many counties the clerk has the weighty duty of managing the official election machinery for state and county elections, which includes handling the filing of candidates' and direct legislation petitions, preparing the ballot, securing the necessary election supplies, and overseeing vote tabulations. (In a few of the larger counties these electoral functions are performed by a separate registrar of voters.) In addition, the county clerk issues marriage licenses to prospective couples.

Virtually all of the counties have in addition to the district attorney, whose jurisdiction is the criminal law, a county counsel whose field of operation is the civil law. The county counsel gives legal advice to the supervisors, other county officers, and to the various special districts within the county and also represents the county or a special district in the courts in a civil suit.

The county superintendent of schools approves the budgets and payrolls, maintains full records, and processes teacher certification for school districts within the county. It is this official's responsibility to see that the state laws on public education are observed by these districts.

These important county officers are elected directly by the people on a nonpartisan ballot and thus are neither subject to central lines of responsibility within the county government nor answerable to political parties. This independence in large part explains why many county officers and agencies seem to the citizen to have an existence of their own, unattached, and almost sovereign in their particular fields of activity.

The Charter County   A state constitutional amendment, adopted in 1911 and revised in 1970, permits a country to frame and adopt its own charter. The charter may be drafted by either the county board of supervisors or by a special charter commission of citizens elected by the voters of the county. After the document is completed it is submitted to the voters in a special election. If a majority votes approval, the new charter is then filed with the California secretary of state and goes into effect.

Large-scale revisions of existing county charters may be drafted either by the board of supervisors or by a charter commission. Individual amendments (or even outright repeal of the whole charter) may be proposed by either the board of supervisors or an initiative petition. All such changes must be ratified by the voters of the county at the polls.

A general-law county that has changed over to charter status is not completely exempt from all state laws governing the structure and operation of counties. For example, all charters must provide for an elected board of supervisors and for an elected sheriff.

Flexibility is allowed the charter county in determining the *number* of supervisors (the constitution specifies only that there shall be at least five), in deciding whether to make the lesser county officers appointive rather than elective, in setting the salary of its own officials, in providing, if it wishes, for a county-manager system of centralized administration, and in consolidating county offices.

Los Angeles in 1912 was the first county to adopt its own charter. Since then ten other counties have successfully completed all the required steps: San Bernardino, Butte, Tehama, Alameda, Fresno, Placer, Sacramento, San Diego, San Mateo, and Santa Clara. (San Francisco is a chartered city-county.)

The tendency is for the more populous, urban counties of California to use charters and for the rural counties to operate under the general law. However, Orange County, the third most populous county in the state, has never adopted its own charter, and the same is true of Contra Costa, Kern, Monterey, Riverside, San Joaquin, Santa Barbara, Sonoma, and Ventura counties, each of which has more than 250,000 inhabitants. On the other hand, Tehama County, with about 45,000 people, has its own charter.

The Problem of Divided Responsibility

One of the greatest shortcomings of county government is its lack of integrated authority and responsibility. Unlike the national government, the typical county does not have one single elected official who has major administrative responsibility. Although the state government in California is headed by a plural executive, consisting of 12 elected officers, at least the responsibility for general executive policy is centered in one person—the governor. The county not only elects many of its subordinate administrative officers but divides its top executive authority among a five-member board of supervisors. If the voters are dissatisfied with the administration of their county, they do not know whom they should hold responsible.

Some charter counties in California, taking advantage of the structural flexibility allowed them by the constitution, have made progress toward centering administrative responsibility. In Los Angeles County, for example, all officers except judges, the sheriff, the district attorney, and the assessor are appointive and are directly under the authority of the board of supervisors.

The legislature has tried consolidating county offices in some of the general-law counties. In five counties the positions of clerk and auditor have been merged; several counties have combined the duties of the sheriff and coroner into one office. Such consolidations, however, are usually possible only in counties of small population.

The Orange County Bankruptcy A notable example of divided responsibility is provided by the bankruptcy of Orange County, disclosed in 1996. Robert L. Citron, the elected treasurer, who had held office for 24 years in one of the wealthiest and most conservative counties in the state and the third largest in population, resigned in disgrace. He later told the court the county's $21 billion investment pool which he managed had lost $1.5 billion in 1994. When the Securities and Exchange Commission investigated the portfolio of investments, they estimated the actual loss at $2.02 billion. Upon learning this, the board of supervisors, fearing a run on the treasury of the county, filed for federal bankruptcy.

Citron, in his testimony, blamed his assistant, Matthew Raabe, for some part in the formation of the plan by which money belonging to cities, school districts and other special districts was siphoned off and invested in a county-run pool, investments that yielded high interest rates (8 to 11 percent) but were also high risk, and many of which failed, causing heavy losses. The result was the largest municipal bankruptcy in United States history.

Several officials were indicted and Mr. Citron, described in the press as a broken man, was sentenced to serve one year in jail and pay a $100,000 fine for his part in the skimming scheme.

(Courtesy Frank Interlandi)

The impact on Orange County was felt in several ways. Cuts were made in social services, especially those in the areas of mental health, child abuse and health care for the poor. A variety of fees for such things as landfill dumping and planning permits, library fines and parking at county beaches and parks were all increased. Some 500 county employees lost their jobs. In all, it cost the county $87 million in fees charged by lawyers, accountants and financial advisors, enough to run the county's district attorney's office for 18 months. Why did this happen?

Sifting through the many documents relating to the bankruptcy, investigators and some legislators came to the conclusion that Orange County was a community without a leader and without accountability. An elected treasurer could act on his own without authority granted by the top elective body—the board of supervisors. Clearly this was a case of divided responsibility.

Some charter counties in California, taking advantage of the structural flexibility allowed them by the state constitution, have made progress toward centering administrative responsibility. In Los Angeles County, for example, all officers except judges, the sheriff, the district attorney, and the assessor are under the authority of the board of supervisors.

The County Administrative Officer

The most effective and widely used means to bring greater integration to county government has been the establishment of some kind of appointive chief administrative officer. More than half of California's counties have created such a position. This officer is appointed by and responsible to the elected board of supervisors. Charter counties may legally establish the position of *county manager*, an official with considerable administrative authority—even the power to appoint and remove the heads of some county departments.[1] Charter and general-law counties may establish the position of chief administrative officer—essentially an agent of the board of supervisors. The principal functions of this officer are to implement the decisions of the board and include the preparation of the county budget. Although there is a legal difference between the *county manager* and the *chief administrative officer*, people generally refer to this official as the "county manager."

Although county administration has been somewhat more effectively coordinated by the county administrative officer, as far as the citizens are concerned the county is still an amorphous body speaking with many voices and, therefore, able to avoid specific responsibility for its actions. The feeling of many residents was voiced in one of the "Letters to the Times" in the summer of 1978:

> Would you buy stock in a $4.6 billion corporation that was directed by five presidents, each with the authority to act independently of each other and who rarely communicate with each other? Common sense tells us that we would not—yet this is the power structure of our largest local corporation— Los Angeles County![2]

THE CITY

The California city or municipality is like the county in some respects. Both are creatures and administrative agents of the state, performing certain basic governmental functions, such as law enforcement, fire control, and sanitation. But the city is less an arm of the state and more a unit of local self-government than the county. Cities are incorporated areas within the larger territory of a county, voluntarily activated by residents within a local community to perform mutually desired services for which coordination and cooperation are necessary. Presumably, cities are agencies rendering

---

[1]Only San Mateo County uses the title of county manager.
[2]Jerry B. Epstein, in the *Los Angeles Times*, August 22, 1978.

needed services that neither private industry nor state and county are capable or desirous of providing.

Communities may decide to incorporate and become a city for many reasons, including the following: to obtain more control over money (after incorporation the city receives a portion of the sales tax and the motor vehicle fees generated within the city boundaries that formerly went to the county to spend anywhere within the county); to reject county plans for land use (most frequently residents of the unincorporated areas have felt that the county allowed too much development or the wrong type of development in their area); to secure a better identity (strong homeowners associations and chambers of commerce and ambitious politicians wish to exercise more leadership than was possible under county organization); and to prevent annexation (many unincorporated areas have been threatened by annexation and merger with neighboring cities).

California has become one of the most highly urbanized states in the nation and now contains more than 450 incorporated cities ranging in population from some 152 persons living in Vernon to the 3.54 million residents in nearby Los Angeles. In true California fashion the founders of some of the more recent municipalities have adopted unorthodox and exotic names such as the City of Industry, the City of Commerce, the City of Hawaiian Gardens, and Paradise.

Proposition 13 has been the cause of an upsurge in the formation of new cities, and since 1978 some 30 new cities have received their charters. This initiative measure removed the financial argument against incorporation because it limited the level of taxes levied against a parcel of property. Prior to the act, cities would add their property tax average to that of the county, thus creating heavier tax burdens for city residents.

In order to meet the present conditions and to provide for the growth and orderly development of cities in the state, the legislature passed the Knox-Nesbit Act in 1962. Although final authority for local boundary change rests with the legislature, the law delegated powers to local agency formation commissions (LAFCO), one in each county to deal with boundary changes. Each LAFCO has five members—two county supervisors, two representatives of the incorporated cities in the county, and a fifth member representing the public, selected by the other commissioners. This body serves as a planning and regulatory agency and ultimately establishes physical boundaries and service areas for every governmental agency in the county—the county, the cities, and the special districts. Among the factors that the commission takes into account when making decisions are natural boundaries, population density, the likelihood of significant growth in the area, the need for governmental services, and the cost and adequacy of service in the area.

With this legislation, when residents of a community wish to incorporate and become a city, they must follow the procedure as shown in the accompanying chart (see Figure 9.1).

Annexation

Those communities that desire to be annexed must first negotiate with the given city to determine the fiscal feasibility and willingness of the city to add this area to its responsibility. If the city approves, a formal request with a plan of providing government services to the people is submitted to LAFCO. If LAFCO approves, the city

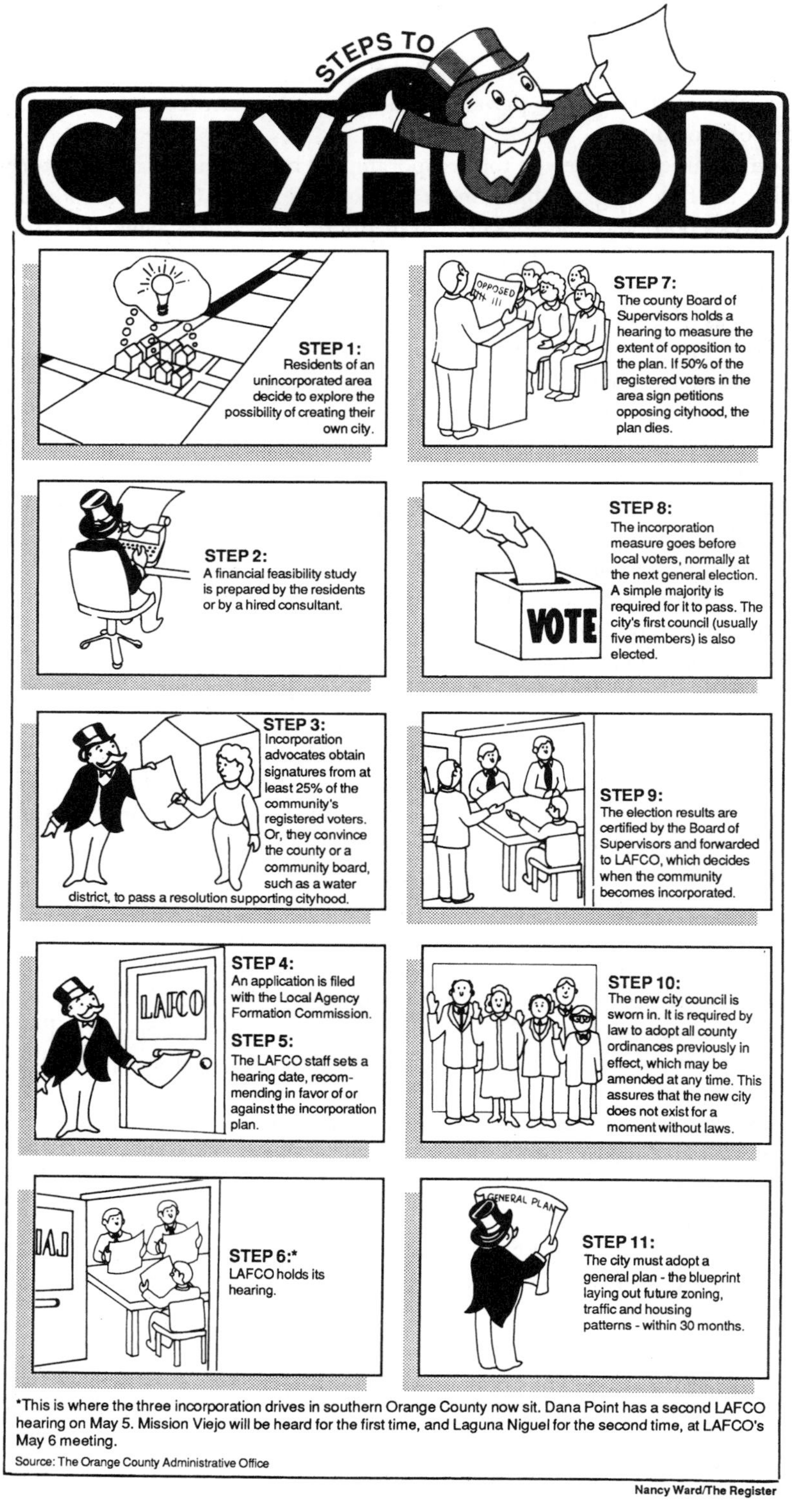

STEPS TO CITYHOOD

STEP 1:
Residents of an unincorporated area decide to explore the possibility of creating their own city.

STEP 2:
A financial feasibility study is prepared by the residents or by a hired consultant.

STEP 3:
Incorporation advocates obtain signatures from at least 25% of the community's registered voters. Or, they convince the county or a community board, such as a water district, to pass a resolution supporting cityhood.

STEP 4:
An application is filed with the Local Agency Formation Commission.

STEP 5:
The LAFCO staff sets a hearing date, recommending in favor of or against the incorporation plan.

STEP 6:*
LAFCO holds its hearing.

STEP 7:
The county Board of Supervisors holds a hearing to measure the extent of opposition to the plan. If 50% of the registered voters in the area sign petitions opposing cityhood, the plan dies.

STEP 8:
The incorporation measure goes before local voters, normally at the next general election. A simple majority is required for it to pass. The city's first council (usually five members) is also elected.

STEP 9:
The election results are certified by the Board of Supervisors and forwarded to LAFCO, which decides when the community becomes incorporated.

STEP 10:
The new city council is sworn in. It is required by law to adopt all county ordinances previously in effect, which may be amended at any time. This assures that the new city does not exist for a moment without laws.

STEP 11:
The city must adopt a general plan - the blueprint laying out future zoning, traffic and housing patterns - within 30 months.

*This is where the three incorporation drives in southern Orange County now sit. Dana Point has a second LAFCO hearing on May 5. Mission Viejo will be heard for the first time, and Laguna Niguel for the second time, at LAFCO's May 6 meeting.

Source: The Orange County Administrative Office

Nancy Ward/The Register

Figure 9.1 Steps to cityhood. (Courtesy Nancy Ward, *Orange County Register*)

holds a public hearing at which time residents of the area to be annexed may be heard. (Should LAFCO disapprove, annexation may not take place, and any new plan must wait at least one year before submission to LAFCO.) If 25 percent of the registered voters and property owners of the city sign a petition protesting the annexation, an election must be held at which time a majority of those voting is necessary to authorize the annexation. If less than 25 percent protest, the annexation takes place without an election.

Types of Cities

The General-Law City The vast majority of California municipalities (470 at the start of 1995) are incorporated under uniform state law provisions. The constitution of 1879 specified that the legislature could not enact a *special* law that granted a charter to a particular city; rather, the legislature had to pass *general* laws that set the procedure whereby the people of any locality that met the requirements could incorporate themselves into a municipality.

The Charter City Once having become a general-law city, a municipality may, like a county, frame a charter of its own and thereby become somewhat more independent of the state legislature. In 1995 there were 87 charter cities in California, the majority of which were in densely populated areas. Almost all cities with more than 100,000 inhabitants are charter cities, Fremont, Fullerton, and Garden Grove being exceptions, and only a few charter cities have fewer than 10,000 inhabitants. Thus, although fewer than one-fifth of the total number of cities are chartered, they contain more than one-half of the state's population.

A city may gain charter status through procedures similar to those available to a county. The document may be drafted either by the city council or a charter commission elected for the purpose. The charter is submitted to the voters of the city, and if it is approved by them it becomes the organic law of the city.

The primary advantage a charter city has over a general-law city is greater *flexibility*—in determining structure, such as the number of council members, and in determining functions. The charter city has considerable power in municipal affairs. Occasionally, however, there have been conflicts with the legislature over the definition of a "municipal" matter. The California courts have grappled with this problem for more than 60 years and have yet to arrive at a satisfactory answer. Their practice has been to decide each case on its own merits. The salary of a San Francisco police officer, for example, is a "municipal" matter, whereas the license fee set for local liquor dealers is within the jurisdiction of state agencies. Furthermore, the California Supreme Court in 1962 declared unconstitutional a Los Angeles ordinance against prostitution on the grounds that it went beyond the provisions of a preexisting state law. Similar problems arose when local authorities sought to prevent card-game gambling.

In spite of the advantages of operating under their own home-rule charters, most California cities, even those that have more than 50,000 inhabitants, have chosen to remain under the general law of the state. One reason is the cost, time, and political wrangling often involved in drawing up a charter. Another is that they have found that the general law itself often allows a city sufficient flexibility to meet the needs of its citizens. For example, a general-law city may elect its council members either at large or by districts; it may set up a city-manager system; it may provide either for the election or appointment of city officials such as city clerk or treasurer; and it may provide for the mayor to be elected separately from the city council.

Members of the city councils of most cities in this category are elected at large, that is, by citywide vote, and serve a four-year term. However, in a 1988 decision by the ninth Circuit Court of Appeals the court held that the City of Watsonville was perpetuating discrimination against its Latino residents by continuing to hold at-large elections for its city council. Latinos, it said, would have a better chance of electing one of their own if the city were divided into electoral districts for council elections. The Watsonville case could bring about a change in the method of electing members of the city council in many cities in California where there is a high proportion of Latino residents.

Forms of City Government

California cities illustrate various types of two main forms of city government: (1) the mayor-council and (2) the council-manager (see Figure 9.2). Either plan may be selected by general-law and charter cities, but charter cities have a greater range of choice in that more variations of the mayor-council plan are open to them.

The Mayor-Council Form   The traditional form of American city government has been one in which a legislative body (the council) and the chief executive officer (the mayor) are elected separately by the voters of the city. Most municipalities in California do not follow this pattern today. In fact, only one-eighth of the California cities should be called mayor-council cities, and each of them varies widely in structure. The main differentiation in this group is between strong-mayor and weak-mayor cities—terms that have nothing to do with the personality of the mayor but rather with the amount of power granted the mayor by the city's charter or by the state law.

In a *strong-mayor city* the mayor is the principal administrative officer, having the authority to appoint many of the city's officials and, under specified circumstances, to remove them. Typically, a strong mayor has a veto power over the ordinances passed by the council. The relationship between the mayor and the council in strong-mayor cities is similar to the relationship between the governor and the state legislature. Los Angeles and San Francisco are among the few cities in California that are considered to have the strong-mayor form of government. However, it is probably more correct to say that these two municipalities *approach* the strong-mayor system; in neither city does the mayor have the authority that other mayors have in some Eastern cities, such as New York and Chicago. (What local official in California has ever had the power in local, state, and national affairs that was exercised by the late Mayor Richard Daley of Chicago?) In Los Angeles the 15 members of the city council are elected by districts for staggered terms of four years each. The mayor, elected at large also for a four-year term, has the power to veto council ordinances, and the budget is prepared under the mayor's authority with the assistance of an appointed chief administrative officer. The appointive power of the Los Angeles mayor is somewhat limited, however. Some of the administrative departments of the city are run by general managers appointed by and directly responsible to the mayor, but 12 of the most important departments, including police, fire, water and power, recreation and parks, harbor, air-

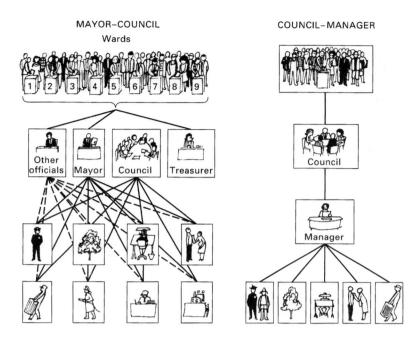

Figure 9.2 Forms of municipal government (*Source:* National Municipal League)

port, and public works, are operated by boards of commissioners. Each board consists of five members appointed by the mayor with the consent of the city council. Commissioners serve longer terms than the mayor, and no board member may be removed by the mayor without the consent of the council. Mayors of Los Angeles for more than 50 years have complained that although the voters of the city hold them accountable for the effective government of Los Angeles, they do not have real power to control the administration, the basic decisions about police and fire protection, and other important matters being made by the semiautonomous commissions.

Most of the mayor-council cities in California fall into the *weak-mayor* (or *strong-council) city* category. Under this plan the council has substantial administrative as well as legislative power. The mayor is primarily a ceremonial figurehead, possessing little if any administrative authority. Usually, this person is a member of the council, selected by fellow members to serve as chairperson and mayor for a one-year term. The mayor presides over council sessions, digs the first shovelful of dirt for new public buildings, and presents visiting celebrities with keys to the city but has no veto or appointive powers. The city's administrative jobs are filled either by election or through council appointments. The mayor, solely as agent of the council and acting under its orders, may undertake to coordinate the day-to-day operations of the municipality, or this task may be undertaken by the city clerk or the city engineer. Some general-law cities have provided by vote of the people that the mayor is to be elected independently of the council and at large; however, they have not substantially increased the mayor's powers.

The Council-Manager Form   The most prevalent type of city government in California is one in which a city manager is appointed by the elected council. California leads all other states in the number of municipalities organized in this manner. More than three-fourths of the state's incorporated cities have delegated most administrative functions to a central office, thus bringing about a more complete integration of municipal activities. A city may choose this plan by a vote of the people or through council ordinance. The typical city manager supervises the administration of ordinances passed by the council and has the power to appoint and remove most of the heads of the city's administrative departments. The manager is selected for an indefinite term and holds office as long as he or she enjoys the confidence of the majority of the council, whether it be for 20 days or 20 years. This system is similar to that of a private corporation—the voters being the stockholders, the council the board of directors, and the city manager the general manager. The mayor in such a city presides over the council and has ceremonial duties.

About 100 California cities have adopted a modified form of council-manager government in which the council appoints an administrative officer somewhat more restricted in functions than a city manager. Such an officer does not have appointment or removal power over all administrative officials and is subject to greater control by the council. This type of arrangement is often a step toward the adoption of a true council-manager form of government.

Most authorities in the field of public administration agree that the manager form of government does much to integrate authority and responsibility in government, thereby improving the services of the city to its people. A professionally trained administrator not required to face periodic public elections is better qualified to execute the policies of the city council and to manage the technical and complex business of modern city government.

THE CITY AND COUNTY OF SAN FRANCISCO

San Francisco is one of the very few city-county governments in the United States.[3] Rather than maintaining two sets of officers performing overlapping functions in the same metropolitan area, the city and county of San Francisco has one board of supervisors (its ordinance-passing body), one police force, and one set of financial officers. Unlike the citizens of metropolitan Los Angeles who, if involved in an auto accident, might have to determine the side of the street they were on before deciding to call the chief of police or the sheriff, San Franciscans know who is responsible for them and to whom they are responsible.[4]

San Francisco's Board of Supervisors consists of 11 members elected at large for four-year terms, 6 and 5 members, respectively, coming up for election every two

---

[3]Denver is also a city-county, but certain cities like Philadelphia, although they have consolidated most city and county functions, still operate with some elected county officials independent of the city government.

[4]There are fine divisions of authority among some San Francisco officials, but they are based on function rather than geography. The sheriff thus acts in civil matters and the police chief in criminal matters. A similar division exists between the city attorney and the district attorney.

years. The major is elected at large every four years and is the city's chief administrative and ceremonial officer. He or she is considered a stronger mayor than the mayor in Los Angeles, since, in addition to having the veto power and authority over the budget, the mayor of San Francisco also has full appointment power over the police commission, the planning commission, and the civil service commission. However, there is one factor that seriously limits the authority of the San Francisco mayor; namely, the city employs a chief administrative officer (appointed by the mayor upon approval by the board but removable only by a two-thirds vote of the supervisors or by popular recall) who has direct supervision of nine other city departments, including finance, purchasing, public works, and public health. Thus the city by the Golden Gate has really two top executives largely independent of each other.

THE CASE OF LOS ANGELES

In 1985, Edmund Edelman, chairman of the Los Angeles Board of Supervisors, maintained "that the merger of the city of Los Angeles and the county would provide the advantages of both forms of government and save taxpayers' money." This would be accomplished by the consolidation of the two separate offices or services (one in the city and one in the county) such as the crime labs, library systems, fire departments, and animal control departments. In 1978 this type of merger was approved by the voters in an advisory referendum, but was never implemented.

Both Mayor Richard Riordan and the City Council of Los Angeles in 1996 attempted to form panels to consider rewriting the 71-year-old governing charter that appears to be too antiquated to meet the problems of Los Angeles. The reform movement was encouraged by the several attempts of San Fernando Valley residents to secede from the city of Los Angeles.

A more modest change was undertaken in 1996 when the board of supervisors voted to designate its chairman mayor of the county. Though no new powers were given the position, it was deemed to be a better reflection of what the person holding it does than the term "chairman."

SPECIAL DISTRICTS

The most varied and least known of all units of government in the state are the special districts. They deal with matters such as water supply, irrigation, air pollution, public education, and flood control—problems that extend beyond city and county boundaries. After all, flood waters originate high in the mountains and in their flow to the river or sea cross areas occupied by many cities and sometimes several counties. This was dramatically indicated by the torrential rains that led to massive flooding in Northern California and the Central Valley at the end of 1996. Damage to cities and on farms across one-third of the state was estimated at close to $2 billion. Forming a third category of local government, special districts are created from time to time as the demand arises and as an alternative to city or county administration.

Number and Types of Special Districts

California has more than 6,000 special districts whose total annual financial transactions amount to more than those of all cities and counties of the state. Then-Assembly Speaker Curt Pringle introduced a bill in June 1995 to shrink local governments in Orange County by more than 30 water and sewer districts into a single entity by 1998. Opponents representing special districts' employees questioned the proposal on the basis this would jeopardize the bond security of the districts and many district employees would lose their jobs. The proposal failed in the Senate.

California's special districts can best be classified according to the function they perform, ranging from public education to cemetery maintenance and mosquito abatement. The most widespread group of special districts is the school districts; so important are they, in fact, that the state controller in financial reports handles them as an entirely separate category from the other special districts. School districts account for more than one-fifth of the total number of special districts in the state, and they spend more money than any other form of local government.

Every square foot of the State of California is included in a public school district of some type. The approximately 1,100 districts in California are classified as elementary, high school, unified (covering both elementary and high school grades), and community college. Sometimes a high school district will include several elementary districts and is, therefore, known as a union high school district. When a district includes territory in more than one county it is called a joint district. Each district has its own governing board, usually consisting of five members; in practically every case they are elected by the voters of the district in a nonpartisan election for a four-year term. (A chartered city may provide for the appointment of its board of education.) Each board hires a superintendent, a professional educator who is responsible for administering the policies adopted by the board. Upon the recommendation of the superintendent the board hires the principals, the teachers, and all other employees of the district. It also adopts the annual budget and establishes the curriculum or course of study. However, the board is governed in almost every detail by state law and is accountable first to the county superintendent of schools but more importantly to one of two statewide boards for the performance of its legal obligations. The state Board of Education, consisting of ten members appointed by the governor, oversees the public schools from kindergarten through the twelfth grade (K–12). Its administrative agent is the state superintendent of public instruction, who is responsible for granting state credentials to teachers and for distributing state funds to the various school districts according to the formula adopted by the legislature. Somewhat lesser control is exercised over the 70 community college districts of the state by the state Board of Governors of the California Community Colleges, also appointed by the governor.

School board elections generally have a low voter turnout. Citizens frequently excuse themselves for not having gone to the polls on the grounds that there was no real contest or significant issue. However, in various localities in California there have been spirited election campaigns for the school board. Sometimes the issues are ideological. Recall elections that have focused on highly contentious issues over curriculum (peace studies, sex education, religion) can and have led to larger voter turnout, but those have tended to be infrequent.

Other Special Districts   California's nonschool special districts, totaling more than 5,000, present an amazing variety. There are currently on the statute books more than 200 enabling acts of the legislature that authorize the formation of the various districts. The state controller lists 57 different *types* of special districts that perform 30 basic activities or functions. (Usually, a special district will perform just one function, but some will conduct several activities simultaneously.)

REGIONAL GOVERNMENT

Local government in California's metropolitan areas is a crazy quilt of counties, cities, and special districts, each with its own taxing authority, administration, and rules. This arrangement creates much confusion for the citizens. For example, it may be legal to park a pick-up truck on the east side of Citrus Avenue but not on the west side, since Citrus Avenue is the dividing line between two municipalities, the westerly one being very opposed to such plebeian vehicles vulgarizing its patrician curbs. However, the water one drinks, the air one breathes, and the highways one travels cross county, city, and special district lines, and the problems of pollution, traffic, and law enforcement must be handled on the basis of an entire metropolitan region.

Urban atomization is most marked in the two largest metropolitan areas of the state. The San Francisco Bay Area includes about 50 incorporated cities, 9 counties, and a host of special districts. Most of the Los Angeles metropolitan area is included within Los Angeles County, but that county contains 84 municipalities, the largest being the city of Los Angeles itself. Some of the other cities, such as San Fernando, are enclaves completely surrounded by the "City of the Angels." A lesser degree of governmental fragmentation is to be found in some of the other cities, such as San Diego and Sacramento.

Many efforts have been made to bring order out of this urban chaos. One result has been the creation of the large regional special districts, such as the Bay Area Rapid Transit District, which furnishes public transportation for the people of several counties, but this expedient does not really solve the problem. The San Francisco Bay region not only has BART but also has several other regional special districts, for example, the Golden Gate Bridge and Highway District and the San Francisco Bay Air Pollution District. Each serves a single purpose, each has its own board of directors, each its own source of revenue, each its own bureaucracy, and each guards its own authority jealously. None can make and enforce a general plan of development that will make the Bay Area the beautiful and livable place it can be.

Planning Commissions

Various measures short of regional government have been adopted to solve the metropolitan problems. In the past 25 years tens of thousands of acres of California's open space, fields, vineyards, and orchards have been gobbled up by housing tracts, shopping centers, and parking lots. This urban sprawl has given birth to a swarm of "slurbs"—"sloppy, sleazy, slovenly, slip-shod semicities" around the metropolitan

BART train with San Francisco skyline and Mt. Sutro in the background. (Courtesy BART)

centers.[5] Therefore, a strong demand has risen for careful planning for the future growth of metropolitan areas to preserve California's traditional beauty while accommodating its population increases. Consequently, a state law of 1953 authorized area planning commissions, one of the first of which was set up in a six-county area around Sacramento. The commission is appointed by the county supervisors and city councils of the region, and it merely makes recommendations to its constituent cities and counties on matters such as land use and zoning. Since that time other measures have been passed by the state legislature that favor regional planning. The U.S. Congress in 1966 added its support by offering national funds for urban-renewal projects, provided there was systematic metropolitan-wide planning for such projects. The result is that most areas of California today are under the jurisdiction of regional planning commissions. This is particularly true of the coastal areas following the passage of the California Coastal Zone Conservation Act of 1972, which created regional commissions with genuine authority to control development within their areas.

---

[5]Samuel E. Wood and Alfred E. Heller, *California Going, Going . . .* (Sacramento: California Tomorrow, 1962), p. 10.

Cooperative Efforts

The need for cooperation in a host of areas has led to councils of government that act as voluntary advisory bodies to their members. Mayors of cities meet periodically to address common problems such as air pollution, traffic congestion, and energy and water policy. Examples include the Association of Bay Area Governments (ABAG), which addresses concerns of San Francisco Bay Area cities and counties, the Southern California Association of Governments (SCAG), and the Sacramento Area Council of Governments (SACG). While helpful these bodies can only *recommend* actions which then have to be ratified by the city council or county board of supervisors.

Another form of cooperation involves cities contracting with counties to furnish city residents with services. A number of these services may be said to be routinely provided, such as the running of elections, library services, tax assessments and collections, and enforcement of state health regulations. In tough economic times some cities have abolished their police forces and contracted with the county sheriff to deal with crime.

CITIZEN PARTICIPATION

Observers of the American political scene have decried the apathy of the average voters toward their local governments. *This* is most unfortunate, since many of the decisions that affect our daily lives are made not in Washington or Sacramento but in our city halls, county courthouses, and boards of education headquarters. Furthermore, if citizens would stir themselves, their impact on the local officials would be more direct and persuasive than on state and national authorities. A delegation of irate homemakers may not be able to affect the course of a bill in Sacramento, but can derail efforts of real estate developers to railroad through the city planning commission a change of zoning that would erect a superfluous shopping center in the middle of a residential neighborhood. (For information concerning the financing of local governments in California, please refer to the discussion in Chapter 10.)

SELECTED REFERENCES

California Department of Education, *Fact Book,* Sacramento: State Printing Office, annually.

Feinbaum, Robert, "Climate Right for Creating New Cities," *California Journal,* October 1987.

Hanley, Craig, and A. G. Block, "Regional Government: Everybody Wants to Land on Boardwalk," in Thomas Hoeber and Larry Gertsen, *California Government and Politics Annual, 1992–93,* Sacramento, California Journal Press, 1992.

Post, A. Alan, *Report of Commission on Government Reform,* Sacramento: State Printing Office, 1979.

Reeves, Scott, "State Mandates Defy Logic," *Fresno Bee,* August 7, 1988.

Ross, Robert, *Perspectives on Local Government in California,* Belmont, CA: Star Publishing, 1987.

Starkey, Danielle, "Counties in Revolt," *California Journal,* August 1993.

State Controller, *Annual Report of Financial Transactions Concerning Cities of California,* Sacramento: State Printing Office, annually.

———, *Annual Report of Financial Transactions Concerning California Counties,* Sacramento: State Printing Office, annually.

———, *Annual Report of Financial Transactions Concerning School Districts of California,* Sacramento: State Printing Office, annually.

———, *Annual Report of Financial Transactions Concerning Special Districts of California,* Sacramento: State Printing Office, annually.

Zimmerman-McKenna, Kathy, "No Cash on the Horizon for Parched Counties," *California Journal,* August 1989.

Chapter 10

Financing California Government

Different than in many recent years, the 1996-97 budget of $63 billion was in balance. With more Californians working and paying taxes there was far more money to go around, reflecting a 9% increase over the previous year's spending.

In the early 1990s the state ran a deficit budget in that it spent more money than it took in and had to borrow from Wall Street. The deficit ran into billions of dollars and the state was also required to pay interest so it was not a practice that the state preferred, but certain obligations were unavoidable. The fact that the state had a comprehensive welfare program and more people, schools, drugs, gangs and earthquakes necessitated large amounts of money to meet necessary obligations.

However, for 1996-1997, income was greater that in past years allowing for that 9% increase over the previous year's budget. This made possible increased expenditures for certain functions.

Governor Pete Wilson advocated a larger investment in education that would diminish class sizes in the lower grades and to emphasize his stand he travelled to Columbia Elementary School in Glendale to sign the new budget. The new budget included a $28 billion education plan that provided $771 million for schools to decrease class size to 20 students in the first and second grades plus either kindergarten or third grade and $200 million for new classrooms.

In addition to the expenditures for primary grades, the budget added $130 million to the budget of the University of California system (UC) and $101 million to the last year's budget of the State Universities (CSU). The Community College system also was a winner with added funding, including money to support 650 new teachers.

Republicans and Democrats who had become accustomed to budget fights seemed pleased with this budget and were delighted to take credit for it.

Another feature of the 1996-1997 budget was related legislation implementing a 5 percent cut in taxes on corporations and banks. Starting January 1, 1997, the tax cut translated into some $200 million in tax savings for business. It was anticipated that more jobs would be created as a result of this cut.

The increase in funds for the new budget was also made possible by Governor Wilson making a number of cuts ("blue penciling") in the budget submitted to him by the legislature. He deleted approximately $82 million by paring out several projects in the districts of Democratic legislators and he eliminated $1 million for earthquake work at the San Francisco City Hall where former Speaker and rival Willie Brown served At the same time, with Republicans in control of the assembly for the first time since 1970, Wilson left intact several of their projects, including $4 million for a science center in Santa Ana and he shifted $147 million from urban schools to suburban and rural areas which are Republican strongholds that traditionally had received less than city schools. Republican Orange County received an extra $10 million, perhaps more than it would have received under formula if both houses of the legislature had been under the control of the Democrats.

The battles resumed with consideration of the $67 billion 1997–1998 budget. Though the economy continued to be robust, Wilson and Democratic leaders in the legislature deadlocked over a number of issues, many related to welfare reform. The governor also pushed for a substantial tax cut and that, too, was resisted by legislative leaders who complained it would hurt education. Complicating matters was a $1.36 billion debt the courts had ruled had to be paid to the state workers' pension fund, money that had been taken during the fiscal crisis of the early 1990s. Wilson, blocked in his dsire to cut taxes and unable to come to terms with labor unions over the schedule of repayment, declared that, rather than paying the pension fund off over several years, it would be repaid in one lump sum. In effect that meant no tax cut, no pay raises for state employees, reductions in some welfare programs for legal immigrants and an increased possibility there would be fee increases for students attending state institutions of higher education. One observer said that this budget, drafted in a time of prosperity, looked more like one designed for a Third World nation.

STATE REVENUE: WHERE THE MONEY COMES FROM

Until 1950 in California nearly all of the state revenue was derived from the general property tax and a poll tax. However, with the coming of industry and the increase in population, additional funds became imperative.

As may be seen in figure 10.1, California presently secures its revenue from several sources, nearly all of which are taxes of some sort. Only about 14 percent of total receipts is not from taxes and comes from such sources as royalties from oil and gas production on state owned land, motor vehicle fees, horse racing fees, medical and board charges from state hospitals, traffic penalties, investment of state funds, fees and tuition at state universities and colleges, and regulatory charges and special fees for businesses and the professions. The remaining 86 percent of state revenue comes from various types of taxes.

The Personal Income Tax

The leading source of revenue is currently the personal income tax. Not as high as the national income tax, it is similar in that the rates vary according to the size of the individual's income. Persons whose annual adjusted gross incomes are below $6,000 (or $12,000 for couples filing jointly) are not required to file tax returns. Those filing returns with an annual adjusted gross income less than $20,000 paid just 1.5 percent of the total income tax received in 1995–1996 while those with adjusted gross incomes

Total Revenues and Transfers

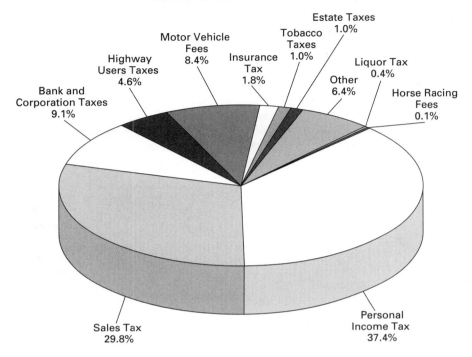

Figure 10.1   Source: *Governor's Budget* 1997–1998, Sacramento, 1997.

over $100,000 paid 53.3 percent of the total taken in. The total amount received by this tax for 1996–1997 was estimated at $22 billion compared with $20.5 billion received the previous year.

Since 1972, California has had a system of withholding for state personal income taxes similar to that used by the federal government. Withholding has prevented some tax dodging, and it provides monthly revenues that help the cash flow of state finances. In 1979, a tax indexing system was passed that uses brackets that are adjusted upward when necessary to compensate for inflation. This measure, as amended by the Jarvis-sponsored initiative of 1982, protects taxpayers from being placed in a higher tax bracket due to higher earnings that provide no greater purchasing power because of inflation.

Because of the growth of California's economy in the 1980s, coupled with a high rate of inflation, revenue realized through the state income tax grew by leaps and bounds. Slowed by the recession of the early 1990s, the personal income tax remains the leading source of revenue for the state, surpassing the amount received through the sales tax.

The Sales Tax

First used in the days of the Great Depression, when other sources of revenue had dried up, the retail sales tax has become a major source of income. A tax of 7.25 percent on the sales price of all tangible goods, except food for home consumption, prescription drugs, electricity, gas and water, ambulatory aids, custom computer programs, and other minor items such as newspapers and magazines is collected by retail merchants from purchasers.

There have been add-ons from time to time. The state added a special half-cent sales tax in the midst of the budget crisis in 1991, a tax the people voted to make permanent in November 1993 with the intent that the added revenues be devoted to public safety programs. As a part of this increase, the sales tax was applied to snack foods, candy, magazines, and newspapers. It quickly became apparent that the line to be drawn between snacks and food was blurred at best. For example, popped popcorn was taxable as a snack; unpopped popcorn was not. The voters resolved this knotty question by approving an initiative in 1992 that repealed the snack tax.

A "use-tax" provision levies a similar tax on goods purchased outside the state for use in California.

With practically no cost of collection borne by the state, the retail sales tax has yielded between 28 and 38 percent of the total state revenue since it has been in effect. For 1996–1997 revenue from the sales tax was approximately $19, billion or approximately 31 percent of state revenues.

The principal objection to the sales tax has been that it is a *regressive* tax; that is, it is not based on a person's ability to pay. It is argued that the tax places an undue burden on large families with low incomes. An initiative measure to reduce the sales tax by 1 percent and to increase business and personal income taxes was placed on the 1958 ballot but was defeated.

Taxes on Motorists

It is expensive to provide adequate facilities for California's highly mobile population. The costs to the state of constructing, maintaining, and policing an extensive network of highways generally exceed $2 billion a year. Californians, as a result, cannot escape paying plenty if they want to drive to work or take a holiday trip. The variety of special taxes and fees levied on motorists has caused the per capita car cost to zoom to the highest in the nation.

Highway Users Taxes   Income from this source goes to a special fund and is generated by the motor vehicle fuel tax (gasoline and diesel). It provides the major amount of money for maintaining, replacing, and constructing state highway and transportation facilities. Close to one-half of these revenues is apportioned to local jurisdictions for streets and highway use. All these taxes bring in about 4.6 percent of the total of state revenue.

The current tax rate for motor vehicle fuel is 18 cents per gallon; aircraft fuel is taxed at 2 cents a gallon; and local transit systems and certain common carriers pay one cent per gallon.

Motor Vehicle Taxes and Fees   Motor vehicle fees consist of vehicle licenses, registration, weight and driver's license fees, and various other charges related to vehicle operation. Vehicle license fees are based on the "market value," which is the cost of the vehicle to the purchaser exclusive of sales tax adjusted by a depreciation schedule and is levied each year. This fee is imposed in lieu of a local personal property tax on automobiles. All of the revenue from this tax, other than administrative costs and fees on trailer coaches and mobile homes, are constitutionally dedicated to local governments.

Registration fees are based on a flat rate of $29 on all motor vehicles. Motor vehicle taxes and fees are collected and administered by the Department of Motor Vehicles and account for about 8 percent of the total revenue of the state.

Bank and Corporation Taxes

Revenue from bank and corporation taxes for 1996–1997 was estimated at about $6 billion, accounting for 9 percent of the state's total revenue for that year. A franchise tax and a corporate income tax are levied at 4.3 percent on profits. The franchise tax is imposed on corporations that do business in California, while the corporate income tax is imposed on corporations that do not do business in the state but derive income from California sources. Banks and other financial corporations pay an additional "bank tax" of approximately 1.5 percent on their net income.

Insurance Tax

A tax rate of 2.35 percent is levied on gross premiums of the majority of insurance written in California. Certain pension and profit-sharing plans are exempt from this tax. Revenue from this source has been increasing gradually and currently totals about $1.8 billion.

Liquor Taxes

Taxes are levied on the manufacturers of all alcoholic beverages. Excise rates vary from $0.20 per gallon on beer and wine to $3.30 on distilled spirits per gallon. Revenue for 1996–1997 was about $2.7 billion.

Horse-Racing Fees

The state government is always a "winner" at the parimutuel horse races. Revenues from horse racing are derived mainly from a fee on the amount wagered, "breakage" (odd cents on each dollar wagered), unclaimed winning tickets, and license fees, fines, and penalties. The total revenues from horse racing have increased during the last few years and now amount to approximately $90 million. About one-eighth of horse-racing revenues are earmarked for distribution to fairs and expositions, for wildlife restoration, and for research and improvement in animal husbandry and agriculture conducted primarily by the University of California and some of the state universities. The rest is returned to the general fund.

Tobacco Tax

An excise tax imposed on distributors selling cigarettes in California has been 35 cents a pack since January 1989 as a result of Proposition 99. At the same time an excise tax was implemented at a rate "equivalent" to cigarettes upon cigars, chewing tobacco, snuff, and pipe tobacco. Effective January 1, 1994, with the passage of the Breast Cancer Act, the cigarette tax was increased an additional two cents a pack.

Twenty-five cents of the total tax is allocated to a variety of anti-smoking programs and other objectives deemed socially desirable under the terms of Proposition 99.

State Lottery

Included with other miscellaneous smaller sources of revenue is the income from the well-publicized California state lottery. A constitutional amendment initiative approved in November 1984 established the lottery. Lottery proposals to raise revenue for the state had been before the state legislature for the previous ten years but had never mustered the necessary two-thirds vote in both houses for passage; and California voters had once before, in 1964, rejected the plan for a lottery. However, in 1983 the California Poll indicated widespread support for a government-run lottery to raise revenue, and Proposition 37 passed with a 16-point margin.

As enacted, Proposition 37 created a state-run lottery with a state commission of five persons appointed by the governor to run it. Revenue from tickets costing a minimum of $1 and sold by retail businesses would be divided as follows: 50 percent for prizes, 16 percent for administration, and 34 percent for public education. Money appropriated for education was to be spent for educating students rather than for construction, buying property, or research. Distributed quarterly, lottery revenues are distributed to public education systems as follows: kindergarten through twelfth grade—81 percent; community colleges—12 percent; California state universities—4.5 percent; and the University of California—2.5 percent.

Put into operation in October 1985, the state lottery totaled as much as $2.09 billion in 1987–1988. But there was a significant drop in sales of lottery tickets in the early 1990s with revenue dropping to $767,625 in 1995–1996. That means of course much less money for the schools and at a time of financial difficulty.

It is claimed that the lottery is a regressive tax because its burden falls primarily on those who can least afford to pay. Low-income players spend a proportionately larger share of their income on tickets with money they should be spending for food and other necessities. Yet demographic studies of seven states with lotteries indicate that 70–75 percent of lottery players are from households with $15,000 annual income or more.[1]

STATE EXPENDITURES: WHERE THE MONEY GOES

Types of Expenditures

The California state budget contains three general types of expenditures, which are referred to as state operations, local assistance, and capital outlay. Funds spent for state operations include those functions that are under direct state control; funds spent for local assistance are funds allocated to counties, cities, and special districts to cover services provided by local governments. Capital outlay designates those expenditures spent for state buildings and facilities.

---

[1]Congressional Research Service, "Overview of State Lottery Operations," Library of Congress #85–52, 1986, p. 25.

Total Expenditures
(Excluding Selected Bond Funds)

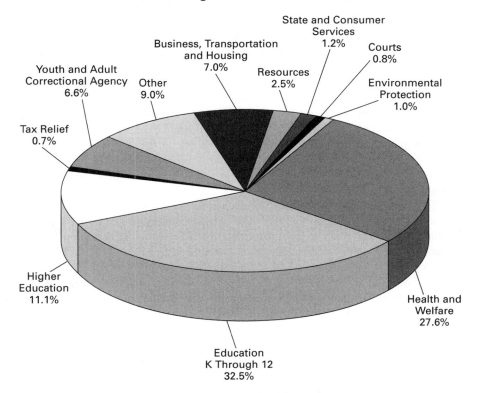

Figure 10.2   Source: *Governor's Budget* 1997–1998, Sacramento, 1997.

In recent years approximately 60 percent of the money collected by the state has been allocated to local governments for designated services (local assistance) such as welfare and education (K–14). Funds spent for state operations themselves, such as the expenses of the legislature, the governor's office, various state agencies, and the state universities and colleges, amount to about 36 percent of the budget. Approximately 4 percent of state operations is presently allocated for capital outlay expenses.

State Expenses

Figure 10.2 shows where the money goes and lists the various major functional areas under state government support. The appropriate percentage of the total budget for each category is also noted.

Health and Welfare   The state expense for 1996–1997 of about $17.5 billion for health and welfare amounted to 27.6 percent of the state budget. The state has funded only about 35 percent of the total welfare cost for California residents, since the federal government paid about 50 percent of the welfare bill and the counties have contributed the other 15 percent.[2] Welfare benefits include family assistance; Aid to the Aged, Blind, and Disabled; general relief; food stamps; Medi-Cal assistance; and various other social services. The largest state expenditure ($16.7 billion) is for the immense Medi-Cal program, which funds medical services for more than 10 percent of California's population. The state also contributes large amounts to the total fund for aid to the aged, blind, and disabled and to the total fund for aid to families with dependent children. The state does not provide money for the food stamp program, which is wholly supported by the federal government.

Education—Elementary and Secondary (K–12)   Approximately 5.5 million of California's school-aged children are enrolled in the public elementary and secondary school system. Another approximately 1 million attend the state's 107 community colleges. In addition, approximately 154,500 students attend the University of California and some 323,000 are enrolled at the campuses of the California State University (CSU) system.

The total expenditure for K–12 education for 1996–1997 was $24.6 billion as compared with $23.8 billion in 1995–1996. Higher education saw no fee increases; funding for the University of California system was increased $130 million to $2.05 billion and funding for the state university system was up $101 million to $1.77 billion. Community colleges got $3.11 billion, up from $2.96 billion.

Beginning in the early 1990s, the state has provided subsidies in the form of financial aid for those students who are academically qualified but cannot pay the full tuition fees. Currently about 36 percent of UC students and 44 percent of those enrolled in the CSU system receive some form of student aid. The Cal-Grant program, for example, provides $33 million a year to assist low- and middle-income students. Other institutions and agencies involved in public higher education are the California Marine Academy, Hastings College of Law, the Post-Secondary Education Commission, and the Board of Governors of the Community Colleges.

Business, Transportation, and Housing   About $3.3 billion (or about 7 percent of 1996–1997 expenditures) is spent by the various departments within the Business, Transportation, and Housing Agency. These funds are used for the general purposes of providing for efficient and safe movement of people and goods within the state, and for promoting a sound financial and business community while protecting the public from economic loss and illegal business practices. The largest expenditure in this segment of the budget (about $2.3 billion) is for providing transportation and highway facilities as administered by the Department of Transportation, popularly known as Caltrans. This department has the responsibility of planning and maintaining California's massive freeway system—the most sophisticated in the world—and is also charged with increasing the use of mass-transit systems by providing research and assisting local governments in right-of-way purchases. The California Highway Patrol, consisting of about 5,800 officers, is responsible for safe, lawful, rapid, and economical use of the

---

[2]The figures cited here are for the 1996–1997 fiscal year. The welfare reform package passed by Congress, signed into law by President Clinton in 1996 and implemented in 1997, had a significant impact on both the percentages and the total amounts shown here as reductions are made in some areas and a share of the total burden shifts from the federal government to state and local authorities.

state highway system and costs approximately $547 million a year. The Department of Motor Vehicles is in charge of the registration and collection of fees for California's more than 26 million vehicles and the processing of drivers' licenses. It costs approximately $531 million each year to operate this department. The remainder of the business and transportation expenditures is spent by the various departments involved in business areas, including the State Department of Banking, the Department of Commerce, the Department of Insurance, the Department of Real Estate, the Department of Savings and Loans, the Department of Housing and Community Development, and the Department of Alcoholic Beverage Control.

Resources   The cost of conserving California's natural resources and improving California's living environment is currently about $1.9 billion a year. The programs funded range from those designed to attain and maintain desirable standards of air and water purity to fighting forest fires, forest management, flood control, water development, oil drilling regulation, and the creation of recreational opportunities. Many boards, commissions, and departments are involved in implementing these programs. The largest share of the resources expenditures, about $288 million, is for the Department of Forestry. The planning, developing, and operation of the state park system consisting of 287 parks, beaches, campgrounds, and historical sites costs some $284 million. The large state water program administered by the Department of Water Resources is financed by revenue from services and through revenue bonds.

State and Consumer Services   Most of the $774.5 million expended for state and consumer services is spent by the various staff and service agencies, including the Department of General Services, the Franchise Tax Board, the Office of the State Architect, the Personnel Board, the Public Employees Retirement System, and the State Teachers Retirement System. These state agencies that perform direct services to the public, such as the Department of Consumer Affairs, the Museum of Science and Industry, the state Fire Marshal, and the Department of Veterans Affairs, expend the remaining one-fourth in this budget category.

Other Expenditures   The funds expended in this category go to support the general government, which includes the legislature, the governor's office, the state courts, and certain other units, including the Fair Political Practices Commission, the Public Employment Relations Board, the Department of Food and Agriculture, the Department of Industrial Relations, and the Public Utilities Commission.

THE BUDGET PROCESS

California's state budget contains a line-item listing of anticipated revenues and expenditures for a fiscal year beginning July 1 and ending June 30. The formulation of the budget by the governor and the legislature involves a rather lengthy process consisting of seven steps as follows: (1) The introduction of the governor's proposal is required by January 10 of each year according to the state constitution. The proposed budget is introduced separately in the senate and the assembly. (2) Review and analysis prepared by the state legislative analyst is made available to the Senate Finance Committee and the Assembly Ways and Means Committee. (3) In March and April budget subcommittees in each house conduct independent hearings on spending proposals for areas of government expenditures such as health, welfare, education, and other government services. (4) In May the State Department of Finance submits its final estimates of revenues for the coming fiscal year to the budget subcommittees. (5) The Senate Finance Committee and the Assembly Ways and Means Committee collect subcommittee reports for incorporation and adoption for each house. (6) The budget is adopted by both houses with two-thirds majorities. Differences are worked out by a two-house conference committee. Adoption by the legislature of a final spending plan has a deadline of June 15, which is missed more often than met. (7) The legislature sends the budget to the governor who has 12 days to sign it. Under the power of item veto, the governor can delete or decrease any individual line appropriations added by the legislature, although the state's chief executive cannot restore any proposals that the legislature deleted. The governor's veto can be overridden by a two-thirds majority vote in both houses of the legislature. (For further discussion of the item veto, refer to Chapter 7, p. 117.)

Overshadowing the deliberations of the legislators and the governor in the budget process is the Gann Amendment to the state constitution limiting state spending.

THE GANN SPENDING LIMITATION

Paul Gann, the coauthor with Howard Jarvis of Proposition 13, organized the campaign for an initiative to limit government spending in California. With the support of many Democrats it qualified for the ballot in a special election in November 1979. Known as Proposition 4, it passed with a large 74 percent majority of the voters.

This proposition placed in the state constitution a provision limiting the amount of tax revenues that state and local governments can spend in any given year to the amount spent in 1978, adjusted annually for population growth and inflation. Thus, if inflation was 4 percent and population growth was 1 percent for a given year, all government spending—including that on education, prisons, and welfare—could grow no more than 5 percent over the base period of 1978. Tax revenues received in excess of the legal spending limit had to be returned to taxpayers.

Two propositions that would have loosened limits on government spending as provided by the Gann initiative were on the ballot in June 1988, but both were turned down by the voters. The voters changed the basis for operation of the Gann initiative in the June 1990 election when, instead of population growth and inflation (which hardly can account for new problems such as the AIDS epidemic or the greatly expanded need for bilingual teachers), the new reference point became changes in personal income.

FINANCING LOCAL GOVERNMENT

Proposition 13 hurled the problem of financing California's local governments into the public limelight. The state's counties, cities, and special districts (including school districts) spend about twice as many tax dollars as the state government, and the expenditures of these entities had more than doubled in the ten-year period from 1967 to 1977. The finances of counties, cities, school districts, and other special dis-

TABLE 10.1   Financial Transactions Concerning
Local Governments in California, 1976–1977 (In Thousands)

	Expenditures	Receipts	Long-Term Indebtedness
Counties	$ 7,172,336	$ 7,366,009	$ 116,340
Cities	4,721,332	5,031,310	3,939,899
Special districts	3,463,584	4,428,975	8,052,845
School districts	8,135,703	8,229,131	4,337,828
Grand total	$23,492,955	$25,055,425	$16,446,912

Source: State Controller, *Annual Reports of Financial Transactions Concerning Counties, Cities, Special Districts, and School Districts of California* (Sacramento: State Printing Office, 1977), *passim.*

tricts for the fiscal year immediately preceding the passage of the Jarvis-Gann initiative are summarized in Table 10.1.

In the years before Proposition 13 the heaviest expenditures of California's counties had been for social welfare and amounted to about 40 percent of the typical California county budget. Other large disbursements had been for public protection (services of the sheriff, district attorney, and the courts) and for health programs. The largest expenditures of California's cities were for police and fire protection and street maintenance. School districts, by definition, spent almost all of their $8 billion budget for public education. The other special districts, having been created for a vast variety of purposes, spent their dollars on many different kinds of activities, ranging from laying sewer pipes to operating airports.

Before Proposition 13 the local governments received a significant share of their revenues from the general property tax. In 1976–1977 the counties received about 40 percent of their income from this source, the cities approximately 27 percent, the school districts more than 50 percent, and the other special districts more than 40 percent (some special districts, such as flood control and mosquito abatement, received almost 100 percent support from property taxes).

THE TAX REVOLT: PROPOSITION 13

In June 1978 California voters approved a ballot measure, Proposition 13, that touched off a tax revolt not only in California but throughout the nation. Property taxes on homes and commercial buildings in California had skyrocketed as a result of the housing boom and the double-digit inflation in the years 1973–1978. Since 1971 property had been taxed at rates ranging from 3–3.5 percent of market value, and that value had been soaring; many homes tripled or quadrupled in value in five years. With new assessments in 1978 some homeowners faced 400–500 percent increases in taxes.

This situation proved to be a real opportunity for Howard Jarvis, a retired millionaire manufacturer in Los Angeles who had been railing against high taxes for 15 years. He enlisted the aid of Paul Gann, who headed a Sacramento area antitax lobby, and they formulated an initiative proposal that would amend the state constitution and reduce property taxes. With the slogan "I'm mad as hell—and I'm not going to take it anymore," the petition received a record-breaking 1.5 million signatures to place it on the June ballot. Despite opposition from Governor Brown and groups such as the AFL-CIO, Southern California Edison, and the Sierra Club, Proposition 13 (the Jarvis-Gann amendment) was approved by the voters with a wide margin of nearly 2–1. This revolutionary measure rolled back property taxes to 1 percent of the assessed value in 1975–1976 and limited annual assessment increases to no more than 2 percent and barred new special property taxes. Furthermore, it prohibited local governments from imposing new taxes without approval of two-thirds of local voters since it also prevented the state from raising new taxes without a two-thirds vote of the legislature. This new amendment chopped $7 billion from the local property tax, the biggest source of revenue for cities, counties, school districts, and other special districts. At the time Proposition 13 was passed, property taxes provided between 55 and 65 percent of the total revenue of California cities and counties and an even larger share of the income for state schools and special districts (see Table 10.2).

However, the effects of this massive tax reduction on local governments were not felt immediately. Because of the existence of a huge budget surplus the state legislature was able to ease the impact of Proposition 13 on local governments by doling out $4.9 billion from the 1979–1980 budget to cities, counties, schools, and special districts. This practice of supplying large funds from the state budget to local governments to fill the gap created by the Jarvis amendment continued during the fiscal years 1980, 1981, and 1982. In 1982 this so-called bail-out reached a peak of $5.9 billion. However, by June 1982, as a result of a poor economy and less federal aid, the state surplus had dwindled from its billion-dollar stature to less than $116 million. A severe recession had seriously reduced income from state sales, personal income, and corporation income taxes.

Yet because of population growth and inflation, expenditures for local governments in California increased from $44.3 billion in 1978 to $71 billion in 1996. To keep up with these pressures, local governments attempted to find new sources of revenue and to make budget cuts wherever possible. Cities were somewhat more successful than other levels of government in charging and raising fees for services such as garbage col-

TABLE 10.2   Property Tax as Percentage of Total General Revenue

	1977–1978— Before Proposition 13	1978–1979— After Proposition 13
Special districts—nonenterprise	73.5%	44.9%
School districts	57.8	25.8
Community college districts	52.2	24.2
Counties	37.0	17.3
Cities	22.8	10.8
Special districts—enterprise	14.7	8.8

Source: California, Department of Finance, Program Evaluation Unit, January 1979.

lection, business licenses, hotel taxes, sewer service, and recreation privileges to increase income. (The voters limited this ability to increase fees by passing Proposition 218 in 1996. See p. 51) But even with budget cuts, cities, along with counties, schools, and special districts, were unable to meet the demands made on them without state aid. County revenues other than state aid fell more than 19 percent between 1978 and 1983. By 1995 the state was supplying 75 percent of all school revenues.

The net result of Proposition 13 was to make local governments more dependent on state aid and, in the process, to take away much of the decision-making power of cities, counties, schools, and other special districts. To voters, Proposition 13 was a simple tax limit. But by limiting local tax power, voters have actually given the state legislature the opportunity to impose more conditions on local government in return for state aid suddenly needed to replace lost property-tax revenues.

Losers and Winners in the "Proposition 13 Game"

As noted in the previous discussion, local governments—counties, cities, school districts, and special districts—were losers as a result of Proposition 13. They lost a major source of revenue since the income from property taxes was drastically reduced. They were forced to cut expenditures and to seek new sources of revenue at the same time to balance their budgets. To reduce expenditures it became necessary to make savings by decreasing personnel and holding the line on the rate of salaries and wages. In addition, some services—for example, library services and recreation privileges—were curtailed. At the same time cities, counties, and special districts raised fees for essential services such as rubbish collection and sewer services and increased rates of licenses and permits.

An excellent study showing who were winners from Proposition 13 was made by Paul Richter, using the period 1978–1983 as a base for his research.

During this five-year period homeowners were the top winners since they received about one-third of the total savings of the first five "Jarvis years." Those who remained in homes they owned in 1978 did better than more recent buyers, since homes are reassessed to market value when they are bought or substantially improved. Owners of commercial and industrial property got 27 percent of the tax savings from Proposition 13, which amounted to nearly $2 billion in the first year. Landlords were also big winners, receiving about 17 percent of the property-tax savings, but only a small portion of these benefits was passed on to tenants since average rents continued to grow from 1978 to 1983. Agriculture received 13 percent of the savings owing to decreased property taxes on agricultural land. However, the Richter study revealed that the gross savings to each of these taxpaying groups was reduced by increases in their state and federal tax liabilities. These liabilities grew since lower property taxes reduced itemized income-tax deductions and increased taxable income. As a result, the federal government became a "winner," claiming about 15–25 percent of gross savings. Ironically, the state gained some 3–11 percent of the tax savings for the same reason.[3]

The tax system created by Proposition 13 was challenged in the courts in the early 1990s on the grounds that two pieces of essentially identical property could be

---

[3]Paul Richter, "Big Winners from California's Tax Cuts," *Los Angeles Times*, June 5, 1983.

'WAIT! Think of the children!'

(Courtesy McClatchy Newspapers)

(and were) taxed at wildly different levels simply because one had changed hands (and thus been reappraised) and the other had not, reappraisal being undertaken only when a property changed ownership. This "dual roll" system was felt by many to be in violation of the equal protection clause of the U.S. Constitution. Opponents maintained no one should pay five or ten times the taxes to receive the same level of services. In June 1992 the Supreme Court ruled otherwise. The Court held the state had a "legitimate interest in local neighborhood preservation" (an issue not raised by the parties in their arguments) and that those buying homes know in advance they will be paying higher taxes and choose to make the purchase voluntarily. To overturn Proposition 13 would result in higher property taxes across the board and might well force many from their homes, precisely what Proposition 13 was intended to prevent.

Same schools; same police and fire protection; same libraries and parks; same water system and refuse collection...

(Dennis Renault, *Sacramento Bee*)

The County—A Big Loser

Decreased revenues for California's counties resulting from Proposition 13 forced a reexamination of the fiscal relationship between state and county governments. For many years the state legislature has required that the state's 58 counties provide and administer statewide programs at the local level without providing enough money to pay all costs. Such state-mandated programs include health and welfare services to the poor; maintenance of rural roads in agricultural areas; and services for city and county residents in the courts, and jail, and juvenile hall; as well as probation, district attorney, public defender, coroner, environmental health, weights and measures, and clerk-recorder services. The county also collects taxes for schools, special districts, and cities.

State and federal governments presently provide about 56 percent of the revenue for California counties, but the cost of these services has been growing faster than the increase in support. In most counties the state-mandated programs now consume as much as 90 percent of the county funds with financial support for local needs such as law enforcement, libraries, and parks continuing to shrink. These mandates, together with the loss of tax revenue from Proposition 13, have meant what one Sacramento lobbyist called "death by attrition" for local governments. Some programs were eliminated, as was the case with Butte County's libraries. Others have been cut drastically, as in Lassen County where an area the size of Connecticut was patrolled by just 13 sheriff's deputies. Cancer-screening clinics and dental clinics were shut down at South Lake Tahoe and Placerville. Nor has it been just in rural counties that cuts have been made. Los Angeles's museums were closed on a rotating basis and hours reduced for all.

To develop at least some additional revenues, counties turned to increasing a variety of fees. There is now an annual $23 maintenance fee for use of trails along the San Gabriel and Los Angeles rivers. Fees on developers have jumped and charges for those using cellular phones have been adopted in several counties. The simple matter of obtaining a copy of a two-page police report can cost upward of $25. And, in a deal with the governor in 1993, the counties receive a portion of the sales tax increase extended by the voters in the special election that year.

SELECTED REFERENCES

Barber, Mary Beth, "Local Government Hits the Wall," *California Journal*, August 1993.

Bowman, David, John W. Ellwood, Frank Neuhauser, and Eugene P. Smolensky, "Structural Deficit and the Long Term Fiscal Condition of the State," in John J. Kirlin and Jeffrey I. Chapman, eds., *California Policy Choices*, Vol. 9, Los Angeles: University of Southern California School of Public Administration, 1994.

California, Governor's Office, *Governor's Budget*, Sacramento: State Printing Office, annually.

California, Legislative Analyst, *Analysis of the Budget Bill*, Sacramento: State Printing Office, annually.

California, Legislative Analyst, *1996–97 Budget: Perspectives and Issues*, Sacramento: State Printing Office, 1997.

Chapman, Jeffrey I., "The Fiscal Context," in John J. Kirlin and Donald R. Winkler, eds., *California Policy Choices*, Vol. 7, University of Southern California School of Public Administration, Los Angeles, 1991.

Goldberg, Lenny, "Spending Limits: Straightjacket for California," *Los Angeles Times*, August 27, 1996.

Leary, Mary Ellen, "The Politics of Tax Repeal and Tax Reform in California," *California Journal*, September 1987.

Mundell, Ed, "Good News: Budget Good for Education," *San Diego Tribune*, July 16, 1996.

Quinn, Michelle, "Have Californians Soured on Their Games of Chance?" *California Journal*, December 1991.

Stall, Bill, and Ralph Frammolino, "Myths vs. Facts of Tax Burdens for Californians," *Los Angeles Times*, October 17, 1993.

_____

Chapter 11

Economic Growth and the Quality of Life

John Q. Commuter sits alone in his car, stopped atop a freeway interchange while traffic on the freeway below him inches forward. His gaze shifts toward the horizon, which is obscured by a grey-brown layer of smog, and then to an orchard struggling to survive against the twin threats of air pollution and the spread of housing tracts in this suburban area. In cars stopped on both sides he sees Hispanics and Asians caught in the same traffic trap. As he waits he glances down at headlines in the morning newspaper carefully folded on the seat beside him. One reports on a new study of prison overcrowding; another proclaims a crisis in the water supply due to a prolonged drought. His car radio is tuned to an all-news station whose stories range from the latest gang killings to the impact of illegal aliens in the state and a newly discovered illegal toxic waste dump. Suddenly his car lurches, not because traffic is moving again, but instead—he realizes with alarm—another earthquake has struck the Golden State.

This scenario may be a bit overdrawn (most commuters listen to music stations and have their newspapers turned to the sports or entertainment sections), but it highlights a number of the problems and issues facing California as it heads toward the twenty-first century: traffic congestion, air pollution, urban sprawl, immigration, crime, water, and the ever-present danger of what scientists call "the Big One," a catastrophic earthquake they believe will strike the state within the next 20 years. To that list might be added a number of issues with which government must deal: the plight of the homeless, the rights of minorities (ethnics, gays, women), energy, providing quality education to an increasingly diverse population.

The challenges posed by these and other issues lie not just in their obvious complexity but in the need to deal with them for a population that has been growing between 400,000 and 600,000 a year. That is the equivalent of adding a Fresno, three Anaheims, or six Berkeleys every 12 months. These new residents must be served, protected, in a whole host of ways dealt with, along with the 32 million already in the state. The burden that places on schools, police and fire departments, sewage disposal, street maintenance, welfare programs, and the like is noted almost daily in the media. California is a great and growing state, but its greatness is threatened by that very growth. In this and the following chapter we will be looking at some of the

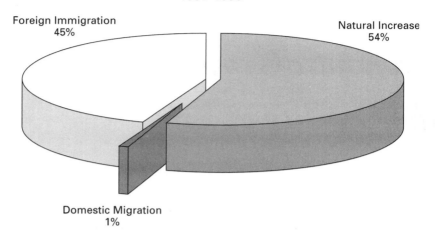

Components of Population Change
1997-1998

Foreign Immigration
45%

Natural Increase
54%

Domestic Migration
1%

Figure 11.1   Components of Population Change 1997–1998.

most difficult of these issues and problems and at some of the attempts being made to deal with them.

Despite the prolonged recession of the early 1990s, California's economic engine remains impressive and had clearly rebounded by mid-decade. Both by the measure of the state's budget and the personal income of its citizens, the state ranks with the major nations of the world. In international trade, California would, as a nation, be in the top ten. Every major agricultural commodity produced in the United States, except tobacco, is grown commercially in California, and the state leads all others in the sales of farm products and food manufactures. It is also number one in the catching of fish. California's wood products industry is the largest in the nation. Only Texas exceeds California in oil and mineral production. Since World War II more than 12 percent of the nation's construction has taken place here—both residential and industrial, including heavy manufactures. Today the state's leading growth sectors are computers and electronics, air transportation industries, plastics, apparel, agricultural services, retailing, business services, and (despite predictions in the early 1970s of a declining population growth rate) residential construction.

California's image of being laid-back, progressive, and a land of opportunity, characteristics that drew millions to the state following World War II, suffered as the recession of the 1990s became prolonged. The state's population grew at an astounding rate, from 10.5 million in 1950 to nearly 32 million in 1996. Growth peaked at 795,000 new residents in 1991. Economic hard times reduced the growth in the early 1990s with the increases for the most part due to natural growth (births over deaths) and immigration from other countries. With the end of the recession in the mid-1990s, growth began once again to increase.

Clearly dissatisfaction with the quality of life in the state also increased. Indeed, most of the dissatisfaction was the result of the uncontrolled growth, for it is the con-

Only God Can Make A Tree.....

..... But Only Man Can Make A Buck.

(Courtesy McClatchy newspapers)

tinuing expansion itself that produces the myth of California's abundance. "There's enough room for everybody and plenty of natural resources just waiting to be exploited, *so everybody come!*" Of course, the more that people come, the more dwellings and roads will be built, the more land will be cultivated, the more local industries will proliferate, the more the economy will become diversified, and the more jobs will be created, producing a steadily expanding economic pie and a bigger slice of the good things of life for each person.

All that growth began to cast a pall (literally) over the California landscape. By the late 1940s smog was a fact of everyday life for many. As the postwar years passed, more and more concern was expressed over air quality, water quality, the problems of toxic wastes, and overuse of pesticides. In 1969, an 800-square-mile oil slick caused by a leak in the Union Oil Company's rig in the Santa Barbara Channel despoiled prized beaches from Goleta to Oxnard. As early as 1972 the state's own Environmental Quality Study Council predicted that, if nothing was done, future Californians would inherit "a great wasteland."

WATER ALLOCATION ISSUES

California's water problem is due to the continuing press of the state's industrial and population growth upon its limited supply of water. In an average nondrought year, about 71 million acre-feet of water fall on California, approximately 37 million acre-feet of which are captured for agricultural, industrial, and residential use. The basic problem (even apart from drought years) is that statewide use-demand now exceeds the amount captured, which means that more dams and reservoir transport systems must be added to the state's mammoth water-harnessing network. But as so often has been the case when new water projects are being considered, efforts to increase the amount of captured water produces bitter disputes between Northern and Southern California, between farmers and city dwellers, between small farmers and large farmers, and between developers and environmentalists.

State, federal, and local governments have been active in constructing reservoirs and dams in California since the early part of the twentieth century. The Hetch Hetchy Aqueduct was built in the early 1920s to transport water from the Sierra down to storage reservoirs in San Francisco; the city of Los Angeles constructed a 283-mile aqueduct from the water-rich Owens Valley down to the semiarid valleys of the populous southland.

The increased demand for water by Southern California in the 1930s led to the construction of the spectacular Colorado River Aqueduct—the longest domestic water supply line ever built—which lifts water 1,600 feet by a series of five pumping plants before transporting it 242 miles across the desert to Lake Mathews, where it is stored for distribution to the five Southern California counties.

In the late 1930s, in response to the drought and to stimulate the economy, work began on the mammoth $793 million Central Valley Project (CVP), constructed and operated by the U.S. Bureau of Reclamation to supply water for irrigation, municipal, and domestic uses; to provide hydroelectricity; to control floods; and to improve navigation on the Sacramento River. The CVP was conceived as a state project but was taken over by the federal government when the state proved unable to finance it. Today the main facilities in the CVP are five Northern California dams (Shasta, Folsom, Trinity, Friant, and New Melonas) from which water is delivered to farmers in the San Joaquin Valley through three canals (Delta-Mendota, San Luis, and Friant-Kern).

The largest California undertaking is the State Water Project, whose 750-mile course of dams and aqueducts, as completed, is the most spectacular water-harnessing system in the world. Originally estimated to cost $1.75 billion and to be built over a period of 25 years, the State Water Project cost more than three times that much by the time it was completed.

The North-South issues are the product of nature's dispensation: 75 percent of the precipitation falls in the northern one-third of the state, but 80 percent of the need for water occurs in the southern two-thirds of the state. In recent decades most of the large water projects have been designed to move the water from north to south. This has stirred northern resentment and fear—resentment at having to pay for facilities that disproportionately benefit the Southerners and fear that in times of drought the North will be left high and dry.

The uses federal water is put to became a heated issue in 1992 when a new federal law, the Miller-Bradley Act, was passed by Congress and, despite major league lobbying by state officials and farm interests, was signed into law by President Bush. It mandates that in normal rainfall years 800,000 acre-feet of water that previously had been available for the most part to agriculture had to be diverted to protect the environment, especially in the Sacramento Delta area. Depleted runs of the winter and summer salmon, the newly endangered Delta smelt, and other species were deemed at risk, and additional flows of water to prevent saltwater from the Pacific from creeping inland were all concerns. How much these diversions will harm the state's multibillion-dollar agricultural industry is an issue. Farmers proclaim catastrophic losses with thousands of acres of productive land lost along with thousands of jobs eliminated, both in the fields and in towns servicing the farmers and their workers. One estimate placed the losses at $1.7 billion. Environmentalists maintain such forecasts are far too gloomy and cite the importance of protecting the environment for future generations of Californians.

Peripheral Canal Issue

The battle over construction of the so-called Peripheral Canal is a prime example of the divisions that exist between North and South over how the state's water resources should be allocated. Proposed as early as 1965, it was intended to make possible the transfer of water from the Sacramento–San Joaquin Delta, which annually produces 40 percent of the state's natural runoff. The Canal would have been linked to the California Aqueduct and would have sent Delta water south to serve the needs of San Joaquin Valley farmers and Southern California. It appeared to have gained final approval when the legislature passed Senate Bill 200 in 1980, but opponents succeeded in securing enough signatures on a petition to put the issue before the voters in the June 1982 election. Opponents of the canal argued it would be extremely expensive to build (one estimate placed the cost as high as $30 billion compared with initial estimates of $3.1 billion) and that it would do great harm to the environment, allowing saltwater from the sea to flow inland. Apparently these arguments worked because the voters rejected the canal with only Southern Californians voting for it.

Loss of the Peripheral Canal is only one of several setbacks suffered by those who would assure adequate water supplies to a rapidly expanding Southern California. Allocations from the Colorado River have been cut by more than half in recent years as demands for that water have increased in neighboring states, most notably Arizona. The federal Department of the Interior has ruled that three Indian tribes living on reservations along the lower Colorado River are entitled to an additional 104,000 acre-feet[1] of its water, enough to meet the needs of 500,000 people in Southern

---

[1] An acre-foot equals the amount of water needed to cover an acre to the depth of one foot.

California. Potentially as serious is a decision handed down by California's 3rd District Court of Appeals in 1988. It held that the licenses awarded to the City of Los Angeles by the State Water Resources Control Board that allow the city to draw water from streams in the Sierra Nevada are illegal. The court's decision was based on a state law which says that licenses for stream diversions can be awarded only if provisions are included to ensure there will be enough water left in the affected streams to sustain the fish living in them. In awarding Los Angeles its licenses, the board illegally ignored this aspect of the law. These canceled licenses could pose a major problem for Los Angeles (however good the news may be for the fish) since nearly 20 percent of that city's water comes from the streams of the Sierra Nevada.

Agriculture

If urban areas need adequate supplies of water, so does agriculture. Agriculture is, after all, a major contributor to the health of the state economy. It is estimated that gross farm income in 1996 amounted to $24.5 billion, making California for the forty-seventh straight year the nation's biggest producer of agricultural products. Of the over 200 crops grown and livestock nurtured in the state, California leads the nation in 53. Half the fresh fruit grown in the United States comes from California. The incredible variety of California agriculture is reflected in its top five cash crops— milk and cream, cattle, grapes, cotton, and hay.

The functioning of this rich cornucopia requires water, a great deal of water. With a population of 32 million, 92 percent of whom live in urban areas, many people are surprised to learn that between 80 percent and 85 percent of all the water used in California goes to agriculture. With a finite—even declining—amount available, con-flicts between farmers and urban areas are to be expected. Agriculture cites its needs and the contributions it makes to the state's wealth; city leaders point to the waste that they say is inherent in the farmer's methods of using water. One bone of con-tention lies in the very considerable subsidy enjoyed by agriculture when it comes to the cost of water. Farmers in the Imperial Valley, for example, pay $10 an acre-foot for their water. Residents of Contra Costa County pay $320, San Franciscans $225, and Angelenos $270. That low cost, some have suggested, encourages waste in the fields and groves, waste that would be reduced if farmers had to pay more. Critics state that furrow irrigation wastes up to 50 percent of the water due in part to a failure to line ditches with cement. Higher costs would make farmers more frugal and efficient, they say, releasing more water for growing urban populations.

Farmers respond that they are careful in their use of water and that agriculture by its very nature requires great amounts of the liquid. They point to the number of gal-lons of water required to grow a pound of lettuce for the fall market (21 gallons) or a pound of sugar beets (28 gallons) or cotton (649 gallons). And a pound of almonds requires 681 gallons. A University of California study found it takes approximately 4,533 gallons of water to feed one person for a single day!

There is another threat to California's agricultural water supply that should at least be mentioned. The growing amount of salt in the underground water tables—a process known as salinization—is taking some 25,000 acres a year out of production in the San Joaquin Valley alone. It is estimated that by the year 2015 another 2.3 mil-lion acres will be lost unless something is done. Urban sprawl with its housing tracts and shopping centers compounds the farmers' problems by swallowing up 92,000 acres of farmland every year. If the process continues at its present rate, within the next 20 years another million acres will have been lost.

Conservation

Most people pay little attention to water supply problems—until a crisis hits. They tend to take for granted their right to water their lawns as much and as often as they like. They assume a glass of ice water will automatically appear when they sit down in their favorite restaurant. The droughts of 1977–1978 and 1987–1994 led to bans on many kinds of water use in a number of areas of the state. San Franciscans, for example, were told they had to cut consumption 25 percent. Hosing down a driveway, if caught doing it once too often, resulted in the violator's water supply being completely cut off. In some areas watering lawns was prohibited, and drinking water in restaurants was available only upon request.

Three approaches to conservation predominate. One is the type of restriction on use just described. A second seeks installation of water-saving devices in showers or in toilet tanks, encouraged by rebates or mandated by building codes for new construction. The third might be termed the "disincentive system." It penalizes high use by making it cost more. Water meters in and of themselves can act as conservation instruments. Fresno and Clovis are neighbors in the Central Valley and enjoy identical climates. Clovis has meters, Fresno does not. Residential water use is 25 percent lower in Clovis.

Of course, having enough water is crucial. Human beings and industry cannot run long on a steady diet of soft drinks. But the quality of that water is also of great importance.

PESTICIDES

In the midst of the picnicking and fireworks that highlighted Californians' celebration of the nation's two hundred tenth birthday on the Fourth of July in 1986, some celebrants suddenly lost interest. Over 500 of them abruptly came down with cases of nausea and vomiting. The cause? Officials traced it to the illegal use of a powerful insecticide, aldacarb, on the watermelons the victims had consumed.

Pesticides are widely used to protect crops from insect damage, improving both production and appearance. Pesticides provide protection against crop losses, add to the nation's food supply, and thus contribute to lower costs for the consumer. However, there are some drawbacks, several of them serious. It is not uncommon to hear complaints about a beautiful, full, red tomato that tastes "funny" or corn on the cob that has a strange chemical flavor. If an illegal and dangerous pesticide has been used, illness can result, as with the watermelons. Overuse can lead to contamination of underground water supplies, posing additional health hazards.

Particularly at risk are those who harvest the crops. Long a focus of criticism by the late Cesar Chavez and the United Farm Workers Union, improper use of pesticides, extended exposure to which can cause cancer, is prohibited by state law. Areas sprayed with them are not supposed to be worked until enough time has passed to make them safe. But how long is "safe"? Seven days? Fourteen? A month? In past years the greatest dangers have come from illegal harvesting when safety standards were ignored. In the 1980s, however, illness was reported in a number of cases in which those levels had been scrupulously observed. The Department of Food and Agriculture reported that 348 farmworkers had been poisoned between 1982 and 1987, and some experts believe that to be but a small fraction of the actual number of cases. Many workers, unless they become violently ill with vomiting and diarrhea, are unwilling to report being sick for fear of losing their jobs.

California used just over 140 million pounds of agricultural pesticides in 1991. That marked a significant reduction from the 310 million pounds used in 1984. If not properly monitored, pesticide residues can easily find their way into the state's underground water supply. With nearly half the population (46 percent) served by underground water, the State Department of Agriculture has made ensuring the purity of those supplies a top priority.

Contamination of underground water supplies is not just a problem for residents of rural areas. Urban populations are at risk as well. Leaking underground storage tanks are a major contributor to pollution, and four out of five of them are to be found in gasoline stations, most of which are in urban areas. In 1985, the State Water Resources Control Board, which has responsibility for water-quality control, reported there were 30,000 of these leaking tanks in the state. In response to the problem, laws were passed in 1983 and 1984 requiring that all underground tanks be registered and periodically tested.

TOXICS

Toxics, or at least toxic wastes, have a bad name. Though a necessary product of industrialization, toxics have long been known to be a danger to human health. There are more than 400 known toxic waste dumps in California. They perform an important service by isolating the public from dangerous materials. But the general impression of them is not favorable for at least two reasons: They hold health-endangering substances, and some of those who operate them have been shown to be negligent. Responsibility for licensing dump sites and monitoring their operations to ensure compliance with state law lies with the Toxic Substances Control Division of the Department of Health Services. Monitoring is no easy task with an estimated 70,000 places in the state generating toxic wastes. And the state's six operating dump sites will be filled to capacity by the end of the century. Finding new sites poses still another headache for government since no one wants such materials deposited in their neighborhoods.

There are many state laws dealing with chemical pollutants. The two best known take somewhat different approaches to the problem. The first is California's Superfund. Established in 1981, it originally operated on an annual budget of $10 million provided from taxes imposed on those generating the waste. However, given some estimates that the cost of cleaning up all the state's chemically polluted sites could run as high as $1.5 billion, depending solely on this source of revenue would have meant delaying completion until well into the twenty-first century. In 1984, the voters approved Proposition 27, the Hazardous Substance Control Bond Act. This law authorized the sale of $100 million in bonds to speed up the treatment of contaminated areas. Although the expense of cleanups is usually carried by the polluter, in 34 cases for a variety of reasons, that has been impossible. Treating them will cost $87 million and will be funded by these bonds.

A somewhat different approach was initiated with passage of Proposition 65 in 1986. The subject of a sometimes bitter campaign, this initiative pitted environmentalists against oil and chemical companies and the state's agricultural interests. The opponents spent four times as much on the campaign, but it passed anyway, demonstrating how difficult it is to fight those who are for clean water (the opposition by inference being against it).

The main provisions of the proposition, as described by the Legislative Analyst's Office, were to prohibit "knowingly releasing into any drinking water in any amount a chemical known to cause cancer or in an amount that exceeds one one-thousandth of the amount necessary for an observable effect on 'reproductive toxicity.'"[2] Critics noted that the term *reproductive toxicity* was not defined, nor were other terms such as *significant risk* and *significant amount of discharge* (as applied to chemicals released into groundwater). The governor is required to publish a list, updated annually, of cancer-causing substances; as of October 1, 1994 there were 402 substances identified as carcinogens, up from 177 six years earlier. In addition, places of business are required to notify employees and customers of the presence of any of the cited chemicals on their premises.

Some toxics are produced naturally. Selenium is such a substance. It has fouled watering places for migrating birds and water fowl. In 1993 one of the largest of the refuges set aside for these birds, over 10,500 acres of wetlands south of Corcoran in the Central Valley, dried up. That caused a migration to other, polluted wetlands that had been contaminated with selenium. The result: dead birds and others born deformed.

And the controversy continues. How much risk is acceptable, and how much are taxpayers willing to pay for further—and sometimes marginal—improvements in health safety? These questions are, of course, not limited to pesticides and toxics. In virtually every area of pollution control the issue of cost and benefit must be addressed. A long-standing example is air pollution.

AIR POLLUTION

Mention smog and most people immediately think of Los Angeles. A temperature inversion puts a pressure lid over the basin and traps pollutants which, after a few days, accumulate to the point that visibility is drastically reduced, eyes begin to smart, and noses wrinkle in distaste. Although some visitors are never aware of it, Los Angeles is located in a beautiful setting, surrounded on three sides by mountains. For much of the year they cannot be seen through the all-enveloping muck.

Los Angeles is, and has been for many years, the most polluted city in the state (and the country, for that matter). However, it is by no means unique in having serious

---

[2]California Ballot Pamphlet General Election, November 4, 1986, p. 52.

air pollution problems. North and south, along the coast and inland, Californians suffer the effects. Some 90 percent of the cities in the state are at one time or another in violation of permissible levels of ozone as set by the federal government. California's pollution, once considered the price that had to be paid for industrialization, provoked many jokes. Today, few find any humor in what has come to be recognized as a condition that is not just inconvenient or an affront to aesthetics but the cause of some major medical problems. It is estimated that some 80,000 Californians die from its effects on the heart and lungs every year. One study found that Southern Californians miss 15 million workdays a year due to air pollution-related illnesses. Another reported that the lung capacity of children living in Los Angeles was, because of air pollution, 10–15 percent less than that of children living in less-polluted areas. Clearly smog debilitates and can kill. Economic costs are also high. Californians spend more for gasoline because devices to control automobile exhaust emissions, needed to limit the damage done to the quality of the air, reduce gas mileage. Regulations on industry, from power plants to paint shops, are often costly to business, and those costs are passed on to the consumer in the form of higher prices. Agriculture suffers as well. Smog causes an annual loss of approximately $1 billion in ruined crops. The yields from grapes, cotton, potatoes, and lettuce are reduced by between 25 and 60 percent, again leading to higher prices to the consumer.

Nor is the situation likely to improve greatly, short of nearly draconian measures most would find highly objectionable. The air in the Los Angeles basin is considered unhealthy one-third of the time, despite decades of strenuous effort to clean it up. Once more, population growth is a major cause. A spokesperson for the South Coast Air Quality Management District (SCAQMD), which encompasses Los Angeles, Orange, and Riverside counties together with the most populated areas of San Bernardino County, has said that pollution generated per person dropped 15 percent between 1977 and 1987, but that the number of people living in the area went up 30 percent. "At that rate," he said, "we'll never make it."[3]

This gloomy picture is not the result of government inaction. The state legislature, in recognition of the fact that automobile exhausts were the biggest contributor to air pollution, passed the Motor Vehicle Pollution Control Act of 1960. It created a board to determine which pollution control devices should be mandated. In 1965 the federal government got into the picture with its Clean Air Act, which led the state to create its own Air Resources Board. In 1977, amendments to the Clean Air Act set penalties for states that did not make "reasonable progress" toward federally approved standards of air quality. When California failed to establish approved methods for smog inspections until August 1983 millions of dollars in federal highway funds and some sewage treatment funds were withheld.

The approved program (biannual inspections are required) came under attack by the federal Environmental Protection Agency (EPA) in 1993. The EPA claimed that the system was riddled with fraud, that having the same facilities test for emissions and make repairs invited cheating and produced evidence from their field personnel to that effect. Instead the EPA demanded the testing be done at 200 state-operated locations with repairs done elsewhere, presumably at the over 9,000 locations where

---

[3] *Fresno Bee,* December 27, 1987.

(Courtesy Frank Interlandi)

service was being provided. Critics claimed that, with over 21 million cars and pickup trucks, limiting the testing to so few centers was ludicrous. The inconvenience of time wasted in long lines and a tripling of the required trips if repairs were needed (first the test, then the repair, and then return for a repeated test) was simply out of the question. In addition, state leaders claimed such a change would cause the loss of thousands of jobs, this in a state still reeling from the recession. Deadlock ensued with the EPA threatening to cut off some $800 million in federal road funds if the state did not comply.

Some urged adoption, at least on a pilot basis, of a system first tested in the Denver area that uses an infrared beam to remotely "read" tailpipe emissions while at the same time photographing the license of the car being "read." That, it was said, would target the worst of the polluters and reduce the time lost and expense involved in taking "Beast" or "Betsy" into the garage if it did not need repair. One study by the state's Bureau of Automotive Repair found 20 percent of the cars on the road produced 80 percent of the smog; most cars run "clean." The infrared beam system was tested in various areas of the state in 1996.

A compromise was worked out between state and federal officials under which 15 percent of California's cars and trucks in very smoggy areas such as San Diego, Fresno, and Vacaville are inspected each year using the testing centers with the remaining 85 percent still tested under the old procedures. Prime targets for the new method: high-mileage vehicles, such as taxis, and older vehicles that cause most of the pollution. Dubbed "Smog Check II," this new approach also entailed more stringent standards for passing the test and led to many complaints from drivers whose vehicles had previously passed with ease. The state's answer: The air is unhealthful and this will help clean it up.

Late in 1996 it was reported that Southern California's "smog season" had been the best in decades. Unhealthful air had been recorded on only 87 days and the state's Environmental Control Agency found air quality 18 percent better in 1996 than in 1994 and 1995.

Much of the credit for this improvement was given to the introduction (and mandated use) of reformulated gasoline. The new product was estimated to improve air quality so substantially it was the equivalent of removing 3.5 million cars from the state's highways. The cost of gasoline went up, in part to reimburse oil companies which had spent $5 billion to convert their refineries to produce the new product. One complaint, that the new fuel resulted in substantially poorer gas mileage, appeared not to be true. Tests by the Automobile Club (AAA) showed a decrease of just 1 percent.

In early 1994 the federal Environmental Protection Agency, under court order following a suit brought by environmentalists, issued a 2,700-page report covering steps that needed to be taken to make air clean in the four-county Los Angeles area by 2010 and in Ventura and Sacramento counties by 2005. The proposed actions covered virtually every possible source of pollution, from cars to airplanes, trains, ships, gasoline-powered lawn mowers, paint sprays, pesticides, and dry-cleaning establishments. Many targets are so-called *small polluters*. These are polluting practices that, in a single case, may not be significant but when taken as a whole are. In this category are volatile organic compounds, or VOCs. These are found in hair sprays, tile cleaners, air fresheners, and floor polish, among other products. Limits imposed in the South Coast Air Quality Management District (SCAQMD) will, by 1998, reduce these emissions by 45 *tons* a day. That compares with an average oil refinery, which emits between 1.4 tons and 3.9 tons of pollutants a day. Small polluters do matter. Other targets of the SCAQMD include gasoline-powered lawn mowers, petroleum-based barbecue starter fluids, and drive-through windows (idling cars pollute at length).

Much of what was included in the federal plan was already part of local authorities' plans but environmental groups claimed progress had been too slow, resulting in the lawsuit. In fact, Southern California has made considerable progress in the fight against air pollution even before the introduction of reformulated gasoline. On a per capita basis, pollution had declined significantly, though there are, of course, many more people. It should be noted, however, that Los Angeles has not had a third-stage smog alert in over 20 years nor a second-stage alert in over 10. In 1996 Los Angeles experienced no Stage One alerts for the third time in four years. San Francisco became a candidate for removal from the Environmental Protection Agency's list of cities with poor air quality in 1994. And there has been a 50 percent reduction in ozone violations over the past 20 years. That is indeed progress, despite the still too often limited vistas experienced by city dwellers.

Still another approach involves what is termed *telecommuting,* the use of remote locations linked to the central office by telephone, computer, and/or fax machines. Typically this has been seen as a single person working out of the home, but some companies and government departments have set up area offices away from their central facility, allowing workers to work together yet with much-reduced travel time and fewer polluting miles driven.

TRANSPORTATION

When Congress passed legislation in 1987 permitting the states to raise speed limits on interstate highways from 55 miles per hour to 65, those portions passing through urban areas were specifically excluded. For most Californians, that exclusion, at least during rush hours, hardly matters. Average speeds on city freeways in California at times when most are either going to or coming from work seem only grudgingly to edge into double figures. Rain, a minor accident, or even a car stalled on the shoulder can easily bring traffic to a crawl or a complete stop.

A number of factors have come together to create what is called *gridlock,* a condition that has become a frequent and frustrating reality for urban commuters. One of the most important—and obvious factors—is the number of vehicles on the roads, each typically carrying only one person—the driver. There are over 17 million automobiles registered in the state and another 5.5 million trucks. Joining them are 2.6 million trailers. The result is traffic overload, which leads to quips such as the one describing the Hollywood Freeway at rush hour as "the longest parking lot in the world."

It was generally recognized from the outset that extensive and efficient transportation was essential to California's economic growth. At the same time it has been a part of the problem of runaway growth, as manifested in issues of energy use, air pollution control, and land use. After World War II the state launched a huge freeway construction program, financed by taxes on motorists. The state Department of Public Works in 1959 recommended a comprehensive system of freeways that by 1980 would connect every section of the state with 12,000 miles of roads, touching almost every town with a population of more than 5,000. The motorist in a hurry to reach San Francisco from Los Angeles would have a choice of five routes, and the nature lover would be able to cross the Sierra Nevada in about ten places. The legislature acted to implement this recommendation by passing the Collier Master Plan for Freeways, which established the California freeway and expressway system and incorporated into it practically all of the important state highways then in operation or projected for the next 20 years.

It became increasingly apparent over the years that no amount of new freeways could ever adequately solve the overall transportation problem. The energy shortage of 1973–1974 further exposed the inanity of bumper-to-bumper rush-hour clogs on the freeways, car after car carrying only one person—the driver. Environmentalists were no longer alone in their complaint that the freeways are turning California into a "concrete desert."

Beginning in 1973, the responsibility for stimulating additional solutions to the growing congestion of the urban and statewide arteries was lodged in the state Department of Transportation (nicknamed Caltrans), which replaced the Department of Public Works. Under Jerry Brown's administration, Caltrans and its director,

(Courtesy Frank Interlandi)

Adriana Gianturco, called a halt to the building of new freeways and advocated the use of public transportation and the building of light rail lines. Automobile clubs, the trucking industry, oil companies, and highway construction firms accused Caltrans of being hostile to the automobile.

Freeway Shortcomings and Some Alternatives

Hostile or not, many transportation experts have concluded that building more freeways will not, in itself, solve the transportation problems facing the state. They stress three main points. The first is that it is impossible to build freeways fast enough to keep up with the increases in the number of vehicles projected for the next 20–30 years. The Little Hoover Commission estimated the number of miles traveled on freeways will be 30 percent higher in 2000 than it was in 1985. This estimate was made long before the onset of the recession of the early 1990s. If there is something good that came from the economic downturn it may have been that traffic, especially in Southern California, became less congested. Fewer jobs meant fewer cars on the road. Caltrans found an 11 percent drop in the amount of time freeway traffic flow slowed below 35 miles an hour in 1992 compared with 1991 and a further decline was experienced in 1993. With the end of the recession, however, a return to extensive gridlock is likely.

Second, freeways are expensive. The Century Freeway, completed in 1993, cost $127 million per mile, or $2.2 billion. It *is* state of the art with roadbed sensors and television cameras to monitor traffic flow and it has a light rail line (the Green Line) designed to carry 100,000 passengers a day by the year 2000 running down its median. The funds required to pay for rights-of-way to help those living in the path of the new freeway to relocate and for erecting sound barriers to protect nearby residents from noise pollution all add to the expense.

Third, other means of moving people are more efficient and practicable. Instead of building more freeways, many urge steps be taken to encourage the use of alternative ways of "getting from here to there."

Carpooling

The logic behind carpooling is straightforward enough: If more people shared rides, fewer cars would be on the road. Fewer cars mean less congestion. One move to encourage ride-sharing, the famous (or infamous) Diamond Lane experiment which reserves a lane for cars carrying two or more people, has met with considerable resistance and a good deal of cheating. (Several drivers were caught using dummies propped up on car seats to fool patrolling police.) At least part of the problem lies with a desire for autonomy ("I want to go where I want to go when I want to") and the fact that a widely dispersed population makes ride-sharing difficult and even impossible as employees converge on their workplaces from so many different locales.

A state law requires that all businesses with more than 100 employees at a single location make every effort to convert solo drivers into carpoolers. As the state neared mid-decade, however, there was little evidence of major increases in joint ridership. In 1992, 77 percent went to work alone; in 1993 that figure rose to 79 percent.

There was a brighter note for proponents of carpooling in early 1997 when it was found that the nearly 200 miles of carpool lanes in the Bay Area were being used at a rate never experienced before. The 316,000 commuters who daily took advantage of carpooling amounted to nearly a tripling of car poolers over a period of five years. An unexpected dividend for one pooler: A matchmaker in his pool set him up with his future wife.

Mass Transit

Most urban planners contend that new mass-transit systems are increasingly necessary not only to relieve freeway congestion but also to provide low-income, non-car-owning families with wider access to jobs, shopping, and recreation in California's cities.

This brings forward other issues: What means of transportation should be used— buses, trains on fixed rails, vehicles operated on air cushions? How shall the routes be determined? Above all, who should pay for transportation—property owners through higher real estate taxes, automobile users through gasoline taxes or license fees, or the general public through increased sales or income taxes?

Proponents of the public's greater reliance on mass transit generally agree that buses, although essential in any comprehensive transportation system, are insufficient for moving millions of people over the long distances of California's great metropolitan areas. They prefer some kind of fixed guideway system: two rail, monorail, air cushion, and so on.

California is not without experience in building rail systems. In the first third of the twentieth century, many of the state's major cities had extensive streetcar lines. In Northern California the electric trains of the Southern Pacific, the Key System, and the Sacramento Northern Railway connected San Francisco with many communities of the Bay region. In Southern California the Pacific Electric was hailed as the world's largest and best interurban railroad, and in 1930 it operated 88 trains daily in each direction from downtown Los Angeles to Glendale and 109 to Pasadena. Northern California was connected to Southern California by almost a dozen daily passenger trains on the Southern Pacific and Santa Fe.

After World War II, however, public transportation systems were allowed to deteriorate, and no efforts were made to replace them; service became less and less frequent, and fares increased; line after line was discontinued. By the 1960s hardly a single streetcar, except San Francisco's cable cars, was operating in California. Today buses are supposed to provide the public with the mobility once gained from streetcars and trains, but passengers often have to wait an hour in the hot sun on a noisy street corner for a bus, and in many areas there is no public transportation at all.

The San Francisco Bay region was the first to meet the new demand for rapid public transit. In 1962 the voters in San Francisco, Alameda, and Contra Costa counties created the Bay Area Rapid Transit (BART) District by approving a $792 million bond issue. The directors of BART decided on the traditional system of cars with steel wheels riding on steel rails with cars operated automatically by computers. The entire system was expected to be completed by July 1, 1971, at a cost of $995.9 million, the debt to be paid off by fares and by a special sales tax levied throughout the district. These targets were missed by a wide margin. The cost mushroomed to $1.3 billion, and it was not until September 1974 that BART trains began to run between Oakland and San Francisco under the Bay (although limited service between Oakland and Fremont began in the fall of 1972).

On a number of scales of performance, the system has worked quite well. In 1995–1996, ridership averaged over 248,000 trips on weekdays with total passenger miles traveled amounting to over 198 million during that period. The trains ride smoothly, frequently, and are generally reliable as they move along the 71.5 miles of track connecting 34 stations. Maximum speeds can reach 80 miles an hour with the average at 36 mph. Stops are usually about 20 seconds long, and trains were on schedule 90 percent of the time in 1995–1996. Its nine-member, popularly elected board of directors, representing the localities of the Bay Area, constitutes a working regional metropolitan government with legislative and taxing powers for its specific functions.

Attempts to match or even approach the Bay Area's efforts in Southern California met with a good deal of voter opposition. A bond issue to finance an 89-mile rail system was defeated in 1968, and other proposals to be funded from increased sales taxes were rejected at the polls in 1974 and 1976.

Undaunted, transit advocates continued their efforts to improve transportation facilities in Los Angeles. A plan approved by the voters in 1980 was scaled down from earlier proposals and is financed by a half-cent sales tax supplemented by federal and state funds and some private financing. Monies are used to improve and expand existing freeways and to build two new rail systems. One is a subway system, known as Metro Rail. The first phase, a 4.4-mile segment called the Red Line, opened in 1993. A second phase that would add a 13.3-mile line linking Los Angeles with the San Fernando Valley at a cost in excess of $2 billion is under construction. A second system financed from the 1980 sales tax increase consists of a 21-mile-long light rail line connecting the Long Beach area with Civic Center. All above ground, this $690 million project (the Blue Line) carries an average of 45,500 passengers a day during the week. The Green Line, which runs down the Century Freeway median, was completed in 1995. Ridership on these three lines nearly doubled between 1994 and 1996, from 50,450 who used them on an average weekday to just over 90,000. Metrolink is a heavy rail system that uses regular train tracks and has five routes that service Los Angeles, Riverside, Ventura, and Orange counties. Its popularity grew enormously in the aftermath of the Northridge earthquake. With freeways unavailable and surface streets jammed, ridership jumped from an average of around 10,000 on a weekday to over 31,000, but dropped back to 19,000 a few months later.

Not everyone supports the emphasis on rail transportation. Critics note that while the Blue and Red lines together with Metrolink carry an average of 75,000 passengers a day, the long-neglected bus system carries some 1.7 million. That, they say, is in large part due to the fact the rail system is focused on Los Angeles as the hub while most people travel elsewhere than to and from downtown Los Angeles. Only 6 percent of workers work there, commuting to other locations in the basin. These critics would use resources to modernize the bus system rather than further expand the rail system.

The Tijuana Trolley in San Diego, Sacramento's Metro, and Cal Train (San Mateo and Santa Clara counties to San Francisco) are examples of mass transit systems elsewhere in the state, none of which pay for themselves.

Changing Work Shifts

Buoyed by the experience of the 1984 Olympic Games, many officials and traffic experts see staggering working hours as a relatively easy and inexpensive way of improving traffic flow. In this way the load on freeways and surface streets can be spread out, lowering volume during peak hours. Los Angeles officials state that, during the Olympics, city roads actually carried 5 percent more traffic than normal, but by staggering shifts and with the voluntary cooperation of 5,000 truckers who agreed to stay off the freeways during rush hours, there was less congestion. Following this successful experience Mayor Bradley convinced the state legislature to permit the city to adopt an ordinance placing ongoing similar restrictions on trucks.

Other Approaches

Some efforts to improve the efficiency of California's transportation system have turned to advanced technology. From "traffic alerts" broadcast on radio and electronic warning signs along freeways (which skeptics maintained often warned of a problem only after you were already in it) to magnetic sensors implanted in roadbeds and remote control television cameras to monitor traffic, advanced technology is being used more and more to regulate movement along urban freeways. A very different kind of experiment is being undertaken in Orange County where four toll roads (sometimes described as "un-Californian," "highway robbery," "unfreeways," and worse) have been or are being built to relieve pressure on the freeway system. Part of their high-tech image comes from the use of *smart cards,* which are inserted into dashboard-mounted transponders that "tell" the tollway computers that the car is using the road, allowing drivers to bypass tollbooths and be billed periodically.

The first of these toll roads to become operational was a ten mile stretch that runs along the middle of I-91, the Riverside Freeway. Four lanes wide, it has proved very attractive to many commuters normally stuck in rush hour traffic. At peak hours the cost is $2.50; at other times it can run as little as 25 cents. For some 60,000 of the 250,000 who use this freeway each weekday, the savings in time and nervous energy spent (some estimate the time gained at up to 90 minutes each way) is well worth the cost.

In the really high-tech category are *smart cars* equipped with on-board computers and television screens displaying maps that tell the driver the least-trafficked way to get from here to there. Then there is the *automated highway,* on which computers and car radars actually control the driving along freeways (that's *really* leaving the driving to us—or Caltrans). At the other end of the technological scale is the antigridlock law that went into effect January 1, 1988. It imposes fines on motorists who become stuck in the middle of intersections, impeding traffic. Intended to improve conditions on surface streets, fines of up to $500 may be imposed for the third offense.

In one way Californians had been receiving a major financial break for years. The state gasoline tax had been raised just once in 20 years, and that from seven cents a gallon to nine cents. The voters, frustrated by gridlock and potholes, approved an increase in the gasoline tax in 1990 (Proposition 111). Starting in 1990 with a 5-cents-a-gallon increase, an additional 1 cent was added in each of the next four years.

In other ways Californians have taken major hits to the pocketbook in recent years. The Los Angeles riots, the disastrous Oakland Hills fires, the Southern California brush fires in 1993 all have had a significant effect on wallets and pocketbooks. Not the least of the monetary shocks were the major earthquakes that have struck the state in recent years.

EARTHQUAKES

Predictions that within the next 20 years or so California will experience a "catastrophic" earthquake—often referred to as the "Big One"—have generated a number of novels and motion pictures depicting the likely consequences of such a massive upheaval of the earth's surface. The descriptions typically feature tall buildings crumbling to the ground, fires fed by broken natural gas lines raging everywhere, structures and people slowly sinking into ground shaken so badly it turns into the equivalent of quicksand, and a tsunami, or tidal wave, crashing across the shoreline, inundating coastal communities. For some, the image of "the late great State of California" slipping beneath the Pacific Ocean apparently holds a certain grim fascination.

Number of quakes since 1800

Number of quakes of more than 5.0 on the Richter scale by decade*

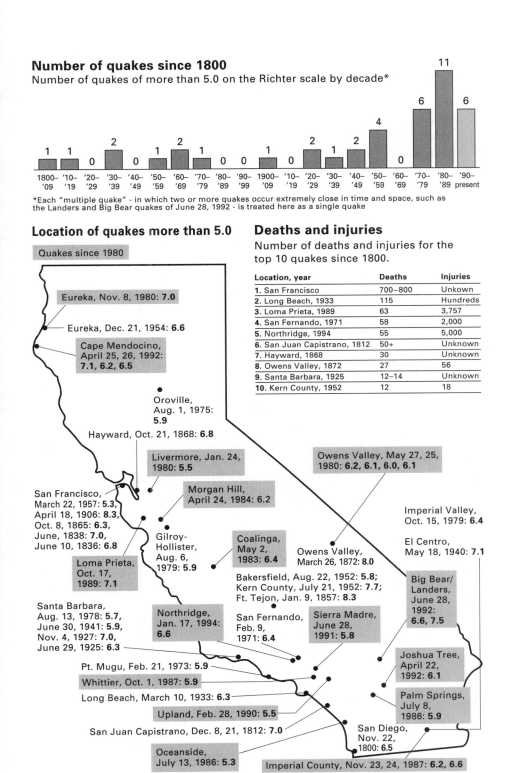

Decade	Count
1800–'09	1
'10–'19	1
'20–'29	0
'30–'39	2
'40–'49	0
'50–'59	1
'60–'69	2
'70–'79	1
'80–'89	0
'90–'99	0
1900–'09	1
'10–'19	0
'20–'29	2
'30–'39	1
'40–'49	2
'50–'59	4
'60–'69	0
'70–'79	6
'80–'89	11
'90–present	6

*Each "multiple quake" - in which two or more quakes occur extremely close in time and space, such as the Landers and Big Bear quakes of June 28, 1992 - is treated here as a single quake

Location of quakes more than 5.0

Quakes since 1980

Deaths and injuries

Number of deaths and injuries for the top 10 quakes since 1800.

Location, year	Deaths	Injuries
1. San Francisco	700–800	Unkown
2. Long Beach, 1933	115	Hundreds
3. Loma Prieta, 1989	63	3,757
4. San Fernando, 1971	58	2,000
5. Northridge, 1994	55	5,000
6. San Juan Capistrano, 1812	50+	Unknown
7. Hayward, 1868	30	Unknown
8. Owens Valley, 1872	27	56
9. Santa Barbara, 1925	12–14	Unknown
10. Kern County, 1952	12	18

Eureka, Nov. 8, 1980: **7.0**

Eureka, Dec. 21, 1954: **6.6**

Cape Mendocino, April 25, 26, 1992: **7.1, 6.2, 6.5**

Oroville, Aug. 1, 1975: **5.9**

Hayward, Oct. 21, 1868: **6.8**

Livermore, Jan. 24, 1980: **5.5**

Owens Valley, May 27, 25, 1980: **6.2, 6.1, 6.0, 6.1**

San Francisco, March 22, 1957: **5.3**, April 18, 1906: **8.3**, Oct. 8, 1865: **6.3**, June, 1838: **7.0**, June 10, 1836: **6.8**

Morgan Hill, April 24, 1984: 6.2

Imperial Valley, Oct. 15, 1979: **6.4**

Gilroy-Hollister, Aug. 6, 1979: **5.9**

Coalinga, May 2, 1983: **6.4**

Owens Valley, March 26, 1872: **8.0**

El Centro, May 18, 1940: **7.1**

Loma Prieta, Oct. 17, 1989: **7.1**

Bakersfield, Aug. 22, 1952: **5.8**; Kern County, July 21, 1952: **7.7**; Ft. Tejon, Jan. 9, 1857: **8.3**

Big Bear/ Landers, June 28, 1992: **6.6, 7.5**

Santa Barbara, Aug. 13, 1978: **5.7**, June 30, 1941: **5.9**, Nov. 4, 1927: **7.0**, June 29, 1925: **6.3**

Northridge, Jan. 17, 1994: **6.6**

San Fernando, Feb. 9, 1971: **6.4**

Sierra Madre, June 28, 1991: **5.8**

Joshua Tree, April 22, 1992: **6.1**

Pt. Mugu, Feb. 21, 1973: **5.9**

Whittier, Oct. 1, 1987: **5.9**

Long Beach, March 10, 1933: **6.3**

Upland, Feb. 28, 1990: **5.5**

San Juan Capistrano, Dec. 8, 21, 1812: **7.0**

Palm Springs, July 8, 1986: **5.9**

San Diego, Nov. 22, 1800: **6.5**

Oceanside, July 13, 1986: **5.3**

Imperial County, Nov. 23, 24, 1987: **6.2, 6.6**

Figure 11.2 Significant California quakes. (*Source:* State of California Seismic Safety Commission)

The causes of earthquakes are reasonably well understood. Some result from the collapse of underground caverns and others from volcanic action. The "Big One," when it comes, will be through the action of what are known as tectonic plates—huge rigid coverings on the planetary surface that float on a soft, plasticlike interior. As these plates move, they push against one another; the pressures generated create mountain ranges—and earthquakes. The most famous example of this in California is the San Andreas fault, which runs 650 miles along the western edge of the state from Southern California to Mendocino. It was this fault that caused the disastrous earthquake of 1906 in San Francisco. The San Andreas fault is, however, only one of many that crisscross the state, each posing in varying degrees the danger of significant damage should the pressures along it grow too great.

Most "adjustments" of the earth's surface do little or no damage. There are frequent "temblors" of less than 4.0 on the Richter scale that result in nothing more than a call to the local fire station or television newsroom. Even those measuring up to 5.5 often result in nothing more than a few broken dishes or soup cans in supermarket aisles. When contemplating the "Big One," a figure of 7.5 or higher is usually predicted. A common misconception is that the figures on the Richter Scale are arithmetic; they are logarithmic. The Palm Springs earthquake of 1986 measured 6.0 on this scale, whereas Eureka's in 1980 at 7.0 was ten times as severe.

Government Policies: Reducing the Risks

There are two major aspects to government planning for earthquakes. The first focuses on actions to be taken before one hits and is designed to minimize its effects; the second deals with the effects after it occurs. Minimizing the effects of earthquake damage involves three factors: land use, structural requirements, and prediction. Land-use laws restrict new construction in known fault areas. The Field Act of 1933 followed the highly destructive earthquake of that year which destroyed or badly damaged a large number of schools in Long Beach and Los Angeles. The Hospitals Act of 1972 was patterned after the Field Act in that it requires that all plans for new hospitals be submitted to the Office of the State Architect, who reviews them in light of the geology of the site. The Alquist-Priola Act of 1972 bans construction of any "building for human habitation" within 50 feet of a known, active fault. Structural requirements are imposed by the California Health and Safety Code. All new buildings must be constructed so as to maximize their ability to withstand the swaying and twisting forces associated with earthquakes. Prediction focuses on trying to anticipate when an earthquake will take place, with the objective of evacuating those in danger before it hits. Although there have been advances in this area (lasers are used to measure minute earth movements, for example), prediction is still far too uncertain. Given the economic and psychological costs of being wrong, officials are unlikely to order an evacuation.

Government Policies: Dealing with the Effects

When dealing with what is termed emergency response planning (ERP), the question shifts from limiting the effects of an earthquake to what to do after one takes place. Those images from the disaster movies are the stuff of policy planning. The Federal Emergency Management Agency (FEMA) lists the many tasks state and local gov-

(Courtesy Frank Interlandi)

ernments should be prepared to perform. With communications disrupted, power generators out and natural gas mains broken, roads obstructed by debris, and structures either badly damaged or destroyed, well-developed plans for dealing with the aftermath of a temblor are essential. Among FEMA's list of tasks are restoring communications to assist in directing postquake activities, clearing roadways so that fire apparatus and medical teams can move quickly to where they are most needed, and providing food and shelter to those whose homes have been destroyed or who are stranded. Local disaster councils are aided by the State Office of Emergency Services in preparing plans for dealing with the effects of a major temblor.

A good deal has been done to prepare for earthquakes in California. There is a consensus, however, that much more needs to be done. But the public has been, for the most part, apathetic when it comes to earthquake preparedness, feeling that when one comes the chances they will be affected are probably slight. More immediate issues such as taxes, pollution, crime in the streets, and potholes are far more likely to capture the public's attention.

A crack in this general apathy was evident in the overwhelming approval given Proposition 77 by the voters in the June 1988 election. Titled the California Earthquake Safety and Housing Bond Act of 1988, it authorized the sale of $150 million in bonds to improve the ability of unsafe structures to withstand earthquakes. Specifically targeted were apartment buildings constructed of unreinforced masonry (brick, cement block), which are most likely to be damaged in a quake. This is no small problem. There are an estimated 60,000 such buildings in the state, 25,000 in San Francisco alone. That they are most "at risk" was shown by the Whittier earthquake in 1987. Of the 700 structures damaged, 80 percent were of unreinforced masonry. The money from sale of the bonds will aid local governments in identifying these hazardous structures as mandated by a state law passed in 1987. The program is administered by the State Department of Housing and Community Development, which makes loans to apartment house owners whose buildings have been found to be unsafe.

The funds came too late to help prevent massive destruction. In October 1989, just as the third game of the World Series between the San Francisco Giants and the Oakland A's at Candlestick Park was about to begin, a major earthquake struck the Bay Area. The Loma Prieta quake measured 7.1 on the Richter scale and wreaked heavy damage, especially in San Francisco, Oakland, and down the peninsula. There were 89 lives lost and $7 billion in property damage. The state passed a quarter-of-a-cent increase in the sales tax to assist local rebuilding efforts, though the amount raised—about $70 million—fell far short of the losses suffered. Much of the damage was to those unreinforced masonry buildings, as had been expected. As many as 2,000 such buildings remained in San Francisco in 1994, but the city's voters passed a $150 million bond issue in 1992 to fund retrofitting of them.

The collapse of the Cypress Freeway in that quake led the state to undertake a major retrofitting of all freeway overpasses throughout the state. The $1.5 billion effort apparently paid off in the devastating Northridge earthquake in January 1994 when all 114 of those overpasses that had been retrofitted survived.

The massive damage that nonetheless resulted from the Northridge earthquake was, in a sense, worse than the Loma Prieta quake. Though fewer lives were lost, 61, the economic costs were far greater. The severe damage done to the freeway system that dominates the lives and economy of the Los Angeles area cost millions in lost time for commuters and truckers forced onto surface streets. Among the six freeways put out of commission were the Santa Monica (the world's busiest and scheduled for retrofitting only weeks later) and the I-5, the state's major north-south artery. Overall, the losses to homes, businesses, and schools and other public facilities were estimated to be as high as $40 billion, making this the greatest natural disaster in the history of the United States. The one beneficiary: the construction industry.

The long-term impact was limited by the speedy response of government at all levels. Federal aid together with state action saw all freeways restored to full operation less than a year after the quake hit. The Santa Monica, which was one of the most badly hurt, was open again within three months.

Perhaps this quake, coming on the heels of the Los Angeles riots, the brush fires that ravaged the area only weeks earlier, and the severe economic recession, did more to raise questions about the image of Southern California as Paradise on Earth that had been promoted for decades by local chambers of commerce. Still, like the residents of San Francisco, called in one television documentary "The City That Waits to

Die," most Angelenos are eternal optimists. It seems unlikely that, even knowing that this one at 6.8 on the Richter scale was relatively mild compared with the promised "Big One," the area will become a wasteland anytime soon.

SELECTED REFERENCES

Assembly Office of Research, California 2000, *Paradise in Peril,* Sacramento: State Printing Office, 1987.

Barber, Barbara, "Transportation in California," *California Journal,* September 1993.

Bowman, Chris, "State Losing Farmlands to Salts, Urbanization," *Fresno Bee,* December 29, 1987.

———, Russell Clemmings, and Alvie Lindsay, "Air Carries Toxic Chemicals Far from Farms," *Fresno Bee,* November 15, 1993.

California Seismic Safety Commission, "California at Risk," Sacramento, 1988.

California Tomorrow, a journal dealing primarily with environmental issues. Published quarterly, Sacramento.

Carson, Dan, "Water Wars," *California Journal,* April 1993.

Cone, Marla, "EPA Smog Plan Just the Start of Negotiations," *Los Angeles Times,* February 21, 1994.

Davis, Phillip, "Omnibus Western Water Law," *Congressional Quarterly Weekly Review,* November 21, 1992.

Herzog, Steven J., "California Water: The New Gold", *Appraisal Journal,* April 1996.

Jarvis, Michelle, "More Care Taken with Toxic Waste," *California Journal,* September 1990.

Kahrl, William, "Court to L.A.: Go Fish on Water Rights," *Los Angeles Times,* July 3, 1988.

Katches, Mark, "Nightmare in Los Angeles," *California Journal,* June 1994.

Olszewski, Lori, "Thirsty Cities Covet Water Used by Farms," *San Francisco Chronicle,* April 17, 1991.

Senate Office of Research, *The Buried Threat: Getting Away From Land Disposal of Hazardous Waste,* Sacramento: State Printing Office, 1985.

Sotero, Ray, "Not Your Average Pothole", *California Journal,* September 1996.

Steen, Margaret, and Mary Beth Barber, "The Squabble over Smog Checks," *California Journal,* September 1993.

Teitz, Michael B., "California Growth: Hard Questions, Few Answers," in John J. Kirlin and Jeffrey I. Chapman, eds., *California Policy Choices,* Vol. 6, Los Angeles: University of Southern California School of Public Administration, 1990.

Vogel, Nancy, "Tapped Out in California," in Thomas R. Hoeber and Charles M. Price, eds., *California Government and Politics Annual, 1991–92,* Sacramento: California Journal Press, 1991.

Wyner, Alan J., and Dean E. Mann, *Preparing for California's Earthquakes,* Berkeley: Institute for Governmental Studies, 1986.

Chapter 12

Major Political and Social Issues

Politics has been described as the art of compromise, a process of give and take. The greater the diversity of the population, the greater the number of competing interests involved in this process. That is particularly true of California where the population is not just growing but growing ever more heterogeneous. Evidence of this increasing diversity can be seen in large areas of most California cities where signs are almost exclusively in a foreign language and shops and restaurants cater to the needs and wants of the foreign born.

If those newly in the country face problems of adjustment and assimilation for which they seek help from government, others, also considered "different" because of the color of their skin or their accent or their sexual preference, increasingly have been turning to the political process in an effort to eliminate discrimination against them. Foremost among their goals is equality. If members of these groups have an interest in reducing pollution or preserving the coastline or ensuring adequate water supplies, and they do, they have an even more immediate interest in pressing for reform in those social and political arenas where they have felt the effects of bias. Their efforts in many cases have not been welcomed. Affirmative action in hiring has been resisted as "reverse discrimination." Or special admissions to colleges and universities to provide greater educational opportunity for minorities have been decried as a lowering of standards. Demands for gay rights have been opposed by those for whom that lifestyle is repugnant.

If the battle continues for blacks and Hispanics and gays, it is for the most part just beginning for others who have seen progress pass them by. They either have chosen not to join in it or do not possess the skills to do so. Many are now turning to "the system," attempting to bring pressure on government for help. Lobbies for the underprivileged, the poor, the unemployed, and the homeless have emerged.

Then there are those who have rejected the system and the society it regulates. They have gone outside the law (are literally outlaws) and have declared war on society. Norms of behavior are ridiculed, and violence escalates as profits roll in. Questions of how to deal with criminals and the root causes of their actions are major concerns of public policy.

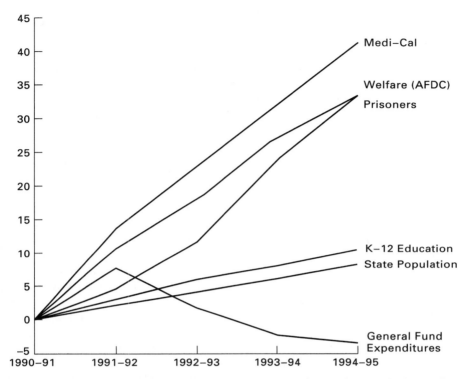

Figure 12.1   Population: State versus programs, percentage growth. (*Source:* "Charting the Course of California's Future," Governor's Budget, Sacramento, 1994)

THE SITUATION OF RACIAL MINORITIES

On the basis of demographics alone, California is a multiracial society. The 1990 census found blacks composed 7 percent of the population, Hispanics 25.8 percent, and Asians/Pacific Islanders 9.1 percent. A third of all Hispanics and 32 percent of all Asians in the United States are residents of California. The native Indian population numbers 242,000. Non-Hispanic whites are still in the majority with 57.2 percent but if population projections hold up there will be *no* ethnic majority group by the year 2000. Los Angeles has been a "minority city" for some time with non-Hispanic whites making up just 40.8 percent of the population. Dan Walters, political columnist for the *Sacramento Bee,* has written extensively of the development of this multiethnic mix as a "two-tier society," one in which the upper tier is made up of non-Hispanic whites and Asians and the lower tier of blacks and Hispanics.[1] Issues of wealth, income, and status all concern the various groups within California's heterogeneous society. Nor have the minority groups lacked for strong leaders in their search for a part of the economic, political, and social "pie" here.

[1]Dan Walters, *The New California,* 2d ed. (Sacramento: California Journal Press, 1992).

The Evolution of Black Power

The period from the late 1950s to the late 1970s witnessed an evolution in the political role of California's black population: From a minority that felt itself essentially a victim of injustice it has grown into a highly activated community at the center of the state's political life. This change has been reflected not only in the methods by which the 2.1 million blacks have pressed their demands on the majority of the population, but also in the responsiveness of California's institutions to these demands.

In 1965 Californians were shocked by the violence of the Watts riots. The focus of black concerns shifted from basic civil rights, school integration, and housing to economic deprivation. The tree-lined streets in Watts with their pleasant, pastel-colored homes and neatly trimmed yards hid the fact that many living there were out of work and living on welfare, that the prices charged in local stores were exorbitant, that there were no motion picture theaters, and mass transit hardly existed.

The shock from the riots was made all the more forceful because Californians had believed their state had one of the best civil rights records in the country, both in the degree of integration and in the upward mobility being achieved; there were more black doctors and lawyers per capita than in other states and more blacks owned their own homes. With their new awareness a number of studies were undertaken. New job-creating and skill-expanding programs by both government and private industry were urged. The hiring of more black teachers in the schools, having labor unions integrate their memberships, and improvement in police-minority community relations were all part of the proposed changes. But the massive programs to build needed housing, schools, hospitals, neighborhood centers, and transportation facilities, which had been recommended by black leaders, did not get sufficient backing.

The problems of south central Los Angeles festered for two decades, to explode in the Rodney King riots in 1992. These riots were set off by the verdict in a case involving a videotaped episode in which it appeared police officers had used unnecessary force in beating a black man who had been speeding and refused to stop. When a jury in Simi Valley (the case had been moved due to pretrial publicity in Los Angeles) acquitted the four police officers involved on all counts, much of Los Angeles—and especially south central Los Angeles—exploded. Smoldering anger concerning allegations of a pattern of police brutality against minorities and suspicion that justice in the courts had a double standard, one for minorities and one for whites was, in many minds, confirmed. (Some whites felt much the same when two black men who had been videotaped beating a white truck driver to near death were later acquitted of all but the most minimal of the charges brought against them.) The old Watts era concerns over price gouging were renewed as many Korean shopkeepers became targets (rightly or not) of black anger. Hundreds of businesses were burned to the ground; looters ran wild, many less interested in the King verdict, it was claimed, than in getting loads of free goods. Clearly racial animosity was not directed solely toward non-Hispanic whites.

The 1970s, in the aftermath of the Watts riots, saw a renewed effort by blacks to use the electoral process to obtain power and status and to bring pressure on government programs. The first major breakthrough was the election of Wilson Riles as superintendent of public instruction in 1970. Riles was reelected in 1974 and again in

Former Speaker of the Assembly Willie L. Brown. (Photo courtesy Speaker Brown's office)

1978. The election of Mervin Dymally as lieutenant governor in 1974 made California the only state with two black statewide elected officials.

Blacks made other significant gains in later years, in Congress and the state legislature. Yvonne Brathwaite Burke was the first black women elected, first to the state assembly in 1966 and later to Congress in 1972. Diane Watson in 1978 became the first black woman to sit in the state senate. Without doubt, however, the most visible and most powerful black politician to date has been Willie Brown, who was first elected to the assembly in 1964 and chosen speaker of the assembly in 1980, a post he held longer than any other person. Forced to seek other office by term limits, he was elected mayor of San Francisco in 1996.

Blacks also began to have considerable success in running for local office. Most impressive was the election of Tom Bradley as mayor of Los Angeles in 1973 (a spectacular comeback after being defeated in his 1969 bid). Three blacks were also elected to the Los Angeles City Council. In the northern Bay Area, Berkeley, Oakland, Richmond, and Albany each elected a black mayor, and Berkeley elected a city council with a black majority.

Meanwhile, mainly as a result of appointments by Governor Jerry Brown when he was in office, the number of black judges on the state bench expanded to more than 45. Of particular note was Brown's appointment of Wiley Manuel as the first black supreme court justice in 1977, but he served only four years (he died of cancer in 1981). Brown later named Allen Broussard, another black, to the high court in 1981. The first black woman justice, Janice Rogers Brown, was appointed by Governor Wilson in 1996. These actions had considerable symbolic significance because they give integrity to the system of law and order that touches the daily lives of blacks. However, the Rodney King riots demonstrated there is much ground yet to cover before full credibility will be accorded the court system by some.

Hispanic Political Power

"It's our turn. It's been 150 years." The rallying cry was that of Abe Tapia, candidate for the Democratic nomination for lieutenant governor in the June 1978 primary against the black incumbent Mervyn Dymally. Tapia lost, but the challenge of this respected Mexican-American political organizer who had loyally stumped the state in previous elections on behalf of the Kennedys, Hubert Humphrey, Jimmy Carter, and Jerry Brown symbolized the rising determination of Hispanic leaders in California and throughout the southwestern United States to take political advantage of the fact that they, not the blacks, are the largest racial minority and that on most indexes of socioeconomic deprivation their situation is worse in California.

Although there are more than four times as many Hispanics as blacks living in California, blacks have historically outnumbered Hispanics in the state legislature and on California's congressional delegation. However, with the redistricting of legislative seats following the 1990 census, several new Hispanic districts were created. That led to four more Hispanics being elected to the House of Representatives and, by 1997, there were 14 Hispanics serving in the state assembly. Another mark of the growing influence of Hispanics was the election of Cruz Bustamante of Fresno as speaker of the assembly.

A major center of political influence for many years was the United Farm Workers (UFW) union and its charismatic leader, the late Cesar Chavez. He was highly successful in his early efforts to organize farm workers and was supported by Governor Jerry Brown in his push for better working conditions for farm laborers. Other organizations have worked toward improving the lot of Hispanics in recent years. The Mexican-American Legal Defense and Education Fund (MALDEF), though headquartered in Texas, has been active in the state as has the League of United Latin American Citizens (LULAC). The Mexican-American Political Association (MAPA) has perhaps been most active in working to promote the participation of Hispanics in politics.

The history of Hispanics in California politics has been, at times, frustrating for those who believe such participation is the key to their future progress there. Despite major efforts to increase Hispanic voting, for example, typically Hispanic turnout is

Speaker of the Assembly Cruz Bustamante. (Photo courtesy Speaker Bustamante's office)

roughly half that of non-Hispanics and blacks. That has been due in part to two factors: age and citizenship. Of the 7.1 million Hispanics counted in the 1990 census, 39 percent were under the age of 19. In 1994 while non-Hispanic whites constituted just 57 percent of the population they cast 81 percent of the votes. By contrast, Hispanics, with 26 percent of the population, cast just 8 percent of the votes. That figure increased substantially in 1996 when Hispanics were estimated to have been 11 percent of the electorate casting ballots.

In the late 1960s a chicano militancy, patterning itself on the militancy of black-power activists, flared up in California under the leadership of organizations like La Raza Unida party and the Brown Berets. Thousands of Mexican-American high school students staged a march in 1968 to protest the inferior educational opportunities provided them in the schools of East Los Angeles. The Mexican-Americans had their own "mini-Watts" in East Los Angeles in 1970, when Ruben Salazar, a *Los*

Angeles Times columnist and the news director of KMEX-TV, was killed. Police disruption of a march of 20,000 Mexican-Americans who were protesting the Vietnam War led to the violence, which in turn provoked a virtual police occupation of the area for over a month. Since then Mexican-American militants have found it more difficult to mobilize followers for direct confrontations with official power.

Though Hispanics still lag well behind non-Hispanic whites and blacks in voter participation and the holding of public office, progress is being made. It is somewhat ironic that this is the case inasmuch as Hispanics held high office early in the state's history. Romualdo Ramirez was elected governor in 1875. Pablo de la Guerra was chosen lieutenant governor in 1861. Andreas Pico was elected to the assembly in 1851. It was not until 1982 that a Hispanic woman was elected to the assembly, Gloria Molina, the same woman who later broke new ground when she was elected to the Los Angeles Board of Supervisors. Still, though progress has been made, Hispanics—with 26 percent of the population—hold less than 3 percent of elected positions in the state.

The greatest progress has been in local government where the number of Hispanics successfully running for city councils, boards of supervisors, school boards, and the like has increased significantly. In 1973 there were 23 Hispanic mayors in California; in 1992 there were 38. In 1973 Hispanics filled 99 city council seats; in 1992 that number had risen to 172.

There have been, and to a degree still are, obstacles to overcome if this segment of the population, referred to for many years as California's "sleeping giant," is to become the potent force it could be.

One such obstacle is the relatively low English literacy rate among Hispanics. Despite the provision of bilingual ballots and increased access to news through Spanish-language radio and television stations, full participation in most instances requires a reasonable proficiency in the use of written and spoken English.

Some of the obstacles are more easily correctable, for example, the failure of the major parties to funnel sufficient financial support to Hispanic candidates. This has been a function of the belief that the Mexican-American is a safe constituency for the Democrats (so why spend any money on them?) and a futile one for the Republicans to capture (so why waste resources?). Studies undertaken by Cal Tech political scientist Bruce Cain in 1987 indicated that, as Hispanics improve their economic circumstances and move into more affluent neighborhoods, they are increasingly likely to change their registration from Democrat to Republican. Other data would appear to support this conclusion. The Southwest Voter Registration and Education Project found that 82 percent of Hispanics making under $10,000 voted for Walter Mondale in 1984, whereas 70 percent of those who earned over $50,000 cast their ballots for Ronald Reagan.[3]

Another obstacle in the past was gerrymandered election districts, which despite reapportionments (see Chapter 6) have not allowed the Hispanics to take proportionate advantage of their population pluralities in many regions. Two cases in 1988 raised the "gerrymander factor" but in different ways. The United States Department of Justice ordered the Los Angeles Board of Supervisors to redistrict on the grounds that no Hispanic had been elected to the board nor had one ever been, despite the

---

[3]*Los Angeles Times,* December 26, 1987.

county's very substantial Hispanic population. In a second case, the federal court of appeals in San Francisco ruled that at-large elections can be discriminatory. The city in question was Watsonville (see page 158).

Immigration, as we will see shortly, became a major issue with the onset of the recession of the 1990s. While polls showed Californians of all ethnic backgrounds, including Hispanics, opposed illegal immigration, there was concern that cracking down on these, for the most part Mexican, immigrants could raise animosity toward those of Mexican descent, especially among employers who faced heavy fines if they "knowingly" hired illegal aliens. The fear was that, to be on the safe side, employers would simply not employ any Mexican-looking applicant. One factor in the increased participation in the electoral process by Hispanics in 1996 was thought to be new federal legislation denying legal immigrants a variety of welfare benefits and the earlier approval by California voters of the anti-illegal immigrant Proposition 187 (see Chapter 3). Several Democratic victories were attributed to Hispanic displeasure over what was perceived to be anti-immigrant policies of the national Republican party. Best known of these: Loretta Sanchez' victory over Congressman Bob Dornan in an increasingly Hispanic district in Orange County.

Another factor in the greater number of Hispanics voting was the action of the Mexican government in passing a law permitting dual citizenship. Many Mexican residents of California had been reluctant to take up United States citizenship for fear of losing Mexican citizenship in the process. That ceased to be a barrier in 1996.

Another emotional issue is bilingualism. Because Spanish is the native tongue, and sometimes the only functional language, of so many Californians, an important political and constitutional issue is the extent to which Spanish should be used as a medium of general instruction in public schools. A related issue is the use of Spanish on official state and local documents (especially election ballots and public signs and announcements of laws and regulations). Under the federal Voting Rights Act of 1975, California counties with a sizable portion of Hispanics have the option of asking voters whether they want their mailed sample ballot printed in Spanish or of simply mailing all voters both Spanish and English ballots. But the counties *must* provide an *opportunity* to voters to receive the Spanish version. In some counties voting officials have had to contend with a nasty backlash from whites who complain that Hispanics who have not learned English are not fit to be American citizens.

The Hispanic community is vitally interested in a wide variety of other public policy issues. Some are specific to their particular interests, but most Hispanics see themselves as part of the larger community as well. They are concerned not just with affirmative action policies, housing discrimination, and other "minority" issues, but with such "general" problems as assuring a quality educational system, improving transportation, and combating crime. As their numbers increase, so will their stake in the resolution of these problems—and their influence in determining how they are to be addressed.

Other Minorities

Californians of Asian ancestry, numbering approximately 3 million, have been systematically denied equality of opportunity at various periods in the state's history: the Chinese in the last decades of the nineteenth century and the Japanese during

World War II. A degree of militancy was generated in efforts to gain a measure of recognition and restitution from federal and state authorities for the forced relocation of Japanese-Americans during World War II. Those efforts met with success when, in August 1988, President Reagan signed into law legislation tendering an official apology for the action and awarding $20,000 in reparations to each of the surviving 60,000 former internees. Two of the leading cosponsors of the bill were the only two members of Congress interned during the war, Robert Matsui of Sacramento and Norman Mineta of San Jose. State action followed which made the payments exempt from taxation.

Asian-Americans have served in a number of prominent positions in the state. March Fong Eu was the first Asian-American to serve in a statewide office (secretary of state). Her son, Matt Fong, became the second Asian-American to hold statewide office when he was elected treasurer in 1994, though he did it as a Republican. Joyce Kinnard in 1989 became the first to be a member of the state supreme court. She was followed onto the court by Ming Chin in 1996. In 1992, Jay C. Kim, mayor of Diamond Bar and a native Korean, was elected to Congress where he joined Robert Matsui of Sacramento and Norm Mineta of San Jose (since resigned) as three of the four Asian-Americans in the House of Representatives (Patsy Mink of Hawaii is the other).

The original Californians, the Indians, are on most indexes of relative deprivation the most badly treated of the state's minorities. As described in Chapter 1, when the Spaniards ruled California the Indians were suppressed within the mission system; under American rule all Indians were deprived of their lands and were forcibly confined to reservations, where they became wards of the national government. Today California's approximately 242,000 Indians have the highest infant mortality and alcoholism rates and the lowest average age of death of any ethnic group. Although those who want to are being encouraged to leave their reservations and to become assimilated into the dominant culture, their actual opportunities for full entry into the majority community remain severely limited. Beginning in the early 1970s, these "forgotten Americans" began to seek ways of pressuring the larger society to rectify the historic inequities foisted on them. The Indians' symbolic occupation of Alcatraz Island, like the confrontation at Wounded Knee, South Dakota, was an early sign of the inevitable growth of militancy among the Indians.

In the mid-1990s a new controversy developed. A number of Indian tribes hit upon a means of transforming their economic status for the better—casino gambling. The legality of such enterprises was challenged by the state of California, more specifically by Governor Wilson and Attorney General Lungren. They contended that the most lucrative of the games played at these casinos, an electronic type of slot machine which provided between 80 percent and 90 percent of the casino profits, was illegal. Casino operators maintained either they were not or the state had no jurisdiction over activities on Indian reservations that were under federal jurisdiction.

There was no doubt the casinos had proved to be an economic bonanza. Over 40 casinos generated hundreds of millions of dollars in profits and provided work for over 10,000 employees, Indians and non-Indians. Some of that money was used in 1996 in a high profile public relations campaign to generate public support for the Indians' position. Radio and television advertisements making the tribes' case featured such Hollywood celebrities as Steven Seagal and Chuck "Walker, Texas Ranger" Norris who called attention to the improved tribal living conditions that had resulted from casino operations. However the United States Supreme Court refused to hear a challenge by the tribes to the state's position thus upholding the ban on video slot machines. In the aftermath, several tribes began phasing out the machines, though the impact on casino profitability seemed likely to be great.

GAY RIGHTS

The nationwide emergence of a gay-rights movement and the resulting backlash finds California, not untypically, a major storm center. Starting in the early 1970s, homosexuals began to organize for political activity. They recognized that their numbers were sufficient to effect an enlargement of civil rights for themselves if only they would follow the example of the blacks, Hispanics, and women and function as a special-interest constituency, supporting candidates for public office who would act to repeal antihomosexual legislation and generally help gays to overcome their status as pariahs in society. The activist stance of the gays, however, has stimulated antigay agitation by elements in the population with more traditional moral views, who believe that equal rights and equal status for gays will weaken the fabric of essential social institutions, such as marriage and the family, and will make it more possible for gays to serve as role models for impressionable children.

Initially operating out of homosexual Democratic clubs in the San Francisco area, by the mid-1970s the gay activists were able to take credit for local ordinances and resolutions that extended fair-employment practices to homosexuals in San Francisco, Berkeley, San Jose, Palo Alto, and other communities.[4] They elected one of their own, Harvey Milk, to the San Francisco Board of Supervisors. Supervisor Milk and George Moscone, the mayor of San Francisco and not a gay, were both shot and killed by an ex-supervisor, Dan White, in 1978. At issue was White's ouster from the Board of Supervisors and his opposition to the political power of gays in San Francisco.

In 1978 the gays received a blessing in disguise: a statewide ballot initiative that attempted to prevent them from teaching in the public schools. The statewide interest and debate over the ballot proposition, like Anita Bryant's campaign in Florida to limit the rights of homosexuals, only allowed the gays to "legitimatize" their cause before the general public and meanwhile intensified their political organizational work in localities more resistant to gays than the San Francisco area.[5]

In 1979 Governor Jerry Brown issued an executive order prohibiting discrimination in public employment based on sexual preference. Since that time California has become among the leaders nationally in adopting policies guaranteeing equal rights for gays.

---

[4]Nancy Friedman, "Gay Power: From Closet to Voting Booth," *California Journal* VI, 10 (October 1975), pp. 341–344.

[5]Interviews with Harvey Milk, May 25, 1978, and with Jim Foster (a gay activist on the California Democratic Party Executive Committee), May 4, 1978.

In 1986 and 1988 the voters defeated initiatives opposed by both gays and the medical profession that would have required disclosure of the names of those with the AIDS virus. (Results of these tests are now confidential.) In his campaign for governor in 1990 Pete Wilson appeared to promise he would sign a gay-rights bill. However, in 1991 he vetoed such a bill barring discrimination against gays in employment and housing and making violations a criminal offense. Violent protests by gays broke out across the state. A more limited bill was signed into law in 1992 which banned discrimination in the workplace only with penalties enforced through civil law. Wilson's signature made little actual difference since a state appellate court ruled in 1991 that discrimination based on sexual orientation was illegal.

In recent years, the AIDS crisis has been foremost in the minds of the gay population. This disease knows no cure and is, without exception, fatal. Those afflicted by it are for the most part, though not exclusively, homosexuals and intravenous drug users. The Department of Health Services reported as of March 31, 1997, there were 99,908 cases of AIDS in the state, up from 47,636 in January 1994; 64,137 died of the disease. Gays have obtained significant state funding for AIDS research, but been less successful in gaining a different objective: an officially approved clean needle exchange program designed to reduce transmission of the virus among drug users. Such legislation has passed the legislature, but was vetoed by Governor Wilson.

The first openly gay politician to serve in the state legislature was elected in 1994. Sheila Kuehl, who gained fame on the old television comedy *The Many Loves of Dobie Gillis*, was elected to the assembly from the 41st district, which includes Santa Monica. She was named speaker pro tem of the assembly by Democratic speaker Cruz Bustamante in 1996.

Gays rallied behind a move in 1996 to have same-sex marriages recognized. With the courts in Hawaii upholding such unions, gays in California fought legislation that would have denied the validity of such marriages. (Under the federal Constitution the civil judgements of one state must be upheld by the courts of the other states and recognition of same-sex marriages in Hawaii presumably would mean these same couples would have to be recognized as married in the other 49 states.) Such legislation passed the assembly but died in the senate. A Field Poll taken early in 1997 found that while a substantial majority of Californians favored awarding gays couples the same rights as heterosexuals in such matters as hospital visitations, medical power of attorney, and conservatorship, by a margin of 56 to 38 they opposed gay marriage.

EDUCATION

In November 1993 the voters overwhelmingly rejected an initiative that would have given vouchers to schools that accepted students whose parents wanted them in a different school (see Chapter 3). That by no means indicated satisfaction with the state of education in California, however. Parents complained of poor scores on standardized tests, a lack of up-to-date texts and computers, and violence in the schoolyard and even in the classroom. The state Department of Education listed the problems most cited by students in 1940 and in the early 1990s. The contrast was—and is— striking.

1940	1990s
talking	drug abuse
chewing gum	alcohol abuse
making noise	pregnancy
running in halls	suicide
out of turn in line	rape
improper clothing	robbery
not putting paper in wastebasket	assault

Many were concerned that on top of all the violence their children were not receiving a good education. The scores on the Scholastic Aptitude Tests (SATs) have been largely stagnant since 1990 with California's test takers ranked thirty-first in the country in mathematics and forty-fourth on the verbal portion of the test. Some of the reasons cited include large class sizes (California ranked last in student-teacher ratio), lack of money (though the state spends approximately 40 percent of its budget on K–14 education, the result of Proposition 98 passed in 1988, it ranked thirty-ninth among the states in the amount spent per pupil), and the fact that minority students who frequently do not do well on such tests accounted for 54 percent of those taking the SATs in California compared with 30 percent in other states.

In some respects the performance of the state's public schools has improved (though a Field survey in 1993 found only 5 percent agreeing that "the public schools are doing the best they can"). Some of that improvement can be attributed to the Hart-Hughes Educational Reform Act passed by the legislature in 1983, which resulted in a longer school year, a longer school day, incentives for school districts to raise teacher salaries, a mentoring system for teachers, and stiffer course requirements for graduation from high school. After a decade, the results were mixed. Scores on the Scholastic Aptitude Tests (SATs) rose but plateaued in the early 1990s. In another positive development, the dropout rate fell to 16 percent from 1986 when 25 percent quit.

Still, parents and others expressed the belief that education was not living up to its job. Several evaluations of the state's schools in mid-decade tended to support these parental concerns. One task force found spending on technology for schools woefully inadequate and compared the lack of computers in the classroom to denying students of an earlier era pencil and paper. With one computer for every 71 students and technology expenditure resting at $3 per student per year, the task force found much that needed upgrading.

A national survey sponsored by *Education Week* magazine and released in January 1997 "graded" California schools in a variety of bases and, with the exception of quality of teaching, found them wanting. Forty-three percent needed significant repairs. School libraries ranked dead last among the 50 states in books per student. Per pupil spending, though increased in 1996–1997 and 1997–1998, remained $1,000 below the national average. In performance, only 14 percent of fourth grade students were found to be "proficient" in reading while only 18 percent of eighth grade students were proficient in math. And just 19.5 percent of those taking the Scholastic Aptitude Test scored above the national average.

A contributing factor is the violence that is common on or near many campuses with gangs often involved. Some schools have banned gang colors; others have prohibited the wearing of clothing with sports logos associated with gang membership. Guns and knives are sometimes present, though that is not the norm. The threat of violence was a major factor behind the voucher movement.

On the plus side are several efforts that promise improvement. Perhaps most dramatic is the plan, announced by Governor Wilson and funded by the legislature, to reduce class sizes, which had grown to the largest in the country, from nearly 30 students per class to 20 in kindergarten through third grade. The 1996–1997 budget included an allocation of $771 million for this purpose and allowed local school districts to hire over 6,500 teachers to staff the 3,800 new classrooms required. Still more funding for lowering class sizes was included in the governor's 1997–1998 budget.

The difficulty of this effort to reduce class sizes is compounded by a rapid increase in student population. The United States Department of Education in 1996 projected an increase from 5.8 million enrolled in 1996 to 6.8 million by 2006. By one estimate there will be a need to accommodate 525,000 more high school students by that time, a need that will require construction of 20,000 new classrooms.

One approach to improving schools that is being tested is the charter school. A charter school is one the state allows to break away from its district (with the district's approval), formulate its own goals, and manage its own affairs, apart from the multitude of state regulations. Volumes containing those regulations, thousands of them, weigh close to 40 pounds and deal with matters from the fundamental to the trivial such as the kind of paint to be used in school bathrooms. The Charter Schools Act permits 100 of the state's 7,000 schools to engage in this experiment with results to be evaluated after five years. Many local educators, fed up with state mandates that they see as micromanagement, welcomed this chance to try a different approach to education. Curricula vary enormously. A school in Oakland emphasizes bilingual education; a Los Angeles area school focuses on personal health and family relationships along with academic subjects.

Two other alternatives are being employed. One was a response to the flexibility promised by supporters of school vouchers. It is embodied in two bills passed in 1993 which, respectively, allow students to transfer to another school in the district or to a school in another district, space permitting. The other has been implemented by districts across the state in the form of magnet schools, which place greater emphasis on a particular area of learning such as science and technology or the arts.

Higher Education

As the numbers of those in secondary education have been rapidly rising, places in the state's public institutions of higher education have been shrinking. An estimate by the U.S. Department of Education foresaw a 34 percent increase in high school enrollments in the 1990s. That, by a separate estimate, meant the need to accommodate a 50 percent growth in the state's colleges and universities between 1991–1992 and 2006, or over half a million more bodies.

The state was moving in the opposite direction in the early 1990s, however. The state's institutions of higher education were "downsizing" due to budget cutbacks. Fewer classes were offered, professors—even some with tenure—were let go, and in some instances whole programs were eliminated.[6] The cuts resulted in dramatically reduced enrollments. The three systems lost 160,000 students between 1992–1993 and 1993–1994 with community colleges suffering the greatest attrition, down 137,000. That was largely due to both across-the-board fee increases and a $50 a unit additional fee for those already possessing a bachelor's degree. Fees were so greatly increased that the tradition of a free college education available to all effectively ended. The University of California Board of Regents went one step further when they not only authorized a $620 increase in student fees for 1994–1995 but also authorized for the first time use of such money to pay for faculty salaries. That broke the agreement under the Master Plan for Higher Education that proposed fees be only for noninstructional "support" services. By the middle of the 1990s the state's economic picture improved to the point that fee increases were halted and there was a modest rebound of enrollments.

A major controversy arose in 1995 in the successful push by Governor Wilson, Regent Ward Connerly (an African American), and others to abolish affirmative action programs at the University of California. Those favoring this move argued that the only criterion for admission or hiring should be qualifications and not race or gender. Those opposed held that elimination of such programs would severely limit minority enrollments, reduce educational diversity, and result in major reductions in the number of blacks and Hispanics enrolled. They pointed out that 95 percent of UC students have grade point averages and test scores that place them in the top 12.5 percent of high school graduates, qualifying them for admission under the Master Plan. Those seeking abolition of affirmative action admissions simply replied it was unfair for a non-minority to be barred from admission in favor of a less qualified minority. The courts delayed implementation of the regents' action to the fall of 1998.

That Master Plan was adopted in 1961 and all three public systems of higher education are supposed to be governed by it. The Master Plan sets down different functions for the University of California, the California State University system, and the community colleges. UC was designated the primary research institution, the CSU has as its primary role teaching, while the community colleges are to provide vocational instruction and an opportunity for those who do not qualify for entry into the other two systems to prove they can do college work, and be able to transfer upon completion of two years of study. UC takes the top 12.5 percent of high school graduates, the CSU the top third, and community colleges accept anyone over the age of 18.

It should be noted that the increasing of fees was accompanied by an increase in financial aid. Approximately one dollar in every three of added revenue has gone to help needy students. However, some argue you have to be very, very poor to qualify and that middle-class parents are the ones being most hurt.

Education at all levels is extremely important for everyone and a good educational system is vital to a growing and vital economy. Particularly in need are those at the lower end of the economic ladder, people on welfare, immigrants, and the homeless.

---

[6]One interesting example was found at the University of California, Berkeley, where introductory Spanish was dropped from the curriculum, this in a state where more than a quarter of the population is of Hispanic origin—and growing.

An area that has been hotly debated has concerned education for those who have recently entered the country.

IMMIGRATION

They are Laotian and Hmong, Filipino and Salvadoran, Korean, Guatemalan, and Japanese, Nicaraguan and Mexican. Theirs are the fear-filled faces of peoples fleeing war in their homelands and the hopeful countenances of those seeking freedom and economic opportunity in another land. They are contributing in a major way to California's recently booming population growth. They are the new immigrants.

There are of course two types of immigrants, legal and illegal. There are also two ways of looking at them: (1) as peoples who can and do contribute to the economic growth and cultural vitality of the nation or (2) as likely to add to the burdens of Americans, who have to compete with them for jobs (and allegedly experience lower pay scales in the process), and as recipients of welfare benefits provided out of their tax dollars.

Just how many immigrants have settled in California in recent years is difficult to determine. However, in 1997 the Immigration and Naturalization Service (INS) estimated that of the 5 million illegal aliens in the country, 2 million lived in California, or 6.3 percent of the state's population. (To put that in context, the next most affected state was Texas with 700,000 illegal immigrants or 3.7 percent of its population.) Most have settled in Southern California. Immigrants, legal and illegal, together make up well over 20 percent of the state's population. An estimated 200,000 legal immigrants arrive annually; another 100,000 are believed to come illegally. The continued growth in the number of illegal immigrants entering the state would seem to indicate that voter approval of Proposition 187, the anti-illegal immigrant proposition, in 1994 has had little if any effect on the flow of such immigrants into the state.

Why do they come? There are both what are called "push" factors and "pull" factors. "Push" refers to living conditions that are so bad people are "pushed" into leaving their home countries. Immigrants from Mexico are pushed by high unemployment, whereas those from Southeast Asia and Central America have fled homelands torn by war. "Pull" factors generally refer to opportunities to better oneself economically, though the freedoms associated with the American way of life are significant for some.

The subject of illegal immigrants became a "hot button" topic with the onset of the recession and became even hotter in 1993 with the sudden influx of Chinese being smuggled into the country by ship. The issue of immigration is complex and involves a number of tradeoffs. Migrants of all types add greatly to the cultural richness of the country. They also in many cases take low-paying jobs that native-born Americans do not want. Some 92 percent of farm workers in California are foreign born, with one estimate that nearly 75 percent of them are in the country illegally. Without them the state's $5 billion in perishable crops would be threatened. Seventy-five percent of the employees in Los Angeles's furniture manufacturing and textile industries are immigrants, many illegal. The hard-working and legal immigrants who have been here more than ten years are slightly less likely to be on welfare than those born here. Hispanic and Asian immigrants have fewer drug-influenced babies, are less likely to have heart attacks or strokes, have fewer out-of-wedlock babies, are much more likely to have two-parent families, and live longer than native borns. Because they will work for lower wages, the costs of much that we consume are lower and thus benefit the rest of the population. So what, then, is the problem (aside from the fact many illegals are unscrupulously exploited by employers who know they cannot complain)?

The costs of illegal aliens became a major issue in 1993 when the federal government was asked to pick up the tab for the cost of educating and providing health care for those illegally in the state. Since immigration is a federal responsibility, that request seemed reasonable to many. It was, however, ignored. The same proved largely true in 1994 when the governor's budget was "balanced" based on substantial federal money ($3.1 billion) for this purpose. What are these costs? Estimates vary and figures change quickly, but there is some agreement that health care costs run close to $1 billion a year. Educating the children of illegal immigrants enrolled in public schools, estimated to number nearly 400,000, runs another $1 billion. Then there are the over 18,000 illegal aliens being held in state prisons at a cost of nearly $375 million a year.

There are several studies that point to illegal aliens contributing more to society than they take from it. No statewide data are available, but one study of Los Angeles County found those not legally in the country paid $4.3 billion in federal, state, and local taxes while drawing only a quarter of that amount in public assistance. Another study, this of San Diego County, found the same pattern. However, in both instances it was determined that most of the tax revenues went to Washington, D.C., and the local governments came out on the short end, in Los Angeles by $807 million and in San Diego's case by about $145 million.

America's tradition of welcoming immigrants to its shores for their contributions, economic and cultural, to the country has never been as unmixed a welcome as often portrayed. But with California facing bad economic times, ever-increasing urban strife, clogged highways, and water shortages, the question of how many more people can reasonably be borne by the state's finite resources is being raised more and more often by environmentalists who point to future growth and proclaim a disaster pending.

What to do to stem the tide of those entering the country illegally has been a major question for years. One approach was used in the Immigration Reform and Control Act passed by Congress in 1986. Under it, those who were illegally here since January 1, 1982, could apply for legal status and amnesty. Of the three million who applied, over half settled in California. As noted earlier, sanctions were to be imposed on employers who "knowingly" hired illegal aliens. Within two years it was clear that (1) employers were seldom being penalized and (2) the flood of undocumented workers was as large as ever.

Other ideas have included creating a "secure" (hard to forge) identity card (much money is being made from the sale of fake social security cards and other forms of identification), building walls or digging ditches along the Mexican border, adding to the number of Border Patrol agents, and using the National Guard. However, the persistence of those seeking entry makes all such measures of at least questionable value. As one waiting to cross the border under cover of night put it: "We'll come back again and again. . . . Until the *migra* (Border Patrol) gets tired or I get old." The lure of jobs is so strong and the penalty for getting caught so weak (a quick trip back to try again) that only with enhanced economic opportunities in their own homelands will the "hemorrhaging border" to the south be likely to stop bleeding.

THE HOMELESS

"Winos," "Junkies," "Crazies"—these are some of the terms traditionally used to describe those living on the streets of the United States. These are the shiftless, the broken, and the alienated of our society, sleeping in shop doorways and public parks, panhandling to support their alcohol and drug habits. Or are they? Well, some are. A Gallup organization survey in 1992 found that a third of the homeless cited alcohol or drug abuse as the primary reason for their homelessness. That means of course that two-thirds are not abusers. A survey for the United States Conference of Mayors in 1993 found that 43 percent of the homeless were families with children, up from 33 percent just five years earlier. Nearly one in five held full- or part-time jobs. Some were the victims of family violence, while others had lost their jobs and had nowhere to go. These constitute the "new homeless" and bear little or no resemblance to long-time residents of skid row or of "bums" riding the rails.

This is not to say that a substantial percentage of the homeless is not made up of the alienated. One cause of the increase in the homeless population is deinstitutionalization of the mentally ill. Believing those people not a danger to themselves or society might be better treated on an outpatient basis, and under court decrees that held their constitutional rights were being violated, mental institutions released thousands of them, only to find many refused to continue treatment. Medication use ceased and behavior deteriorated. The mayors' survey found 27 percent of the homeless were mentally ill, but over half appear to be victims of social and economic forces beyond their control. Alcoholism and drug abuse were also factors in up to 40 percent of the homeless population. Of course there are some who apparently prefer that lifestyle, but the majority appear to be the victims of social and economic forces beyond their control.

Two Programs

Local communities throughout the state have attempted to address the problem of homelessness. Some, like Santa Ana, have attempted to keep the homeless from sleeping in parks or business area doorways. Others have tried periodic sweeps of places where the homeless stay, removing their possessions. Two dramatically different approaches to dealing with the homeless were to be found in San Francisco and Santa Monica.

When Frank Jordan was elected mayor of San Francisco he promised to clean up the problem of the homeless. Tourists were being frightened by the sometimes unkempt, odor-bearing, aggressive panhandlers. Merchants complained that even those who simply slept in commercial areas were hurting business. A city report concluded the cost in lost business was running about $200 million a year. In August 1993, Jordan ordered the police to cite or arrest homeless people who were sleeping in parks, blocking sidewalks, or aggressively panhandling. During the first few months of the program, called Matrix, over 3,000 of the homeless were cited, moved, or arrested. Fines for violators ran $76. Civil libertarians objected to Matrix as harassing and intimidating people down on their luck. The intent, they said, was to drive these unfortunates from the city. The mayor maintained it was to clean up the area but also help the homeless get into social programs designed to help them.

A THOUSAND POINTS

(Dennis Renault, *Sacramento Bee*)

In Santa Monica the approach was quite different. There, the welcome mat was put out as city leaders felt compassion for and a desire to help the homeless. The city spends $1.1 million a year to provide services for the homeless. There are ten feeding centers, seven overnight shelters, three day-care centers, five mental health centers, and two missions. In addition, there are shelters for mentally ill women and for drug abusers. Critics complain the cost is much too great for a city of 90,000 to bear. They say there is little reason to believe the social programs are getting many people back into the mainstream of society. And they maintain all that these services do is attract more of the homeless and point to some 4,500 homeless people living in their city, giving it the highest per capita homeless population in the state, if not the nation.

Both approaches underwent change over time. Willie Brown, campaigning for mayor, bitterly opposed Matrix and vowed to end it if elected. He did, though some residual effects remained. However, when the ban of sleeping in the parks was removed the number "camping out" skyrocketed, especially in Golden Gate Park where they were said by city gardeners to be "out of control". In Santa Monica most of the welcome mat remains out, but a portion of it has been withdrawn, in the neighborhood of Third Street Promenade. It seems teenage street urchins were harassing shoppers, panhandling, and blocking the entrances to businesses. The city council passed an ordinance prohibiting people from sitting or lying down on the Promenade between 6 A.M. and 1 A.M.

Perhaps this illustrates that Mayor Willie Brown was right. When asked about what was happening in San Francisco with respect to the homeless and what to do about it, he replied, "I don't have an answer. It may not be solvable."

How many homeless are there in California? The 1990 census counted just 48,886, but everyone, including the census takers, agrees that figure is woefully short of the actual number. Most estimates run between 100,000 and 250,000. In addition to local programs, there are an even dozen state programs to deal with the homeless population. They range from one operated out of the Department of Social Services that provides assistance to those on the Aid to Families with Dependent Children program through one run by the Department of Mental Health that assists local government in helping the emotionally ill, to a third that underwrites the operation of emergency shelters through the Department of Housing and Community Development.

Hope and even faith are characteristic of many in the ranks of the homeless, the new migrants, and those on the welfare rolls. They have hope that the system can be made to work for them and faith that their futures will be better than their pasts. For them, "the system," if it failed them then, is still regarded as a means of serving them now. Others have opted out and, in effect, have declared war on the system and the society it regulates.

DEALING WITH CRIME AND THE CRIMINAL

"Two killed in Drive-by Shooting," "Judge Orders Early Release of Felons Due to Overcrowding," "Epidemic of Crack Use Reported," "Gang Related Violence Escalates." Headlines like these have become almost commonplace. Carjackings are no longer news unless someone dies. Gang turf wars have "graduated" from tire irons and chains to AK-47s and Uzis as members fight over the buying and selling of drugs. Violent crime tops the list of things Californians worry about. What to do about it became the big issue of the mid-1990s.

Three Strikes and You're Out

As with immigration, politicians sought to outdo one another in their concern for and toughness on crime. The kidnapping and subsequent murder of 12-year-old Polly Klass from her home in Petaluma shocked the nation, raising concerns that even the

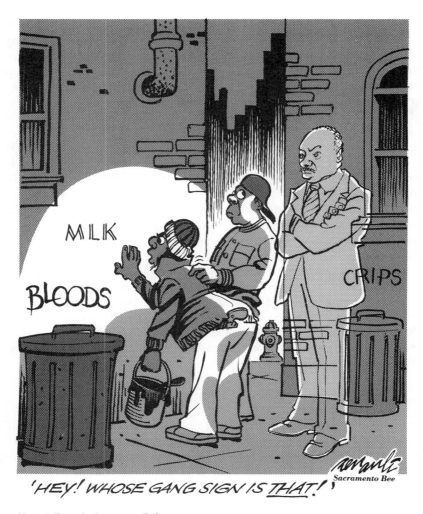

'HEY! WHOSE GANG SIGN IS _THAT!_'

(Dennis Renault, *Sacramento Bee*)

most "secure" spots were not very secure at all anymore. The fact that her admitted killer was a convicted felon recently released from prison after serving 8 years of a 16-year sentence for, yes, kidnapping, gave momentum to a number of efforts to come down hard on repeat offenders. One such effort was the "Three Strikes and You're Out" proposal. Patterned after a similar initiative adopted by the voters of the state of Washington and pushed by the father of a Fresno teenager, Kimber Reynolds, who was killed by another repeat offender in 1992, it received strong public support. The legislature passed "three strikes" legislation and Governor Wilson signed it into law in March 1994. It doubles the sentence for a second offense and for the third felony the effective term is life without possibility of parole. It, along with other proposals, substantially reduces the amount of time a prisoner can get off his or her sentence for "good behavior." Had it been in effect, neither of the men involved in the two murders just cited would have been on the streets. Opponents pointed to the fact the law does not require the third conviction be for a *violent* felony, claiming that writing a bad check could result in a life sentence. Others noted that the overwhelming majority of felony cases were settled out of court by plea bargaining.[7] With a third conviction automatically resulting in life behind bars, few, they said, would opt for a plea bargain to a lesser felony. The results, the critics said, would be to overwhelm the court system, with an incredible backlog of cases becoming inevitable.

Court rulings changed and/or clarified the original law. One found that a felony conviction for a crime in another state could be counted as a "strike" in California. That made supporters of the law happy, but another set of decisions did not. These allowed considerably greater judicial discretion in application of the law when dealing with what are described as "wobblers" (actions that might be considered misdemeanors or felonies). A 1996 decision held this to be true for cases involving public safety (a felony if it did, a misdemeanor if it did not). A January 1997 ruling expanded that to include cases that could be felonies or misdemeanors but did *not* involve public safety. The decision was based on a case where a man was riding a skateboard on the wrong side of the street and, when arrested, was found to have drug paraphernalia and a small amount of methamphetamine on his person. The court found application of a misdemeanor more appropriate "in the interests of justice." Such discretion exercised by prosecutors had already led to widely varying results, however. In San Diego County strict application of the three strikes law has resulted in life imprisonment for some felons with no history of violent behavior while in Alameda County someone accused of the same crime has not been subjected to the three strikes standard.

Prisons and Prisoners

The question remained, however—just how many people the state should put in prison and for what offenses. In 1980 the state's prison population was less than 25,000; by mid-1996 it had passed the 150,000 mark and was growing at a rate of 200 a week. The overcrowding rate, at 184 percent, will grow far higher unless new prisons are built or, as suggested by some, alternative ways of dealing with nonviolent criminals are found.[8] Home incarceration with electronic monitors for nonviolent offenders has been tried in several jurisdictions, for example. The cost of keeping so many off the streets has escalated. At $24,000 per prisoner per year, the budget has reached nearly $4 billion a year and, at the current rate of increase it is predicted such spending will soon surpass that on higher education.

Those costs aside, the public clearly wants to see violent repeat offenders spend more time in prison. The average time spent "inside" for murder is just over 16 years. Rapists average four years, one month. Some have urged "one strike and you're out" for rapists and child molesters. But that again raises questions of cost as well as a concern that a single false charge could lead to life imprisonment.

---

[7]Of 1,700 violent felony cases in Alameda County in 1993, between 100 and 150 went to trial, the rest were plea bargained. Approximately 90 percent of such cases were plea bargained in San Francisco that same year.

[8]At the beginning of 1994, 12 new prisons were being planned and it was thought another 20 might be needed when the impact of "three strikes" was fully felt.

This stress on stronger punishment by Governor Wilson and those who sought to replace him as governor in 1994 has a long tradition in California. The political success of Ronald Reagan and George Deukmejian reflects the general public sentiment. Jerry Brown, with the exception of his opposition to capital punishment, also took a hard line against crime.[9] There has been, nonetheless, a good deal of controversy over how to deal with crime and those convicted of crimes in recent years.

The Death Penalty

For many years perhaps the central focus of the law-and-order debate in California was the propriety of the death penalty. His avowed opposition to it hurt Pat Brown in his attempt to gain a third term as governor in 1966. His son Jerry, equally opposed, might have suffered the same electoral fate as his father had he faced stronger opposition in 1978. Those favoring capital punishment contend that, as the ultimate sanction, it deters crime. It also, and obviously, ensures absolute protection to society from dangerous and violent criminals who might otherwise be paroled. Opponents deny that the death penalty deters, citing studies comparing states with and without it, studies that appear to show it has no effect. They point out that because humans make decisions, mistakes occur and they cannot be rectified once this most severe of sentences is carried out. Nor, they say, do most murderers kill again. None of these arguments has proved persuasive to the general public, which continues overwhelmingly to support the death penalty. More than any other single factor, the belief that three justices of the California Supreme Court either refused to permit the carrying out of the death penalty (Rose Bird) or were very reluctant to do so (Joseph Grodin and Cruz Reynoso) in 1986 led to their failure to be confirmed to new terms on the court. In June 1988 the voters approved a ballot proposition that extended the death penalty to include unpremeditated murder when committed against a peace officer.

The question of deterrence is clouded by the infrequency with which the death penalty has been applied. In a move to expedite cases (some have been pending for a dozen years or more), the state supreme court ruled in 1993 that inmates who claim their constitutional rights have been violated are limited to one appeal. A second appeal is only allowed when the petitioner can show a "fundamental miscarriage of justice" has occurred.[10]

Two Systems of Sentencing

A change made in 1977 in the way convicted criminals are sentenced has helped add to the overcrowding problem. Until that year California operated under a system known as indeterminate sentencing. That means that a judge would impose

---

[9]Members of both political parties reacted to the public's outrage over crime and passed a number of anti-crime laws that took effect in 1995. Two are worthy of special note. One involved the amount of time that a sentence could be reduced for "good behavior" from 50 percent to 15 percent. The other was in response to increasing and increasingly violent juvenile crime and lowered the age at which a juvenile can be tried as an adult from 16 to 14.

[10]*In re Clark.*

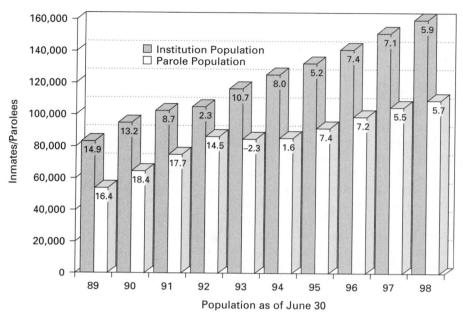

**Department of Corrections
Institution and Parole Population Growth**

Figures in the bars represent the percentage change from the previous year.

Figure 12.2   (*Source:* Budget Summary Highlights, Department of Finance)

"the sentence required by law," typically five years to life. With time off for good behavior, a person serving such a term could be released in 20 months. If the prisoner proved uncooperative or violent, the time behind bars could be extended indefinitely. The rationale behind this system reflected the rehabilitation school of thought. Good behavior, such as participating in projects beneficial to society and education programs, would be encouraged by rewarding it with shorter time served.

Liberals opposed indeterminate sentencing, saying it was unfair to send someone to prison with no idea of how long the individual would be there. Conservatives disliked it because they felt it could be used as a safety valve by which overcrowded facilities could be relieved of pressure by releasing those who might still be a threat to society.

These objections, together with the public demand that government "get tough" on crime, led to the adoption of determinate sentencing in 1977. This system, which applies to over 90 percent of criminal offenses committed in the state (first degree murder is an exception), ensures that convicted criminals will serve a specific time behind bars. It is grounded in the belief that prisons are not very good at rehabilitation and better suited to punishment and keeping society safe from dangerous felons. In theory, determinate sentencing meets the concerns of both liberals and conservatives. In practice, there have been some problems. Knowing that no matter how much trouble they caused their terms could not be extended led to a quadrupling of prison violence over a six-year span. Short of conviction for an act committed in prison (which is difficult to obtain given the reluctance of prisoners to inform on their fellows), nothing can be done to extend their stay. Also disquieting are some notorious cases in which those convicted of truly horrible crimes have been turned loose, their sentences having been served, with no assurance they will not commit like crimes again. In one instance a man who picked up a young hitchhiker, raped her, and cut off both her arms below the elbow, leaving her to bleed to death, was released despite a loud public outcry and no indication he felt any remorse. The determinate sentencing law required he be set free after serving eight years and four months in prison. Polly Klass's abduction and murder in 1993 raised again the issue of whether violent—and unrepentant—offenders should be released or made exceptions to the determinate sentencing law.

SELECTED REFERENCES

California Journal, June 1993 issue, has several articles on aspects of education in California.

California Tomorrow, "Crossing the Schoolhouse Border," San Francisco, 1988.

Carry, Bill, and Lou Cannon, "Hispanics Building a New Power Base," *Washington Post,* October 9, 1978

Chiang, Harriet, "3 Strikes: A Tale of Two Counties," *San Francisco Chronicle,* September 23, 1996.

Gaston, Beth, "California's Shotgun Approach to Helping the Homeless," *California Journal,* June 1990.

Gianturco, Adriana, "Prison Construction," *California Journal,* June 1985.

Hero, Rodney E. and Caroline J. Tolbert, "Race/Ethnicity and Direct Democracy: An Analysis of California's Illegal Immigration Initiative," *The Journal of Politics,* 58, August 1996.

Locke, Laura A., "Crime Knocks Education Out of the Spotlight," *California Journal,* February 1994.

Scott, Steve, "The New Legislature," *California Journal,* Janaury 1997.

Starkey, Danielle, "Immigrant Bashing," *California Journal,* October 1993.

———, "Pete to Immigrants: Don't Huddle Here," *California Journal,* March 1992.

Starkey, Danielle, and Vic Pollard, "The Prison Dilemma," *California Journal,* April 1994.

Maharidge, Dale, "Did 1992 Herald the Dawn of Latino Political Power?" *California Journal,* January 1993.

McLeod, Ramon G., and Tim Schreiner, "Ethnic Economic Gap Remained Wide in '80s," *San Francisco Chronicle,* May 11, 1992.

Skinner, Casey, "To Jail or Not to Jail: Seeking Alternatives to Hard Time," *California Journal,* November 1988.

Shuit, Douglas P., and Patrick J. McDonnell, "Calculating the Impact of California's Immigrants," *Los Angeles Times,* January 8, 1992.

Taub, J. S., "Gay Politics," *California Journal,* November 1993.

Warner, Mary S., "The Rise of Blacks in the Politics of California," *California Journal,* August 1978.

Toward the Twenty-First Century: Possible Reforms

In the thirteenth edition of *Politics and Government in California* we wrote the following:

As Californians move closer to the twenty-first century, a number of ideas are circulating concerning how to make their governing system more effective, efficient, and responsive. A common complaint (except among those who prefer that government do less) is that the system, as now constituted, simply fails to work well all too often. Or when it does work, it sometimes works in ways the public does not care for.

In the period since that was written little has taken place to cause us to be more optimistic that reforms to improve the workings of the system will be implemented, at least not if left to the tender mercies of the state's elected officials. That is of course not true of all elected officials. Some, like Secretary of State Bill Jones, a Republican in the executive branch, and Patrick Johnston, a Democratic member of the assembly, have worked diligently to correct some of the deficiencies and/or abuses. However, reforms proposed by commissions, academic panels, advisory groups or individual citizens have not fared well. The most sweeping reform of the last few years was contained in an initiative, Proposition 208, which attempted a drastic alteration in campaign financing. As this is written even that is under court challenge. As a general rule—and this must not be applied to all elected officials—those who gain office are inclined to resist changes because they do not want to change a system under which they were successful. For them the old adage "if it ain't broke don't fix it" is sound advice, even if in other respects "it" may seem to be in terrible shape indeed.

It might be well to review those reforms listed in the previous edition to see how well they are faring.

The most radical of the ideas that have been floated in recent times is an old one: dividing California into two or three states. This idea has a long history and typically in the past has seen division taking place along the Tehachapi Mountains between Los Angeles and Bakersfield. Such a proposal actually passed in 1859 with 75 percent of Californians endorsing the idea. Congress balked.

The most recent proposal, pushed by then-Assemblymember Stan Statham of Redding, would have divided the state in three with a northern state starting at the Oregon border and running just short of San Francisco and Sacramento, population 2.35 million; a central state that includes those two cites and runs to the Tehachapis, population 10.1 million; and a southern state reaching from those mountains to the Mexican border, population 17.85 million.

Arguments for such a splitting up of the state include a belief it has become too big to be governable, that San Diego, Fresno, Sausalito, and Redding have little in common with each other and that division would give the area more clout in Washington by giving the area six instead of two senators. Opponents argue that California's diversity is one of its strengths and problems could arise with respect to services and resources such as water. And, they say, Congress is not likely to approve the change in any event.

With Assemblyman Statham's loss in his attempt to attain higher office (he was defeated for the Republican nomination for lieutenant governor in the 1994 June primary), the steam promptly went out of this movement. It cannot be assumed we have heard the last of it since it has reappeared with some regularity over the course of the state's history.

A second proposal would create a unicameral legislature, replacing the present two-house system. It is argued by some, most notably by former Independent State Senator Lucy Killea, that the rivalry between the assembly and senate makes it more difficult to pass legislation, each unwilling to give credit to the other's initiatives. Proponents also argue a unicameral system is both more efficient with less duplication of effort and likely to be more responsive to voters' desires with smaller districts making communication between constituents and elected officials easier. By combining the two houses into one of 120 or more seats the resulting smaller districts would also make campaigning less expensive. Opponents point to the desirability of looking twice at legislation before sending it on to the governor. They see a benefit in duplication. And they deny the assertion by those favoring the change that the two houses are pretty much alike. Each actually, they say, is different and sees things through different eyes, a valuable check.

A variation on the theme that the legislature needs changing is a proposal that the state adopt a parliamentary system. With the governor chosen by the legislature (very possibly a unicameral legislature), the kinds of deadlocks that have developed in recent years with a governor of one party and the legislature controlled by a different party might be avoided. If the system followed the British model, a governor who went against the will of the majority party in the legislature would be removed from office and a new election of all members of the lawmaking body would be called. No more long-distance feuding such as characterized the relations between the Democratically controlled legislature of the 1980s and much of the 1990s and governors Deukmejian and Wilson would be possible.

These last two ideas have struck anything but a responsive chord in either the minds of legislators or the general public. Polls consistently show John Q. and Mary Citizen have no interest in any radical changes in the state's governing system. They may be—and often are—unhappy with the way government works in Sacramento, but they blame the associated problems on those holding office, not on the system itself. A series of public hearings by the legislatively created Commission on Constitutional Reform found not just apathy but active resistance to these proposals.

A fourth proposed change involves the two-thirds rule. It is most obvious in two areas: legislative approval of the state budget and voter approval of local school bonds. The arguments for change focus on the undemocratic nature of the two-thirds requirement. In budget negotiations it gives a sizable minority veto power over majority will. Those favoring the rule argue that is precisely what it should do in forcing the majority to compromise with the minority and not allow that majority to run roughshod over their opponents. With respect to school bonds, the argument is similar but focuses often on the need for new school construction (a topic discussed briefly in Chapter 12). Often a bond measure will be widely approved with well over 60 percent of the vote but fall shy of the 67 percent needed. This gives a minority, often composed of those with no children or grown children who see no personal benefit, the power to prevent new construction. Those who support this "super-majority" rule argue that paying off bonds comes largely at the expense of property owners who must be protected from a majority bent on spending their money. Some have offered a compromise that keeps a super-majority but lowers it to 60 percent.

Again, while this idea has generated less vigorous opposition, it has made little impact on the public's consciousness and seems unlikely to find its way into law anytime in the near future.

Earlier a number of other ideas concerning reform were recounted. In addition to efforts to reform campaign financing, a topic already touched upon here with Proposition 208, changes in the way propositions are treated, including restoration of the indirect initiative, were discussed. New ways of dealing with our overcrowded courts and prisons were covered. The conflict between development and the environment was given attention (especially in Chapter 11) as well as concern over the quality of education being provided by the state's public schools (in Chapter 12). The fact is that California is facing monumental problems/challenges as it moves ever closer to the twenty-first century. Growth and the challenges associated with it would seem to call for more government action to manage that growth. In many cases the public has taken that task into its own hands through the slow growth movement that has sprung up in virtually every corner of the state. Local initiatives have set limits on the number of new units that can be built.

Meeting these problems/challenges effectively requires imagination and strong leadership. And to accomplish that may involve the biggest challenge of all facing our elected leaders, restoring in the public faith that our elected officials in government can and will act in the interests of all the people of the state, not just in their own interest or the interests of those who make the largest campaign contributions.

Index